MAKING IN SCHOOL AND PUBLIC LIBRARIES

....

BY

Kristin Fontichiaro, Tori Culler, Caroline Wack, Amber Lovett,
Sophia McFadden-Keesling, Ben Rearick, Alyssa Pierce,
Kamya Sarma, Sarah G. Swiderski, Nicole Sype

....

EDITED BY

Kristin Fontichiaro, Caroline Wack,
Tori Culler, and Nicole Sype

Copyright © 2020 by the authors
Some rights reserved

This work is licensed under the Creative Commons Attribution-NonCommercial-NoDerivatives 4.0 International License. To view a copy of this license, visit http://creativecommons.org/licenses/by-nc-nd/4.0/ or send a letter to Creative Commons, PO Box 1866, Mountain View, California, 94042, USA.

Published in the United States of America by
Michigan Publishing
Manufactured in the United States of America

DOI: https://doi.org/10.3998/mpub.11500417

ISBN 978-1-60785-558-3 (paper)
ISBN 978-1-60785-559-0 (e-book)
ISBN 978-1-60785-566-8 (open-access)

An imprint of Michigan Publishing, Maize Books serves the publishing needs of the University of Michigan community by making high-quality scholarship widely available in print and online. It represents a new model for authors seeking to share their work within and beyond the academy, offering streamlined selection, production, and distribution processes. Maize Books is intended as a complement to more formal modes of publication in a wide range of disciplinary areas.
http://www.maizebooks.org

CONTENTS

PART I: ESTABLISHING YOUR MAKERSPACE

Chapter 1: The Roots of Our Maker Movement — 3
Kristin Fontichiaro and Caroline Wack

Chapter 2: Purposefulness — 35
Kristin Fontichiaro and Sophia McFadden-Keesling

Chapter 3: Setting Up a Makerspace — 53
Kamya Sarma and Kristin Fontichiaro

Chapter 4: "Help! My Principal/Director Says I Need to Start a Makerspace!": Figuring Out What to Buy — 75
Kristin Fontichiaro

Chapter 5: Making and Learning — 83
Amber Lovett and Kristin Fontichiaro

Chapter 6: Measuring Learning — 105
Kristin Fontichiaro and Amber Lovett

Chapter 7: Beware the Magical Object: Don't Expect Tools to Be Teachers — 113
Kristin Fontichiaro

Chapter 8: Should Your Makerspace Have a 3D Printer? Maybe   119
Kristin Fontichiaro

Chapter 9: Grantwriting   127
Kristin Fontichiaro

Chapter 10: Visual Documentation in Makerspaces   133
Kristin Fontichiaro

Chapter 11: Written Documentation in Makerspaces   141
Kristin Fontichiaro

Chapter 12: Sustaining a Makerspace   149
Kristin Fontichiaro

Chapter 13: Learning from Peers: Maker Idea Swap   155
Ben Rearick

Chapter 14: Makerspace Tune-Up   161
Kristin Fontichiaro

Chapter 15: Makerspace Tune-Up 2.0 for Schools   171
Kristin Fontichiaro

PART II: PROJECTS AND PROGRAMS

Chapter 16: Junk Box Provocations   181
Kristin Fontichiaro

Chapter 17: Toy Takeapart   187
Kristin Fontichiaro

Chapter 18: Paper Circuits   203
Tori Culler and Caroline Wack

Chapter 19: Cardboard Challenges   217
Tori Culler

Chapter 20: Knitting and Crochet   227
Tori Culler

Chapter 21: Sewing — 235
Tori Culler

Chapter 22: Fashion Hacking — 247
Alyssa Pierce

Chapter 23: Costume Creation Lab — 253
Kristin Fontichiaro

Chapter 24: Photography — 263
Sophia McFadden-Keesling and Kristin Fontichiaro

Chapter 25: Zines — 277
Kristin Fontichiaro

Chapter 26: 20 Ways to Make a Zine — 285
Sarah G. Swiderski

Chapter 27: Button Making — 293
Nicole Sype

Chapter 28: 3D Modeling and Printing — 301
Caroline Wack

Chapter 29: Robots — 317
Caroline Wack

Chapter 30: Design Thinking and Design Challenges — 327
Ben Rearick

Chapter 31: Design Thinking Game — 335
Kristin Fontichiaro

APPENDICES

Appendix A: What's in Your Community's Dream Makerspace? — 339

Appendix B: Project Personnel and Partners — 349

Image Credits — 353

Index — 355

From 2012-2019, our work has incorporated everything from Arduino microcontrollers and Raspberry Pi minicomputers to old-fashioned engineering tools like these donated NoEndz building materials.

PART I
ESTABLISHING YOUR MAKERSPACE

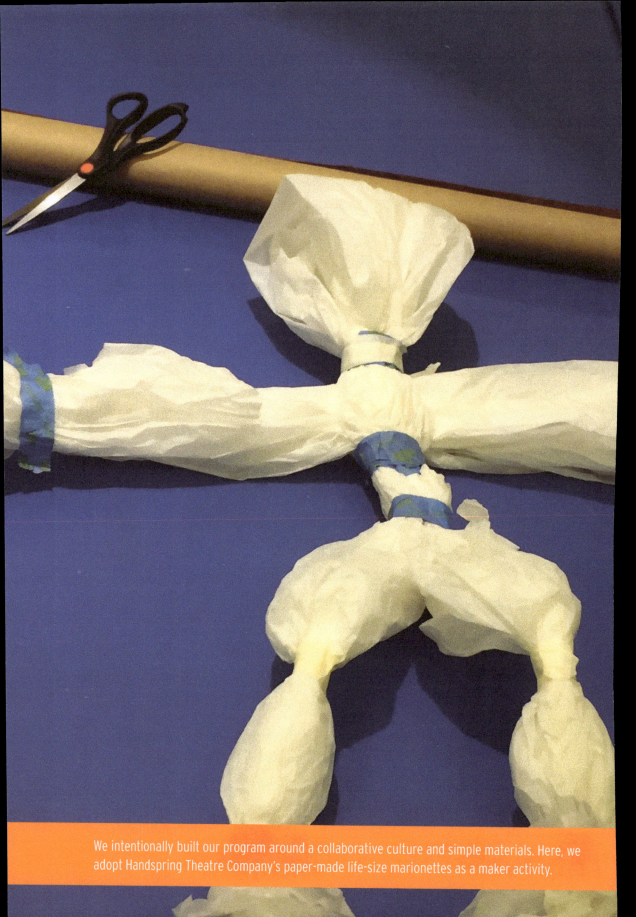

We intentionally built our program around a collaborative culture and simple materials. Here, we adopt Handspring Theatre Company's paper-made life-size marionettes as a maker activity.

CHAPTER 1

THE ROOTS OF OUR MAKER MOVEMENT

Kristin Fontichiaro and Caroline Wack

HOW WE BEGAN

The Michigan Makers project, later absorbed into the Making in Michigan Libraries project funded by the Institute of Museum and Library Services grant RE-05-15-0021-15, was born from post-class conversations with Kristin and eventual Michigan Makers co-founders Terence O'Neill, Shauna Masura, and Samantha Roslund in the weeks leading up to the 2012 release of the Raspberry Pi microcomputer. At that time, most maker work was happening in community makerspaces or in home economics, industrial arts, shop, or other vocationally-focused hands-on courses. While educational technology was firmly established in K-12 schools, more attention was focused on Web 2.0 applications like blogs, wikis, and podcasts than on learning to code.

Those who created Raspberry Pi saw it as the 21st-century version of the BBC Micro of their own youth, a low-cost way to get more kids doing programming. From their perspectives being involved in computer science at Cambridge University, they had seen that while earlier computer science students had come to campus with experience actually *programming*, the incoming students were more likely to have experience with ed tech tools or creating web pages using HTML. The inventors felt—as many still do today—that there was an impending shortage of computer programmers. To combat this, they created the Raspberry Pi: a simple, cheap computer that students could play with and program (Severance and Fontichiaro 2014). By removing the barriers to entry, they hoped to build up a next generation of students and employees with in-demand tech skills.

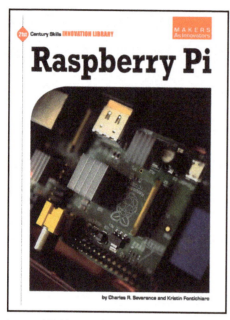

In a publishing project parallel to our IMLS-funded work, we showed off our early enthusiasm for the low-cost Raspberry Pi with this Cherry Lake Publishing title, part of the first maker series for youth.

In our late-night conversations, Michigan Makers' founding members were similarly optimistic; the idea of a $35 minicomputer that could fit in one's pocket felt revolutionary to us. Then something strange happened: the Raspberry Pi launched, and while K-12 initiatives were the *company's* goals, there was a surge of buyers with quite different expectations. Adult makers leapt at the chance to embed tiny computers at the core of new inventions, from sensors that could identify whether someone was lying in bed to cameras that automatically collected environmental data (Severance and Fontichiaro 2014). The portability and low cost of this small, powerful computer made it an inventor's dream.

This was when it really hit us that there was a group of passionate hobbyists out there that were using tools like the Arduino microcontroller and Raspberry Pi, in addition to traditional tools like woodworking, welding, and sewing, to create new inventions for fun or profit. These hobbyists were building loose coalitions and organizations, pooling funds to purchase expensive fabrication equipment ranging from laser cutters to 3D printers to classic welding tools to industrial-strength sewing and embroidery machines. These communities were not merely about stuff, however; they saw themselves as creating a new culture of inclusion and sharing. Open-source, collaborative work was fundamental. Sometimes these organizations had a strong focus on programming and were known as hackerspaces; others called themselves makerspaces.

As we began to search for (and find!) these spaces, we realized how much of the early makerspace activities came from our own area of Southeastern

Michigan. For example, Maker Faire™ Detroit was only the third large-scale Maker Faire™, and our home of Ann Arbor shares the title of first-ever Mini Maker Faire™. Our maker-focused work was inspired by early work in the Southeast Michigan area: Mt. Elliott Makerspace in Detroit, Ann Arbor's All Hands Active, and MakerWorks in Ann Arbor. (While the for-profit TechShop makerspace in Dearborn existed, with multiyear support from Ford Motor Company to enable its employees to participate at no cost, we did not have firsthand interactions with them.) The region's passion for the maker movement makes sense given its manufacturing industry—this is a part of the country that knows how to fix things. In our Midwestern childhoods, it was not uncommon for (mostly) men to open up their car hoods in the driveway and for neighbors to come over and collectively problem-solve how to repair or soup up the vehicle. Dale Dougherty, founder of Maker Faire™ and *Make* magazine, often pointed to a 1960s Chevrolet film, *American Maker*, which tied America's handcrafting heritage to today's vehicles.[1]

Jeff Sturges at the now-disbanded Mt. Elliott Makerspace worked in the basement of a church in a once-prosperous but now declined neighborhood in Detroit. There he helped kids and adults explore entrepreneurship, 3D printing, and, perhaps most critically, bike repair. One of their policies was that any kid who could take a bike apart and put it back together again—with the help of volunteer mentors—could own it. For an impoverished neighborhood, a bicycle unlocks access to a far broader community and can literally change the worldview of a kid. To walk into his space and its yellow walls felt like an embrace. Looking back, Kristin clearly remembers her first visit after encountering Jeff's work in a webinar and thinking, "I want to make a space that feels just like this."

Josh Williams introduced us to the underground hacker and maker culture (literally, it was located in a downtown Ann Arbor basement) of All Hands Active. While Jeff's space was explicitly about welcome and exploration for all ages, All Hands Active was home to some fledgling businesses as well as many gamers and programmers. When Arduino founder Massimo Banzi was in town for a lecture, we took him to All Hands Active after dinner, and hardly a soul looked up from the glow of his or her laptop! As with Mt. Elliott Makerspace, however, Kristin always felt welcomed by Josh.

Our third local influence was MakerWorks in Ann Arbor, founded during the heart of Michigan's—and then the nation's—economic downturn. MakerWorks was public-facing for classes, tours, and community events, but it also

---

[1] You can view this at https://www.youtube.com/watch?v=F3KHfvTDGn0.

nurtured local makers who made not just for fun but as their core business. It was Dale Grover, the co-founder (with Tom Root, who brought over the lean management practices from his other role as co-founder of Zingerman's Mail Order, a high-end food purveyor based in Ann Arbor), who told Kristin that makerspaces were about three things:

1. **Tools**—the equipment, often too expensive or too bulky for someone to own individually.
2. **Support**—staff, volunteers, teachers, and mentors who can help novices grow in expertise. Support also includes equipment repair, which, in the movement's early days, was a Sisyphean task—3D printers were notoriously finicky!
3. **Community**—a sense of collective enterprise, open-source sharing of ideas, and communal celebration of success.

Other frameworks include the *Maker Movement Manifesto*, written by Mark Hatch, then-CEO of TechShop.[2] Hatch (2015) includes the following elements in his manifesto: make, share, give, learn, tool up, play, participate, support, and change. Though phrased very differently, you can see the same principles underlying this and the MakerWorks framework: both emphasize that making does not happen in a vacuum, but rather it is a communal, collaborative process that happens in the presence of tools. Hatch's manifesto also emphasizes play, which we at Michigan Makers took to heart—working with younger makers, it can be helpful to rely on the sense of wonder and experimentation. That sense of play can be powerful when sustained into adulthood!

The early years of the maker movement were defined by a sort of techno-social optimism—the idea that making would be a great equalizer and opportunity-giver. Consider these words from the introduction of Dale Dougherty's *Free to Make*:

> "[The Maker Movement] is changing how we learn, work, and innovate. It is open and collaborative, creative and inventive, hands-on and playful. We don't have to conform to the present reality or accept the status quo—we can imagine a better future and realize that we are free to make it. Making is the mother of all possible futures." (2016, xxi)

This starry-eyed vision of the future and makers' place in it characterized many early publications about makerspaces and maker culture: leaders

---

[2] TechShop was a makerspace chain that closed all locations in 2017.

of the movement heralded the advent of a new industrial and cultural revolution that would lead to a more creative, capable population.

Other publications also rode this wave of techno-optimism. Makerspaces could be a powerful personal and professional accelerator, they argued. In David Lang's *Zero to Maker: Learn (Just Enough) to Make (Just about) Anything* (2013), for example, Lang finds himself temporarily unemployed. He describes walking into a TechShop commercial makerspace and, within months, acquiring enough informal learning to contribute significantly to an underwater drone initiative.

From the perspective of libraries, one thing that is important to keep in mind when discussing early community makerspaces is that they required individuals to pay for their materials and explorations (or, in the case of Maker-Works, to volunteer in the space in lieu of financial payment). The wide variety of products that were invented in the early years of the maker movement include an accessible sous vide machine, a cheaper 3D printer, and the educational tool LittleBits (Dougherty 2016).

As makerspaces moved into schools and libraries, however, the financial costs of equipment acquisition, materials cost, and instructors were generally absorbed by existing library budgets. While there are some exceptions, this shift has been underappreciated in discussions of library makerspaces. When individuals foot the bill for their experiments, there are limits as to who can afford to engage in makerspace activities. This restricts innovation to those with disposable income. On the flip side, libraries operate under frugal program budgets designed to accommodate many makers . . . but with smaller projects. One large, well-funded library system told us informally that they budget approximately $2 per participant per program. When I relayed that to a small rural library, they responded by saying that their budget was more like 50 cents. It is difficult to envision market innovations emerging from $2 budgets!

While the messages of inclusion were present, and there was a genuine and oft-repeated desire that making should be inclusive of gender, materials, tools, and communities, the reality is that such inclusion did not pan out consistently in community makerspaces. Later, initiatives such as GirlsWhoCode.com and San Francisco's Double Union, for women and those who self-identify as non-binary, filled some of this gap. But it emphasizes why, beginning around 2012, the adoption of makerspaces in schools, school libraries, public libraries, museums, and academic libraries is so critical to this decade's definition of makerspaces and making itself.

Early library adopters included the University of Nevada-Reno, where Tod Colegrove's team saw that engineering students had little access to fabrication tools. They installed a widely-used 3D printer (Fisher 2012). New York's Fayetteville Free Library began a Fab Lab (unaffiliated with the broader Fab Lab Foundation's partner organizations) based on 3D printing, but it was also the first to hear its community's desire for sewing-based practices. Westport Public Library placed a makerspace in the middle of the stacks and installed a maker-in-residence under the staff stewardship of Bill Derry (Kaminski 2012).

Though not a library, the Pittsburgh Children's Museum created MakeShop through an intensive research-to-practice loop that later was shared with leaders from a variety of cultural heritage institutions. Targeting learners as young as three, the space had dedicated staff and uses an exploratory model that allows users to create using "the same materials, tools, and processes used by professional artists, builders, programmers, and creators of all kinds." In addition to open-ended play, the MakeShop offers workshops like Toy Takeapart, exploring circuitry, and working with textiles ("MakeShop" n.d.). Other early library makerspace publications chronicling making in libraries included Caitlyn Bagley's 2014 *Makerspaces: Top Trailblazing Projects*, John Burke's 2014 *Makerspaces: A Practical Guide for Librarians*, and Leslie Preddy's 2013 *School Library Makerspaces: Grades 6–12*. (Bagley and Burke's books include information on Michigan Makers in its first year.) Check these books out for more on how libraries were approaching makerspaces in the early years.

When K-12 schools became involved in the maker movement, it was often through exposure to Gary Stager and Sylvia Libow Martinez's *Invent to Learn*, which partnered creative, open exploration with the existing "constructionism" mindset of MIT's Seymour Papert. This book advocated for open exploration disconnected from the standards-based, test-driven education that had otherwise dominated the K-12 landscape. Suddenly, schools and librarians were rapidly adopting making. In our conversations with school and public library personnel, their making initiatives came from a variety of impulses, working solo or in tandem with one another:

1. An expansion of existing educational technology initiatives, particularly in the area of computer programming and coding
2. Librarians seeking novel ways to add value to their communities or to expand their existing patron base
3. Pressure from administrators, colleagues, patrons, or directors to keep pace with other institutions
4. Librarians seeking projects to justify their ongoing relevance in times of budgetary restrictions

5. Libraries positioning themselves to support national interest in STEM, including the implementation of the Next Generation Science Standards
6. In rare cases, libraries reconceptualizing themselves to provide alternate workforce preparation or retraining skills

These needs had some overlap with the community makerspace movement, but also pushed the movement strongly toward coding and STEM exposure and away from the free-wheeling, individualistic creations of community makerspaces. For example, an early commercial makerspace model, TechShop, declared bankruptcy in 2018. In June 2019, word spread that Maker Media had stopped operations and laid off the entirety of its staff. Maker Media, run by Dale Dougherty, who as we mentioned earlier was considered the father of the maker movement, had an overwhelming impact on the movement. Its publications and events not only ushered in making as a 21st-century phenomenon but also served as a central hub for makers to find and share ideas. At the time this book was published, Maker Media was responsible for *Make* magazine, a popular blog, and several maker-themed books. Its most public-facing work was to create, license, and organize Maker Faire™. At the time this book was published, its fate remained uncertain.[3]

Paradoxically, maker initiatives tied to established organizations (and the free utilities, space, oversight, and budget that accompany them) have exploded, with schools and libraries as the primary organizations taking up the banner. Differences in who is considered a maker, how much making costs, long-term sustainability, and legacy beliefs about what schools and libraries "are for" have arisen. From art and engineering departments on college campuses to public library story times, the narrative has shifted from a rambunctious group of skilled outsiders hacking together parts and funds to make wild inventions (Dougherty 2016) to making as an expected component of schools and libraries. The focus has shifted from community-based work in groups to how to scale activities so that they can be both facilitated and attended by beginners. Well-intentioned amateurs are often learning just enough new content to stay ahead of those they serve.

This has led to some awkward moments for makerspaces in legacy institutions. The narrative of STEM (science, technology, engineering, and mathematics) or STEAM (STEM plus art/aesthetics) took hold in schools and

---

[3] See, for example, https://techcrunch.com/2019/06/07/make-magazine-maker-media-layoffs/.

libraries, and some of the whimsy, playfulness, and making-for-the-sake-of-making has faded. In order to scale up, some of the individualistic nature of early maker narratives has been replaced by activities that are low-cost or easily taught to a large group at one time.

OUR WORK

This brings us back to our own Michigan Makers and Making in Michigan Libraries projects. As you will note, our work began with a more technological focus but, as our work with children continued, we leaned more and more into non-digital materials. From its earliest iterations, we consistently prioritized participant agency, self-determined activity choice, community, and creativity, and we saw that those goals were sometimes better met with non-digital, non-STEM tools: children were more engaged and creative. STEM topics may have brought families in the door, but students of all ages often opted for art and handicraft if given a preference. Sewing machines have proven especially enticing, especially to boys. As a result, you will notice in this volume that we repeatedly return to low-cost materials like cardboard, fabric, and junk for this reason. We had freedom to make this decision because our work occurred outside of regular school hours or in public library settings, and we therefore had no duty to achieve curriculum objectives. Your institution may have different objectives from ours (though we do encourage transparency in the mission-setting, as you'll read later in this volume, because "makerspace" means different things to different people!).

East Middle School Media Center, Plymouth, MI

This is the project described early on in this chapter. As one of the earliest youth-based makerspace projects, we focused on the new technologies of Arduino microcontrollers and Raspberry Pi, with a strong emphasis on bringing together the school's gifted population. The librarian, Rachel Goldberg, had been hosting informal lunch-hour coding activities with kids, and our after-school program built on her existing work. It didn't take long for non-digital items to sneak into our work, though!

Activities at East included, on a rotating basis:
- Setting up a Raspberry Pi
- Programming with Scratch
- Wrapping holiday gifts

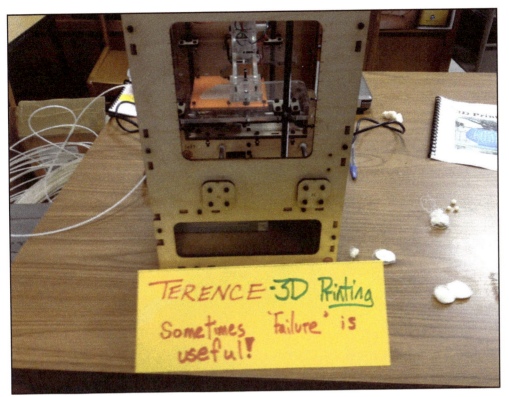

Enjoying the process was an early goal of Michigan Makers at East Middle School.

- Machine sewing
- A contest to conceptualize an app
- Squishy Circuits
- Stop-motion animation designed in PowerPoint
- Photo editing
- Creating a comic
- Minecraft
- Game design
- ComicCon event

We began each session by writing a "menu" of two to five activity options on the board, an activity we carried into our later work with younger learners. This gave students a chance to consider what they wanted to work on. At first, we designated a certain number of "slots" available for each activity, but we soon realized that this was not necessary. For the final 10 minutes, students reflected in composition notebooks about what they had learned and created that week. Those notebooks also hosted our experiment using digital badging and the Badg.us platform (no longer operational), which let us print out badge stickers to acknowledge skill achievement as well as track accomplishments digitally. We ultimately found the work of creating and managing badges to be more ambitious than our busy all-volunteer team could keep up with, but looking back at this 2012–2013 initiative makes us eager to experiment with skill tracking in the future.

Squishy Circuits exploration during our first Michigan Makers year, at East Middle School in Plymouth, Michigan.

A critical factor in this site's success was that it attracted highly-motivated, highly-intelligent students who had near-perfect attendance. This was an affordance we did not always have; we worked in a total of three middle schools over time, and inconsistent attendance was the norm in less-affluent settings. Founding members were involved as mentors, so there were numerous mentors (approximately one mentor to four students), meaning that strong relationships could develop over time. This helped establish a sense of trust and familiarity, which was also helped by the students' existing bond with Ms. Goldberg. In some cases, students served as peer mentors for one another. Because of these factors, this group was able to have extended projects that stretched across weeks, something we could not achieve in other settings.

This project was funded in part by a $1,000 grant to East Middle School from the Michigan Association for Computer Users in Learning and an approximate match from start-up funds provided by the University of Michigan School of Information. All labor was voluntary.

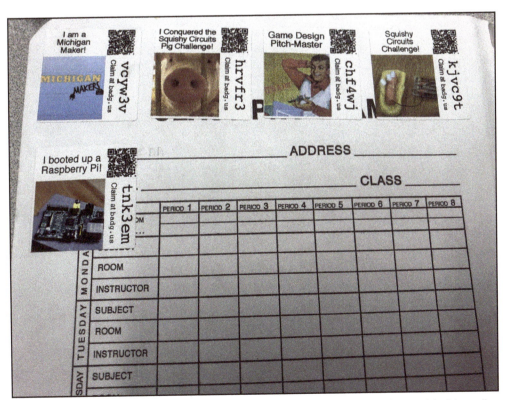

At East Middle School, we used Badg.us to generate physical badges that correlated to online accounts. Unfortunately at the time, the effort of starting up a new program with no paid staff made this effort fall by the wayside.

Michigan Makers, Mitchell Elementary School Fourth and Fifth Grade, Ann Arbor, MI

The awarding of an internal grant from the University of Michigan's Third Century Initiative allowed us to hire student staff for the first time alongside volunteers and gave us funds to acquire additional supplies and equipment, including LittleBit and a MakerBot Replicator 2 3D printer. We approached Mitchell Elementary because it was, at the time, a lower-achieving school (this has since been reversed!) and because several other university initiatives were clustered there. We worked with approximately 25 fourth and fifth graders in a weekly after-school program that was hosted either in the library or the art room. As with East Middle School, we had many "regulars," though attendance could be erratic. With this population, we found that activities that stretched across weekly meetings were difficult and works-in-progress would be forgotten by the next week, so we shifted to activities that could reach closure by the end of our 75-minute sessions.

Activities here included:

- LittleBits
- LEGO
- Using the Silhouette Cameo to create stickers and T-shirt stencils
- Comics creation
- ComicCon
- Machine and hand sewing
- Fleece scarves
- Snap Circuits
- Squishy Circuits
- Origami
- Gliders
- Hour of Code
- Junk box
- Photo editing
- 3D printing and limited modeling

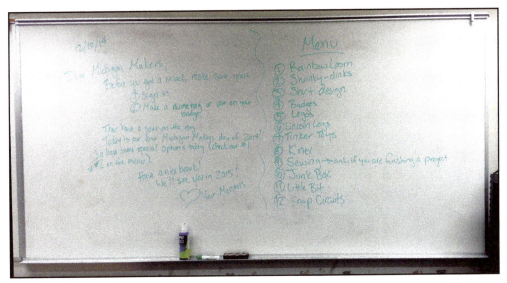

A sample whiteboard from Michigan Makers at Mitchell Elementary School, Ann Arbor, MI, with a letter to attendees and a list of available activities. Our very eager makers would rush in the door and demand to know the day's activity–having this information posted in advance helped us have a gentler start to events.

As with East Middle School, we posted an activity menu, but we added a friendly letter previewing the day. This letter was based on the school's adoption of the Morning Meeting model (Kriete and Davis 2014). We followed a slightly different sequence at this site. As school got out around 4pm, we asked students to sign in and sit on the provided carpet. Once seated, they received a snack (cheese sticks, carrots, fruit, popcorn, or gummies). Our opening meeting was called to order by one of the facilitators beginning to sing, to the tune of the 1970s "I'm a Pepper," this song[4], with the students joining in.

> I'm a maker (point to self)
> You're a maker (point to someone else)
> He's a maker (point to a male)
> She's a maker (point to a female)
> Wouldn't you like to be a maker, too?
>
> Be a maker, Michigan Makers
> (more quietly) Be a maker, Michigan Makers
> (almost inaudible) Be a maker, Michigan Makers

---

4 The original commercial is available at https://www.youtube.com/watch?v=jvCTaccEkMI.

We chose this type of greeting—knowing it was dorky—because it felt friendlier than, "OK, everybody, pipe down so we can get started!" and because its decreasing volume was a gentler way to take kids down to silence. We then asked what people had made over the past week and explained, demonstrated, or displayed that week's activities. Then, we released kids to explore the stations. We stopped about 15 minutes before the event ended at 5:30 to clean up and have a brief closing meeting where kids could show off their creations.

Kristin has always described this group as, "You just turn on the spigot and creativity comes out." This group had a very deep hunger for engagement, stimulation, and playfulness. Never was this more evident than in junk box creations, where kids often made gifts for family members, teachers, or one another; designed their own games; created displays for their collectibles; and more. This was the first site when we started to harbor a hypothesis that there was something about making with physical objects one can take home that seemed to awaken some unfinished business of childhood. Their something-from-nothing making often felt overwhelmingly more important to the students than any digital tool we put in front of them. This may be attributable to the fact that the Ann Arbor Public Schools have an excellent digital literacy curriculum, and so kids were "tired" of screens. But we could not shake the feeling that they were desperate to play and, as kids primarily from low-income families, they understood that if you wanted toys, you needed to make them yourself. In fact, we think this is why clean-up time was always difficult—kids just couldn't stop themselves from creating.

With the exception of clean-up, this group excelled at self-regulation, and this was the era in our work where we felt we best approximated a community makerspace feel. We could set out multiple stations—with some staffed by mentors who could guide in new challenges, and some DIY stations like LEGO or the junk box—and not assign students to groups. Kids—like members of community makerspaces—could determine what to work on and when. Behavior problems were a rarity and tended to be isolated to those kids who already had a track record of behavior problems. (That being said, we also saw that making could center some kids who otherwise struggled during the school day!) More often than not, Kristin found she could step back from time to time and realize that every kid was engaged without her needing to intercede.

This phase was funded by the University of Michigan's Third Century Initiative (which included a budget for us to host our first workshops for librarians and educators), the U-M School of Information's Founders Fund, and was already under way when we received funds for the Making in Michigan Libraries project sponsored by the Institute of Museum and Library Services, which continued Michigan Makers funding for several years while taking on statewide professional development about maker culture.

Michigan Makers, Mitchell Elementary School Third Grade, Ann Arbor, MI

A disadvantage of working in a school with other U-M initiatives was that there were too many activities tugging at the fourth and fifth graders! We were asked to shift our work to third graders. We kept the same basic flow for beginning and ending the session. However, this group's younger age meant that they had less well-developed independent work skills, and our model of multiple activities format did not work as well. Though we often had more mentors with this group than we did with fourth and fifth graders, our experience was that this group needed more guided instruction time and less time making their own choices until they settled into a routine. With this population, we also realized how important it was that every child get some exposure to key activities. It can be difficult for children to make authentic choices if they do not have prior knowledge about their range of options. Therefore, we often divided the 25 students into two groups, with one group learning an activity one week, and then swapping instructors the following week. This was useful for onboarding new mentors—they could watch a more experienced mentor the first time around and teach it themselves the next time—but took away some of the spontaneity we had become accustomed to. The DIY stations (like the junk box) became a "what you can do when you finish the group activity" instead of a main activity. Some of our activities with this group included:

- Zine making
- Cardboard challenges (well-loved)
- Hand sewing felt finger puppets
- Puppet stages (made from cardboard, also well-loved)
- Board game design
- Junk box
- Citizen science (Michigan ZoomIn project at Zooniverse.org)
- Toy takeapart

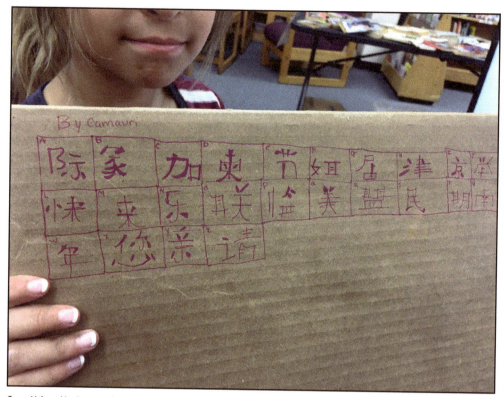

One thing that surprised us about working with third graders was how much more time it took for them to settle into an activity. Multiple exposures to materials was a useful strategy for this group. It took until the last day for the maker of this "Chinese language keyboard" to develop the perseverance . . . and then, look out!

- Finger knitting
- Electric bracelets
- Button maker

Our work with Mitchell Elementary was profiled in a 2017 *School Library Journal* article (Matteson 2017). The profile perfectly describes one of the biggest lessons we learned from working with this age group: ". . . making isn't always about skills and future career aspirations . . . Sometimes, it's about having time to self-soothe: to become quiet with one's self; to take pleasure in materials for materials' sake." At this age, just letting children explore and have fun made for the best learning environment.

This phase was made possible in part by the Institute of Museum and Library Services via the Making in Michigan Libraries project.

Family Events, Benzonia Public Library, Benzonia, MI

As part of the IMLS-funded Making in Michigan Libraries project, we partnered with two public libraries over the years for extended engagement. Our first partner was Benzonia Public Library, a small, Class I library in an agricultural, artisanal, and tourist community near Traverse City, Michigan. It has a service population of approximately 2,000 year-round and seasonal residents, though its imaginative programming and friendly vibe have begun to draw patrons from beyond as well.

We began by hosting one of our nine three-day workshop series there, then began visiting nearly monthly for the next few years. This allowed us to develop warm and collegial relationships particularly with library director Amanda McLaren, maker coordinator Jimmy McLaren, and assistant director Michelle Leines, as well as volunteers and community members. It also allowed us to build on previous activities and have multiple interactions with attendees.

Benzonia already had some maker activities under way. For example, its Repurposeful Librarians—staff members Kathy Johnson and Michelle Leines—used donated or low-cost materials to create holiday and home

Some of the wares for sale by Benzonia's Repurposeful Librarians, made of donated materials.

decor items to sell at craft fairs. The proceeds benefited the Friends of the Library. They also planned workshops focusing on handmade items ranging from knitting to paper folding. A community favorite was Power Tools for Women, led by the local hardware store manager. In this workshop, participants created a short stack of donated books as a lamp base, then drilled through them and threaded lamp hardware. The result? A one-of-a-kind bookish lamp (see previous page)! The Library had also begun its Benzie Guild of Makers project for upper elementary students, which *School Library Journal* profiled in 2018 (Hinton 2018).

Director Amanda McLaren was in her first years of leading the library, and she had a laser-sharp focus on activities that would support the youth and families of the community. As a result, our activities there focused primarily on schoolchildren and families. Because this site was nearly 250 miles from our campus, our interactions there were not weekly but formed around special events. We want to be clear that these events were collaboratively designed, *not* us bringing an event to their community, and we believe this contributed to the mutual satisfaction of the relationship. It also helped us *combine* skill sets rather than sticking with the projects and concepts we were most comfortable with.

These special events included:

- Photo classes with a professional photographer (see related chapter in Part II)
- Costume Creation Lab, a chance for families to make Halloween costumes out of fabric, cardboard, or existing costumes (see related chapter in Part II)
- Cardboard Challenge, with sponsorship from the local recycling center and a roomful of cardboard collected by Jimmy McLaren (see related chapter in Part II)
- MakerFest, a series of stations set up for guided or DIY exploration, ranging from T-shirt stencils to machine sewing to robots, for a target audience of families and community members
- Behavior Incentive Day, a MakerFest-type event where Library staff, U-M staff, and volunteers hosted a variety of STEM and arts and crafts stations, including toy takeapart, zines, LEGO, eRoominate, an electric keyboard, free drawing, and paper flashlights (see Part II)

- Board Game Design Night, a potluck event where families were guided into using junk, leftover game pieces, and a sample game board to create and test an original board game. Custom game pieces could be created using Shrinky Dinks and 3D-printed game piece bases
- Christmas Magic, part of a weekend of pre-holiday celebrations in early December that included a sing-along, gift-making, and a puppet show by local favorites Dr. Fizz and Boomer the Rat (Jimmy McLaren and son Finn)
- Kids Fun Day Carnival, an event run by high school athletes with activities organized by the Library, our team, and other community groups that had an attendance of over 300 (not bad for a service population of 2,000!)

What we learned from this public library maker partnership was the significant impact that a community-focused director makes on library programming; the critical role that a creative, inventive, and resourceful maker staff member has on program success; and the importance of seeing each event as part of a larger arc of library priorities, not as standalone events.

This partnership was made possible in part by the Institute of Museum and Library Services and funds from the Friends of the Benzonia Public Library.

Building a Space from Scratch: Niles District Library, Niles, MI

Niles District Library (NDL) is located in southwestern Michigan, directly north of South Bend, Indiana. The library is a bustling hub for the community, with a wide range of intellectual, social, and entertainment activities. We met the Niles staff when they agreed to host three days of our Making in Michigan Libraries workshops in 2017. One of our strong memories of that week was the number of patrons who dropped into our workshop space looking for events that had been temporarily relocated to accommodate us. We were "interrupted" so many times that we knew this was a library that was offering what its community wanted. There is a strong social justice stance at this library, and the staff has tremendous dedication to those patrons in need of social services. (In fact, they would later receive a substantial grant to explore the role of social workers in their library and with their partners.) Seeing these strengths, we jumped at the chance to be a part of their process of forming a space. Whereas Benzonia's maker work was already established and ready for events, the work in Niles focused much more on building

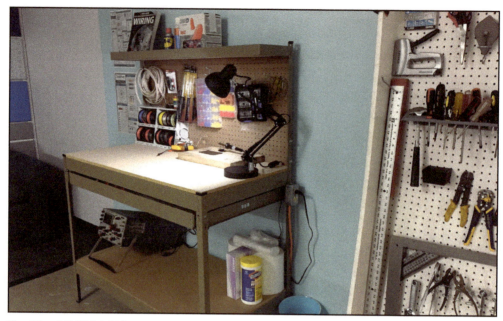

The Niles (MI) District Library's SkillShare space during renovations. This space was primarily built with existing library inventory, such as leftover chairs and room dividers, spruced up with fresh paint. Makerspaces don't have to be fancy!

a permanent space—and all the issues related to that, including permissions, partners, activities, marketing, and more.

Southwestern Michigan, like much of the Midwest, had a more profitable economic past than it has in its current post-industrial state. Much of the housing stock is older, and with a median home price of $79,000 according to the 2017 American Community Survey (ACS), it is difficult for homeowners to accrue additional real estate value over time. However, it is also a surprisingly young community, with the 2017 ACS reporting a median age of 35.4, and one of limited financial means (2017 ACS data estimates a per capita income of $18,725 and a median income of $31,844). Younger patrons moving into aging home stock with relatively low incomes was identified as the population in greatest need of maker activities, and the library intentionally focused its earliest efforts on DIY repair for this population. During one of Kristin's visits, she found that the library staff had installed a fake drywall wall so people could practice nailing to the studs, hanging pictures, spackling, and paint! They would carry this out via a physical space—underutilized storage space in the basement they retitled SkillShare—and a series of shelves to host a circulating Library of Things.[5] Both had their roots in the donated collections of founding staff member Laura Hollister.

---

5   https://www.nileslibrary.com/?s=skillshare.

An example of the problem-solving focus of SkillShare at the Niles District Library.

SkillShare acquired a couple of repurposed tables and chairs, an electrical bench, a standing-height cutting table, a pegboard of tools, some vintage industrial sewing machines, and a few hearty volunteers. As part of the Making in Michigan Libraries project, we supplemented these donations with hand and power tools, additional lighting, and sewing notions for in-library use.

The Library of Things, at the time of our latest visit, made available for checkout items like these, some of which were donations and some of which were funded by Making in Michigan Libraries:

- Board games
- Drywall repair kit (inspired by historic flooding in the city)
- Basic toolbox
- Beverage dispensers for parties
- Musical instruments

Each of these Library of Things items was added to the library catalog to facilitate discovery and circulation.[6]

---

6 http://ndl.michiganevergreen.org/eg/opac/results?_special=1&tag=245&subfield=h&term=Things&locg=21.

Working with our graduate student research assistant Jean Hardy, the library let us in on its goals and ambitions. Jean brought his expertise on organizational management, branding, and policy development to the library and gained insight on the challenges of establishing a new initiative on a limited budget and without dedicated program staff. Now that the program is up and running, tasks of running and promoting the space and its collection have become part of a library staff member's regular duties.

NDL narrowed their target audience to young adults aged 18–35, pinpointed that general DIY skills were what they were interested in and needed to learn, and then created their makerspace workshop to meet those needs. But drawing in that audience required a bit of sleight of hand. To draw in this age group, we designed a high-profile workshop focused on kids and toy takeapart. And guess who came along? Their parents, our target audience. NDL staff was able to circulate among the parents as the kids were busy at work. By the end of the afternoon, parents had stepped forward offering to edit video and teach sessions for the adult workshops!

Here are some of the questions Niles traversed as it planned its space. We include them here as they may inform your own decision-making.

Who are we trying to serve?

The original focus was DIY repair and an intergenerational model that harvested the expertise of more experienced makers in mentoring novices; however, they found that youth- or craft-focused events could be a stronger draw.

What problem are we trying to solve?

This was a critical consideration that Niles recognized from the beginning: that library initiatives cannot be designed in a vacuum. They were thoughtful and conscious of potential users and impact on those users. While there were some pivots and experiments as time went on, the staff never lost sight of what SkillShare and Library of Things were for.

How many hours a week is the space open to select items for checkout or use equipment in-house?

The initial goal was to have drop-in hours with a helpful volunteer, but these did not yield enough attendance. A structured, event-based program was more effective. Checkout of Library of Things has limited but advertised hours.

How do we staff events here?

The original vision was akin to, "If you build it, they will come," from *Field of Dreams*. There was hope that having a *space* would inspire others to volunteer as mentors, teachers, or coaches. While an optimistic and exciting viewpoint, this organic approach moved slowly and was time-intensive for staff. An events-based model with library staff proved more fruitful.

How do we circulate items?

Thinking about how to circulate a collection of objects given the library's small staff was no small consideration. The time it takes to inventory a board game once it is returned, for example, should not be taken lightly. NDL's Laura Hollister did a great deal of background research into other tool libraries to learn from how they circulated unusual materials. The Library had to discuss everything from who would help patrons find and select items to how to designate items in the catalog to inventory issues and potential issues of liability and waivers.

How can we use this initiative to deepen our relationship with existing partners? Become available to new and potential partners?

We saw how infectious the Library's vision was once they got people in the space. For example, we threw a youth-themed toy takeapart event together.[7] At first glimpse, it might seem like this was not connected to the DIY repair mission. But . . . it got *parents* of the target age group in the space. At this single event, one parent offered to edit video to promote the space, another volunteered to teach a workshop or two, and a visiting foundation representative saw the hustle and bustle and encouraged the Library to apply for additional funding. Additionally, there were other potential partnerships brewing around the shared need for good space to support the community.

What do patrons want? What do they show up for?

The event for children and additional craft-themed events drew a much larger audience initially than the DIY repair workshops. Tracking attendance over time helped the staff realize where it was striking a chord with its community.

How and where do we market events?

When the projects began, Hollister set up a standalone calendar and events page for SkillShare but quickly realized that this placed information and events too deep in the website for patrons to discover. Integrating events

---

7 See https://impact.govrel.umich.edu/making-in-michigan/ for an overview of this event.

into the overall Library calendar was more fruitful. Facebook posts were also surprisingly effective, as was a video display (on the main floor, near the entrance and the circulation desk) that showed what was happening in SkillShare in real time. Tapping community influencers, such as the head of Niles's large homeschooling network, were also effective.

What are the potential liabilities? What kinds of permissions and release forms are needed?

The Library staff thought deeply about the fact that their space would have "dangerous" equipment (like power tools and an industrial serger) available for in-library or at-home use and strategized with their attorney about what kinds of release forms or permissions statements would be helpful protections.

Since our time with Niles District Library has ended, we have been excited to see their continued media coverage and increased community awareness and buy-in.[8] For example, their efforts were written about by the *Niles Daily Star* (Hammon 2018):

> Thanks to the efforts of the Niles District Library, those looking to spare their wallet and learn to be handier around their home can gain the tools during a new workshop series called SkillShare.
>
> For the past month, volunteers have been lending their skills to locals, teaching them how to do everything from household repair and maintenance to skills in the kitchen. The workshops are free and open to the public [. . .]

This work was made possible in part by the Institute of Museum and Library Services and the University of Michigan School of Information Founders Fund.

Michigan Makers Family Nights, Ypsilanti District Library, Michigan Avenue Branch, Ypsilanti, MI

In the spring of 2019 we moved Michigan Makers to the Michigan Avenue branch of the Ypsilanti District Library to host weekly maker workshops for families. We quickly discovered that just because we put "Family Night" on the poster did not mean that only families would show up—that particular library has a population of kids that hang out at the library after school, and

---

8   See https://www.wnit.org/educationcounts/s/increased-millennial-usage-of-libraries.html for an example of media coverage of the Niles District Library.

when they saw our activities and smelled the pizza that we brought each week, they wanted to join in. (The pizza was inspired by the library's earlier iterations of Prime Time Reading, family-based literacy nights that included dinner.) Not wanting to bar children from entering, we had to adapt our activities so that they were possible for parent-child teams as well as the older children who were there without parents.

Our calendar of activities for the Ypsilanti Family Night was determined before the semester started and included activities like:

- Toy Takeapart
- Circuits
- Slime
- Board Game Design
- Making Music
- Puppets
- Robots on Parade
- Cardboard Construction

We also left ourselves a little wiggle room with some activities with vague names like Surprise, Inventor's Challenge, Valentine's Day Fun, and Finale of Favorites. We could slot in activities for these weeks depending on staff capacity and available materials, and we found that the flexibility was really nice for a group of busy maker mentors. If it was a busy week where our prep time was limited, we could adjust the activities accordingly!

A typical weekly session of 90 minutes started with 10–15 minutes for dinner, an explanation of the activity, and then devoting the rest of the time for children and families to complete the activity while Michigan Makers staff observed and helped out. We found that setting aside time for group instruction, rather than just letting people walk in and begin on their own, resulted in more focused work time. We also found that after instruction, this group of children and parents would often combine or modify activities in ways that we had not predicted. We were thrilled to see the creative connections that came out of this group of makers!

This work was made possible by the Institute of Museum and Library Services and the University of Michigan School of Information's Founders Fund.

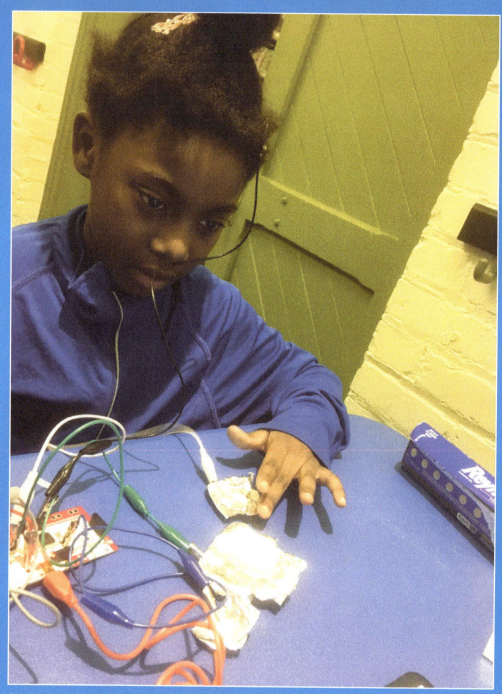

One Ypsilanti District Library maker adapted Makey Makey by clipping one of the wires to her hair and pretending that she was making music with her mind. We loved seeing the twists that each individual child put on the activities that we planned!

Senior Summer Camp, Ypsilanti District Library's Michigan Avenue Branch

As an eight-week pilot project at the very end of Making in Michigan Libraries IMLS funding, our goal with Senior Summer Camp was to build on doctoral student Killian Carucci's work bringing making into a New Jersey long-term care facility[9] and Kristin's personal experiences with senior living facilities. In Killian's work with older seniors in a residential facility, she saw that making could be a way of re-empowering women who, without traditional access to stores, were able to solve real challenges—like a desire for new home decor (solved by 3D printing a vase), a need to repair torn linens (solved by using the space's sewing machine), or a tendency to lose one's sweater (solved by using an electronic embroidery machine to monogram it). The importance of social bonds between mentor and maker were critical components to success in that venue.

Partnering with Joy Cichewicz, the branch manager at Ypsilanti District Library's Michigan Avenue Branch (our partner for Michigan Makers family nights), we set an eight-week agenda with a variety of high-tech and low-tech tools. Tools and projects were selected based on what had been successful in Killian's earlier work as well as the skills, interests, and inventory of the two organizations. While we set a weekly project, we also kept available materials from previous sessions. Our advertised schedule was as follows:

- Week 1: Card making using Silhouette die cut machines, introduction to 3D printing
- Week 2: Photography with smartphones and iPads
- Week 3: Book making
- Week 4: Jewelry making, leather painting, button and magnet making
- Week 5: Digital painting
- Week 6: Cork and leather "woodburning"
- Week 7: Glass mosaics
- Week 8: Maker's choice (glass mosaics)

Based on our evening events, we knew that finding and building an audience would take time—and it did (we had *very* small attendance). We also

---

9 See https://www.mycentraljersey.com/story/life/2018/07/26/reformed-church-home-old-bridge-makerspace/818451002/ or her 2019 CHI paper with Kentaro Toyama, "Making Well-Being: Exploring the Role of Makerspaces in Long Term Care Facilities" at https://dl.acm.org/citation.cfm?id=3300699 for more on this work.

anticipated that most attendees would come from nearby retirement facilities in what is a primarily lower-income African American neighborhood. It wasn't until our first session that we realized that we had layered our expectations with an implicit sense that the attendees would be, as they were in Kristin and Killian's past experiences, over 70, less tech-savvy, and with physical challenges. We carefully considered everything from making a tripod available in case holding a phone was difficult to using digital painting as an arthritis-friendly way to create art.

Instead, we found that the camp attracted vibrant, active, newly-retired seniors—all Caucasian and middle class. One had just retired from an IT job, in fact! The intimate group size fostered savvy conversations, customized activities, and a sense of camaraderie that we enjoyed very much . . . it just wasn't what we anticipated, and we had a nagging sense of missing our target audience.

While the research data collected during this project had not been fully analyzed at the time of production, we do have some practical insights to share here.

Seniors are recognized as an underserved population in libraries . . . but libraries are struggling with how to solve it. Public librarians we have talked with tell us that programming for senior citizens is a gap in their service model. Much more work is needed in libraries to explore how we can best support those aged 65 and up and whether that work should happen within the library or in partnership with residential communities.

Having some events for niche audiences may pay dividends. Many in the maker movement—including ourselves, at times—have extolled the virtue of multigenerational learning. That being said, this experience hints that there may be emotional safety in attending a workshop just for people "like you."

Many of today's seniors in our area are living longer, with better funds and health care than a previous generation . . . and that is a factor worth exploring. Because Ypsilanti was a place where unions were strong (primarily in manufacturing and academia), many of today's retirees—even those considered working class—had great health care benefits, the promise of a pension and Social Security that made retirement in their 60s a reality. There are many here who are retiring very much in the prime of their life, with decades ahead of them. This generation likely remembers their parents not having a similar safety net and were eager to grab the opportunities of retirement when they arose. We would have done well to consider a more nuanced definition of senior citizens. At a minimum, it would have been beneficial for us to distinguish between those in active retirement and those who are slowed by advancing age, physical challenges, or cognitive decline. Needs for the newly-retired, especially those who are still physically mobile, able to drive, and/or still healthy, are distinct from those with physical or cognitive issues. The women we worked with (and we are mindful that our sample size was small) weren't looking to fill endless boring hours, as those in physical decline often complain. Instead, we were one of many activities they were interested in, along with taking community college courses, figuring out how to transfer their smartphone photos, and considering a side hustle.

Marketing matters. Calling this event series "Senior Summer Camp" seemed like a fun way to signal our playful approach. Kristin clearly remembers mentally discarding "Senior Citizen Summer Camp" as a title because it sounded . . . boring. While the descriptive text said this event was for those 55 and up, we wonder if we picked the wrong event title and whether those skimming the list of events thought this was for seniors in high school. Also, the Library uses 55 years as the entry point for senior activities, which may contribute to why we saw younger retirees and not older ones at our events.

Great partners make a difference. In our case, we had Joy as a vibrant and active partner. She had artistic skills, networks, and inventory different from

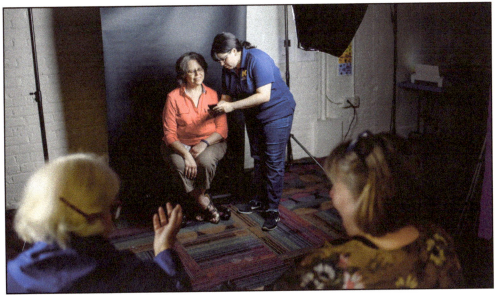

Doctoral student Killian Carucci, who has an undergraduate degree in photography, and Joy Cichewicz of the Michigan Avenue Branch of the Ypsilanti District Library, confer on a portrait during Senior Summer Camp.

our own. As librarians, it's often tempting for us to think we can do everything ourselves ... but if you can find a community partner with complementary skills, the result can be so rewarding. Joy exudes creativity, radiance, and an empowering one-on-one connection, and that kept the room from feeling empty even when attendance was low.

We know that this pilot project is a baby step into making by and with senior citizens, but we include it here because we believe that there is potential for future exploration.

HOW THIS BOOK IS ORGANIZED

All of these experiences led to the creation of this book. Written contributions have been made by some of the many graduate students who have worked on our project. You will see repetition of key beliefs and times that our perspectives overlap or diverge.

The first part of this book, "Establishing Your Makerspace," goes over some of the big-picture discoveries we've made as we've run makerspace programs throughout the state of Michigan that we hope will help you set up your space. We discuss selecting equipment, devising educational plans, assessing learning, funding your makerspace, and defending your makerspace to community members and stakeholders.

The second part of this book gives ideas for different activities that you can run in your makerspace. These are all activities that we have had success with in the Michigan Makers program. We'll discuss equipment you'll need and modifications you can make to adjust activities for different audiences. Finally, the appendices list equipment and tools you might consider adding to your makerspace, as well as giving more information about all of the partner sites that we've worked with over the course of this project.

We hope you'll drop us a line at contactmichiganmakers@umich.edu with your thoughts and with your own project ideas!

REFERENCES

Bagley, Caitlin. 2014. *Makerspaces: Top Trailblazing Projects*. Chicago, IL: ALA Techsource.

Burke, John. 2014. *Makerspaces: A Practical Guide for Librarians*. Lanham, MD: Rowman & Littlefield.

Dougherty, Dale. 2016. *Free to Make: How the Maker Movement Is Changing Our Schools, Our Jobs, and Our Minds.* Berkeley, CA: North Atlantic Books.

Fisher, Erin. 2012. "Makerspaces Move into Academic Libraries." *ACRL TechConnect.* Retrieved from https://acrl.ala.org/techconnect/post/makerspaces-move-into-academic-libraries/.

Hatch, Mark. 2014. *The Maker Movement Manifesto: Rules for Innovation in the New World of Crafters, Hackers, and Tinkerers.* New York, NY: McGraw Hill.

Hinton, Marva. 2018. "Making the Difference." *School Library Journal*, 64(5), 25+.

Kaminski, Robin. 2012. "Westport Public Library Unveils 'Maker Space.'" *The Hour.* Retrieved from https://www.thehour.com/westport/article/Westport-Public-Library-unveils-Maker-Space-8165089.php.

Kriete, Rozanne, and Carol Davis. 2014. *The Morning Meeting Book.* Turner Falls, MA: Center for Responsive Schools, Inc.

Lang, David. 2013. *Zero to Maker: Learn (Just Enough) to Make (Just about) Anything.* Sebastopol, CA: Maker Media, Inc.

"MakeShop." n.d. *Children's Museum of Pittsburgh.* Retrieved from https://pittsburghkids.org/exhibits/makeshop.

Martinez, Sylvia Libow, and Gary Stager. 2013. *Invent to Learn: Making, Tinkering, and Engineering in the Classroom.* Torrance, CA: Constructing Modern Knowledge Press.

Matteson, Addie. 2017. "Invention." *School Library Journal*, 63(2), 39.

Preddy, Leslie. 2013. *School Library Makerspaces: Grades 6–12.* Santa Barbara, CA: Libraries Unlimited.

Severance, Charles, and Kristin Fontichiaro. 2014. *Raspberry Pi.* Ann Arbor, MI: Cherry Lake Publishing.

For a workshop at the Benzonia Public Library (BPL) in northern Michigan, we asked participants to verbalize their makerspace's purpose by imagining that their institution was the cover story for *Make* magazine. This is BPL maker coordinator Jimmy McLaren's design.

CHAPTER 2
PURPOSEFULNESS

Kristin Fontichiaro and Sophia McFadden-Keesling

If you've picked up this guide, it's likely that you either want to start a successful and sustainable maker program or you're already facilitating one and are hoping to glean some tips about how to do it better. Over the past many years, we've started up, run, or observed maker programs in a variety of environments. We've had some stumbles and some successes. We've also talked with a lot of people in schools, libraries, and community makerspaces about where they've found success. And here is one of the biggest secrets to a successful maker program: before you rearrange a room or scroll through a catalog or print up posters, taking the time to ask yourself some fundamental questions is one of the best things you can do.

All maker facilitators (and their bosses!) should be able to answer questions like these:

- Why are we doing this?
- What is this space or program for?
- Who is our target audience?
- What do they want to do here?
- What do we want them to do, create, or learn here?
- What will success look like?

These questions can seem like an impediment. Many of us get excited about doing this work when we see cool tools and engaged people, so our instinct is to grab our credit card and just get shopping! That's human—and we ultimately want our patrons or students to feel that excitement when they walk into our programs, classes, or spaces. But stopping to ask questions like these—as we showed with the Niles District Library in Chapter 1—can help you define where you are going, share that vision with others, and give you a rudder to guide you when the waters get choppy. Instead of thinking of tools first, try thinking about your community instead. What do makers in your community want, need, and aspire to become? The answer to these questions can help you determine your makerspace's *purpose*.

WHAT DOES YOUR COMMUNITY WANT, NEED, AND ASPIRE TO?

At first glance, asking about wants, needs, and aspirations can seem like asking the same question multiple times. Let's unpack those terms:

Wants tend to be things people desire in the moment: I want my library or school to keep up with the times, I want a 3D printer, or I want kids to be exposed to more STEM. These can be helpful for you to know about because they represent gut-level goals or initial steps that may bear fruit. However, *wants* are not always reliable barometers for measurement: you might later discover that these expressions are more nuanced than they appear or that desires can be mercurial. Many makerspaces have fumbled when they have only addressed *wants* for precisely this reason: community members said they wanted a makerspace (who wouldn't?), but this did not always equate to actual visits or repeated usage.

Needs tend to be articulations of necessary items: I need to repair my pants, I need a replacement part for my dishwasher, I need to meet this standard in the Next Generation Science Standards, I need my child to be challenged, or I need to stop losing my sweater. These tend to be more basic and core to our functioning, and if we can fulfill people's *needs* and solve their problems (by guiding someone to a sewing machine to fix the pants, teaching someone how to 3D model the dishwasher part, helping a teacher fulfill curriculum requirements, or helping someone embroider their name on their sweater), then the maker tools, supplies, and expertise we are offering are both meaningful and more essential. This is an important consideration for determining the long-term value of your makerspace.

PURPOSEFULNESS 37

Clarifying people's **aspirations** in your community is another way to frame what would be most useful and beneficial in your makerspace. This method is endorsed by the Harwood Institute (https://harwoodinstitute.org), the design firm IDEO (http://www.designkit.org/methods/2), and University of Michigan researcher Kentaro Toyama (2018). Aspirations help us see where community members want to be in the future. For example, "I want there to be good jobs so my children stay in this community" is an aspiration.

For her mock *Make* magazine cover, an educator at our workshop at the Benzonia Public Library envisioned an after-school discovery space.

So is, "I want young families to move to our community." These are wishes that may take some time to fulfill. But they tend to have a strong emotional quality that, if you can connect to them, can help you get buy-in to your program. When you can link your program to these long-term visions, you can gain support.

Public Data

We can learn about our community or service population's wants, needs, and aspirations through many means. First, it's important to know, as the show *Sesame Street* often asked, "Who are the people in your neighborhood?" What can you discover through public data about who you are serving? Tools like ESRI Tapestry[1], The U.S. Census, and the Annie E. Casey Foundation's KidsCount portal[2] can help you see patterns relating to population, age, housing, household demographics, commuting time, health, and more. Why might you do this work for a maker program? Well, if you discover that there are many single-parent households in your community, you might get an inkling to explore whether quality after-school programs would be a valued event type. Or you might think about having preschool creativity programs on the weekends, when some parents don't have to work. Data won't tell you what to do, but it will help point you toward valuable questions to engage with.

Design Thinking

You can also engage in the Design Thinking process to learn about your community. As described later in this volume, Design Thinking is a flexible set of strategies that helps you investigate a concern, see how various stakeholders respond to it, design and test potential solutions, and refine those solutions based on feedback. To learn more, see these two free guides from IDEO on how to engage stakeholders in conversations: Design Thinking for Libraries[3] and Design Thinking for Educators[4]. Both guides have customized the IDEO process for particular audiences, but community makerspaces can also adapt these protocols for their own use.

---

1 Input a zip code at https://www.esri.com/en-us/arcgis/products/tapestry-segmentation/zip-lookup and gain access to local statistics and consumer profiles.
2 See https://datacenter.kidscount.org.
3 See https://designthinkingforlibraries.com.
4 See https://designthinkingforeducators.com.

For a community workshop at the Pickford Community Library in Michigan's Upper Peninsula, Making in Michigan Libraries workshop leaders Amber Lovett, Kamya Sarma, and Quenton Oakes set out stamp pads and alphabet stamps and invited participants to share the values they wanted to see in a community makerspace.

Community Conversations

Another way of exploring community wants, needs, and aspirations is to adapt the Harwood model of Community Conversations[5], which provides pre-made sequences and scripts you can use to converse with community members about wants, needs, and aspirations in a focus group–like environment.

Discussions with Peer Institutions and Individuals

You can also use informal conversations to discover possible avenues your makerspace could take. If you're at a public or school library, talk to people in your school district, senior centers, and patrons. Ask a vendor at the farmer's market or a cashier when you check out at the grocery store. Keep the questions focused on what would enhance the community, not your space, to keep the range of responses you get as broad as possible.

Conferring with Parents, Guardians, and Caregivers

When trying to create or enhance a makerspace for children, try to discover what their parents and guardians care about. At the end of the day, it's those

---

5 For a version customized for libraries, see http://www.ala.org/tools/sites/ala.org.tools/files/content/LTC_ConvoGuide_final_062414.pdf.

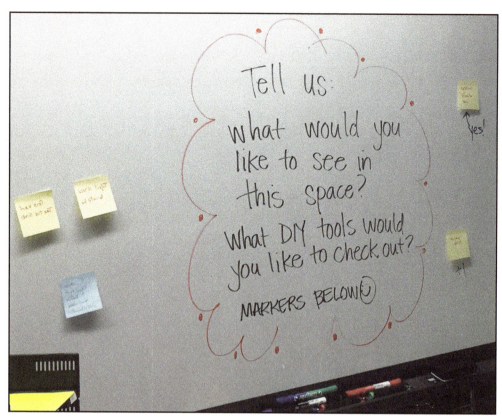

Setting up sticky notes or a whiteboard and inviting feedback can be a simple way for community members to contribute ideas, shown here at the Niles (Michigan) District Library.

caring adults who decide how their children's time is spent and what the family priorities are. By talking with educators and studying the schools' curriculum (usually found on a district's website), you can discover where there may be gaps in the formal curriculum, opportunities to enhance what's happening in the classroom, and what tools and experiences already exist in the school so you can minimize overlap and save money. Ask them what they would want out of a makerspace. Find out what they already make, what they would like to make, and what they didn't know they wanted to make. An interesting observation here, though: over the years, we did notice that parents were more enthusiastic about STEM-themed programs, even though in our interactions with children, they often sustained interest in analog activities for longer.

Library Circulation

If you have a well-balanced library collection, look at sections that deal with DIY: books, DVDs, magazines, etc. DIY material may be spread across different formats, genres, and Dewey numbers. Do a bit of digging. Follow the numbers.

See what materials are being checked out the most. What's circulating? That may be what your community is interested in. See what niche areas you have and where there are areas of overlap. This method isn't foolproof (people can't check out materials you don't have, so there may be bias in your circulation statistics toward topics already in your collection), but it is a good starting point.

Curriculum Connections

If a curriculum focus is needed, review available curricular materials and talk with teachers about desired engagement or extension activities. If your school or local district has adopted the Next Generation Science Standards[6], then you know that there are eight Science and Engineering Practices (SEPs) that underlie every grade level. These practices were ported over from the National Research Council's earlier *Framework for K-12 Science Education: Practices, Crosscutting Concepts, and Core Ideas* and later folded into the Next Generation Science Standards. One possibility for a multigrade makerspace in its formative months is to focus your efforts on these eight practices, knowing that you can make a positive impact across grade levels.

As the SEP's documentation states, "The practices are what students DO to make sense of phenomena. They are both a set of skills and a set of knowledge to be internalized. The SEPs reflect the major practices that scientists and engineers use to investigate the world and design and build systems" (NGSS n.d.).

By going deep in the following eight areas, a library makerspace can make a meaningful and sustained contribution to students' learning journeys without exhausting you in the process:

- a) Asking questions and defining problems
- b) Developing and using models
- c) Planning and carrying out investigations
- d) Analyzing and interpreting data
- e) Using mathematics and computational thinking
- f) Constructing explanations and designing solutions
- g) Engaging in argument from evidence
- h) Obtaining, evaluating, and communicating information

Please see page 42 for a small poster about those eight practices.

---

6 See https://www.nextgenscience.org.

ESTABLISHING YOUR MAKERSPACE

SCIENTIFIC AND ENGINEERING PRACTICES

3. Planning and carrying out **investigations**.

5. Using **mathematics** and **computational thinking**.

8. **Obtaining, evaluating,** and **communicating** information.

2. Developing and using **models**.

7. Engaging in **argument from evidence**.

1. Asking **questions** (in science) and defining **problems** (in engineering).

4. Analyzing and interpreting **data**.

6. Constructing **explanations** (in science) & designing **solutions** (in engineering).

National Research Council 2012. A Framework for K-12 Science Education: Practices, Crosscutting Concepts, and Core Ideas. National Academies Press, p. 42. http://nap.edu/catalog/13165 Images from TheNounProject.com and used with a Creative Commons license.

These eight cross-cutting Scientific and Engineering Principles are integrated at all grade levels of the Next Generation Science Standards, adopted by many American states.

Another way to think about potential curriculum connections is to employ Liz Kolb's Triple E Framework[7] as you evaluate potential activities. This field-tested framework has helped thousands of K-12 educators gain clarity as they try to differentiate between tech-based *activity* and tech-based *learning* by evaluating tools' abilities to enhance, extend, and engage. The framework helps teachers make more powerful choices that lead to a more powerful impact. Take a look at page 44 to view Kolb's model. Replace the model's word "technology" with the word "makerspace" as a way of evaluating the potential impact of stations, tools, or opportunities you are considering.

Asking Youth

If your approach is extracurricular, then your goal is to discern youth interests. One way to do this is by putting up a bulletin board. It can be blank save for a question like, "What do you like to make?" Another option is to put up images of types of projects (e.g., origami, LEGO construction, comics, knitting, or sewing projects) and ask students to sign their names next to ideas that interest them. Be aware, however, that if your library is in a low-income neighborhood where funds for at-home hobbies may not be available, your potential makers may not have extensive exposure to potential tools, projects, or materials. In that case, consider making a "best guess" list and ask for opinions. You might even set aside time just for patrons to explore while they are visiting the library for other reasons, prior to any formal programming.

Connect to the Strategic Plan

A great way to connect your goals to that of your district (or, if you work in a public library, your local schools) is to find your district's strategic plan. Sometimes these are easy to find on the district web page, but you can also do a Google search for "[Your School District] Strategic Plan." This will most likely bring up the plan on the first search page. These are documents that set the priority goals for a school district, looking about five years into the future. Are there goals that you are well-positioned to support? To partner with the district on? Keep in mind that some grants require evidence of partnerships, so merging the needs and aspirations of school districts with those of public libraries may increase your chances of funding. If you do find points of connection, you can then refer to the school district's strategic plan in your future outreach and public relations.

---

7 See https://www.tripleeframework.com.

Triple E Framework

Enhance
1. Does the technology tool aid students in developing or demonstrating a more sophisticated understanding of the content?
2. Does the technology create scaffolds to make it easier to understand concepts or ideas?
3. Does the technology create paths for students to demonstrate their understanding of the learning goals in a way that they could not do with traditional tools?

Extend
1. Does the technology create opportunities for students to learn outside of their typical school day?
2. Does the technology create a bridge between school learning and everyday life experiences?
3. Does the technology allow students to build skills, that they can use in their everyday lives?

Engage
1. Does the technology allow students to focus on the task of the assignment or activity with less distraction (Time-on-Task)?
2. Does the technology motivate students to start the learning process?
3. Does the technology cause a shift in the behavior of the students, where they move from passive to active social learners (co-use or co-engagement)?

Instructional Strategies: Co-Use, Guided Instruction, Interactive modeling, Turn & Talk, I do, we do, you do, Gradual release, Think, pair, share

Liz Kolb's Triple E framework (shared with permission) has been extensively field-tested as a powerful lens for examining the impact of the proposed tech-based activity. If you replaced the word "technology" with "makerspace," where would your proposed projects lie?

LEARN WITH THE UNIVERSITY OF MICHIGAN WITHOUT LEAVING HOME!

Public Library Management

- Are you a new public library manager or director?
- Just want to test the waters to see if moving to management is right for you?
- Want to show your supervisor you're ready for more responsibility?
- Need professional development for a new employee?

Join Kristin Fontichiaro and Lionel Robert, professors at the University of Michigan School of Information, and public library leaders Josie Parker and Larry Neal, in high-quality professional development geared toward public library managers. Study for free or pursue a Verified Certificate to highlight the knowledge and skills you gain. Choose one course or the eight-course Professional Certificate.

COURSES
- Identifying Community Needs
- Managing a Diverse and Inclusive Workplace Personnel Management
- Budgeting and Finance
- Infrastructure Management
- Strategic Planning
- Grant Writing and Crowdfunding
- Public Library Marketing and Public Relations

To find available courses, please visit **edx.org** and search for "PUBLIC LIBRARY MANAGEMENT"
Contact: **publiclibrarymanagement@umich.edu**

 SCHOOL OF INFORMATION
UNIVERSITY OF MICHIGAN

 ACADEMIC INNOVATION
UNIVERSITY OF MICHIGAN

This free course at EdX.org, led by this book's lead author, will help you gain insights about your community.

Additional Resource for Community Needs Work

If you seek additional strategies and coaching to help you learn more about the wants and needs of your community, check out this MOOC (Massive Open Online Course) on "Identifying Community Needs for Public Library Management," on page 45.[8] The MOOC covers how to find demographic and personal data from online sources; conduct environmental scans; lead focus groups and interviews; analyze data to find patterns, overlaps, and gaps in available community services; and synthesize your findings in a report.

SETTING YOUR VISION

Once you know who your community is and what it needs, you're ready to create a vision statement. Doing so will help you synthesize and articulate the needs you've uncovered, the decisions you have made, and perhaps most importantly, how you will define success. This may seem silly—after all, you're the one in charge, so you know this already, right?—but the articulation of a vision will really help you communicate your plans to a supervisor, administrator, educator, grant funder, or community member. It can form the basis of what's commonly known as an "elevator pitch," a short paragraph that you keep in your mind whenever someone asks, "So what is this? And why are we doing this?"

We've learned from experience that the word "makerspace" can mean wildly divergent things to different people. I once fielded a call from a thoughtful, savvy school librarian who was panicked that the administration's maker mania was going to wipe out her library program entirely—she imagined they were planning to replace all things library with all things maker, because that was her mental mindset: makerspaces don't have library stuff in them. As so often happens, the administrators had been wowed by a few maker sessions at a recent conference and wanted to jump on the bandwagon. I asked her to describe what this anticipated takeover would look like. As we talked, she said that what they wanted was some Makey Makey kits on the tables. Wait—just that? We realized that this wasn't the takeover she worried about. She had become overwhelmed by their (undoubtedly forceful) enthusiasm, but given some time to reflect, her common sense told her that she could easily please them and use it as a way to request other things she felt were more suited to the space. She could actually *build* on what they wanted instead of feeling like her information literacy and research curriculum was about to be scrapped. All because this savvy librarian took time to stop and clarify.

---

8 See www.edx.org/course/identifying-community-needs-for-public-library-management for all courses available in the University of Michigan School of Information's Public Library Management certificate.

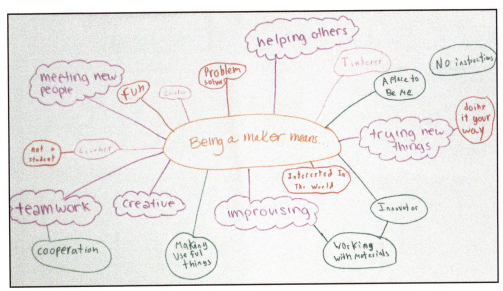

In our first Michigan Makers year, librarian Rachel Goldberg asked students at East Middle School in Plymouth, Michigan, to create a mind map for the word "maker." The exercise helped us solidify our group's collective identity.

Crisis averted . . . but boy, did we learn a lesson about the emotional power of the word "makerspace." A community makerspace likely feels and looks like a mashup between a wood shop, a craft room, and a computer lab. In a classroom, "makerspace" could be the addition of science kits to the curriculum, plus a few bookshelves of tinkering kits and materials to keep kids engaged during downtime. In a public library, it might mean launching new programming related to STEM and/or a set of circulating science or art equipment. In a school library, it might range from centers designed for mental relaxation to cardboard boxes awaiting transformation to digital fabrication tools like a 3D printer. Be sure you have a common definition up front and that you agree on what success looks like: More students entering the science fair? More creative energy in the room? More bodies in the library? Some relaxing down time for stressed, highly-academic students? At this stage in the game, it's tempting for both administrators and educators to fast-forward right to a shopping list. But if you keep the conversation focused on desired skills and outcomes at this stage, you'll gain a sense of intentionality in your planning that will pay real dividends down the road.

You can type your goals up yourself or borrow the maker vision template shown on page 48.

We have worked with hundreds of educators and librarians using this template, and what we find is that it's relatively easy to fill in the observed need

MAKER VISION

Based on _____,
I see that our students/patrons need opportunities to_____.

Therefore, we'd like to launch a maker program that will give them the chance to _____.

In this program, we will prioritize _____.

We will know that we are successful if _____.

We used this visioning worksheet in workshops with educators and librarians. We found that the final prompt was the most difficult for participants to grapple with.

and the resulting action step. But almost every time, we discover that people need a lot of time to determine what success looks like. So often, people are attracted to makerspaces and the maker movement because they feel the energy in the room or in photographs—they see activity happening and get excited. But figuring out what the ultimate outcome is of that effort is a larger question to wrestle with. Ultimately, that outcome should drive the decision-making for the space moving forward.

Some readers may be familiar with the Backward Design approach popularized by Wiggins and McTighe, in which they advocate beginning with the end in mind (2005). If patrons seek careers compatible with stay-at-home parenting, and you could support their craft entrepreneurship (such as opening an Etsy shop), then success could be measured in successful sales. If, instead, your school's need is to improve behavior, then your goal is better-behaved students. You can then create a program that focuses on meditative tasks like sewing or knitting that calm students and help them to focus. And you will know you are successful if you see a reduction in behavior reports about the participating students. In other words, need, purpose, and success become tightly intertwined.

Your maker vision will never be a static document. As your work welcomes new audiences, or new students enter your school, or a new apartment building is built in town, your program will inevitably continue to grow and change. So make it part of your ongoing practice to review your vision (you may find it useful to couple this with the "Makerspace Tune-Up" chapters later in this book). Tie it to an event like payday or the first day of school to help you remember.

CONCLUSION

What you'll find, as you dig in and do this work, is that you will feel a growing sense of importance and seriousness about what you are doing in your space. You're no longer occupied with buying the latest gizmo or chasing the newest trend. You will find that you are more seriously weighing options because your work is in the service of something bigger. And that sense of purpose is ultimately what will lead and sustain your space.

REFERENCES

Hammon, Kelsey. 2018. "Library Workshop Series Offers Skill Sharing." *Dowagiac Daily Star*. Retrieved from https://www.leaderpub.com/2018/08/27/library-workshop-series-offers-skill-sharing/.

Next Generation Science Standards (NGSS). n.d. "Science and Engineering Principles (SEP)." Retrieved November 11, 2018, from https://www.nextgenscience.org/glossary/science-and-engineering-practices-sep.

Toyama, Kentaro. 2018. "From Needs to Aspirations in Information Technology for Development." *Information Technology for Development*, 24:1, 15–36, DOI: 10.1080/02681102.2017.1310713.

Wiggins, Grant, and Jay McTighe. 2005. *Understanding by Design: 2nd Expanded Edition*. Association for Supervision and Curriculum Development.

Setting this makerspace in a neighborhood library helped instructors frame the library as a place of exploration and discovery.

CHAPTER 3
SETTING UP A MAKERSPACE

Kamya Sarma and Kristin Fontichiaro

COMMON EXPECTATIONS, COMMON VISION

Every makerspace has a purpose rooted deep in the needs of the community. It has an identity of what it supports and what it does not. Before setting up a makerspace, it is important that this identity and the vision of the makerspace is communicated unequivocally to the community. Being forthright at the very beginning can help avoid miscommunication, misrepresentation, and conflicts down the line. It will also help identify appropriate funding sources and donors while getting started. (See the "Grantwriting" chapter for funding ideas.) It is important to not lose sight of the mission and goals of the makerspace in order to remain true to what the community needs. A mutual agreement on the expectations creates a strong foundation for the makerspace.

If you are creating a standalone space, then you will want to make sure that you share those expectations broadly and repeatedly over time. If you will be doing maker-type activities in a more traditional format, such as during a school library's fixed schedule or a public library's one-hour event slot, it can still be helpful to set some norms up front. Identify the set of behaviors that will be supported (such as encouraging conversation between makers) and those that will not be entertained in the space (such as removing tools from common work areas or using power tools without training). For youth and adults alike, an orientation session that can walk them through these expectations will ensure that there is no misunderstanding later on. Having these expectations visibly displayed in a makerspace will also help the facilitators engage with and manage the members better. Remember that in many cases, particularly in schools and libraries, signaling what you *can* do that is traditionally not allowed (e.g., talking with one's neighbor, making one's own decisions) may be more important for setting a thriving maker culture than listing what is forbidden.

INFRASTRUCTURE

The first thing to consider before setting up a makerspace is where it will be located. It is common for makerspaces to be part of another organization, like a school or a library. In the case of the Mt. Elliott Makerspace, one of the nation's first makerspaces with a youth audience in mind, it was at the basement of a church in a low-income Detroit neighborhood. Affiliations to larger organizations can aid in bringing a steady stream of members who

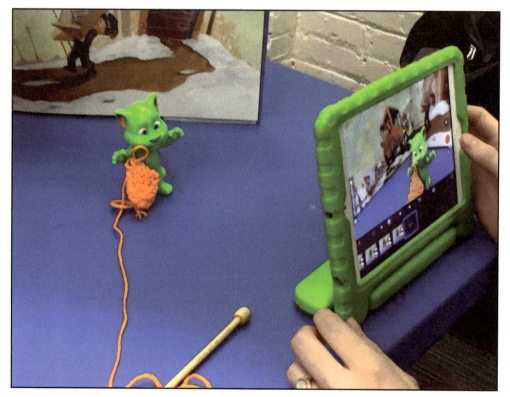

Our workshops at the Ypsilanti District Library took place in a basement multipurpose room. We discovered that some messy activities did not work well in this space, but activities like finger puppets and stop-motion animation were very successful.

already frequent the space. However, it is also important to understand that the target audience for the makerspace might be different from the people who visit the parent organization. Matching these two as closely as possible can maximize the utilization of the makerspace by the community members. The neighborhood that the makerspace is located in, its surroundings, and how accessible a makerspace is also play a major role in determining who the members will be. The location also dictates the kind of activities that the makerspace can support. For example, loud and noisy woodworking tools—and the resulting sawdust!—may not fit into a makerspace situated in a library. Activities involving paint or laser cutters will require proper ventilation and suitable flooring. There are definitely ways to work around any of these problems, but it is always better to be aware of them.

Mobile Carts

It is to be noted that, while having a permanent space certainly has its advantages, a makerspace can also be mobile. Several makerspaces successfully function as curated sets of tools on carts that can be transported and rolled into any space. For example, at the Butman-Fish Branch of the Public Libraries of Saginaw, in mid-Michigan, the staff brings in a cart of craft supplies on wheeled shelving during events. Each in a series of plastic boxes on the shelves holds a single material, such as popsicle sticks.

Rotating Collections in Storage Tubs

Similarly, some libraries have created a rotating collection of maker- and STEM-themed storage totes that are transported between branches or schools for activities. One library acts as the hub for the other branches, conducting inventory, replacing consumables, offering training for staff, and providing simple instructions in each tub. A makerspace can also exist as a hybrid of the two; parts of it mobile and the rest in a physical location. Hence, taking a look at the community's needs and determining the best way to meet them is absolutely crucial for this first step. In a professional development workshop many years ago in Plano Independent School District in Texas, many librarians agreed to each purchase one type of tool (such as Makey Makey, LittleBits, cardboard construction, etc.) and rotate it among the school libraries each month. That way, each library only paid for one tool but gained access to many others: a great, cost-efficient way to minimize up-front costs while testing a variety of possibilities on real students.

Tools like Snap Circuits, shown here in use at a Michigan Makers event at Ypsilanti Community Middle School, are easy to pack away and exchange with other organizations.

Makerspaces on the Road

Some maker and STEM programs are located in motor homes, custom vans, or even converted travel trailers that transport equipment and hands-on activities. For example, thanks to funding from the Herbert H. and Grace A. Dow Foundation, two Saginaw, Michigan, institutions have mobile motor homes that serve as mobile makerspaces. Delta College's STEM Explorer Lab[1] introduces middle and high schoolers to a range of activities that represent the programs available in their community college setting, from first aid

---

1 See http://www.delta.edu/community/youth-programs/stem/stem-explorer.html.

to 3D printing to virtual welding. Across town, Saginaw Valley State University tours its Mobile Research Lab to community locations. While it has hands-on activities such as exploration with pond samples, microscopes, and 3D printers, it isn't just an educational space—it serves as an in-the-field research lab for students and faculty.[2] In 2017, Baltimore County Public Schools in Maryland converted an unused school bus into a portable makerspace[3] with a focus on the district's priorities of coding, robotics, circuits, and engineering tools like LEGO. Fort Hays State University in rural Kansas has made a maker van a critical element in its broader regional outreach plan.[4]

How Much Space? How Can We Best Use It?

The next step is to assess how much space is available and how to make the most of it. At Gretchko Elementary in West Bloomfield, Michigan, the teachers have established a fully functional makerspace for the kids in an extra-wide hallway that connects two wings. The hallway had previously been unused instructional space, but because it was wide enough to accommodate both storage and materials use, it remained safely within fire code requirements. Other teachers there turned what was once a quiet reading corner into L-shaped bookshelves with bins containing materials and the floor as a workspace. At the Zauel Branch of the Public Libraries of Saginaw, a couple of closets have been remade into makerspaces. The doors were removed, and a few shelves were added: some for storage, and others for a table at which to do origami or sew on a small machine. At the time we visited, one was themed toward youth and the other toward teens. Prompts and instructions were printed and posted to facilitate independent interaction, while the open doorways made it possible for circulation staff to keep tabs on makers.

SPACE

Think outside the box: look for any nook or cranny that can be turned into a standalone maker station or a place you can stash materials to be pulled out at event time. Starting small will also enable you to test the waters and change things along the growth of the makerspace without incurring a huge setup cost up front.

As you can see from the models described above, space often determines how your program is structured. Visitors to large public libraries often envy

---

2 See https://www.svsu.edu/dowsciencesustainabilityeducationcenter/mobilelab/requestsvsumobileresearchlab/.
3 See https://www.schoolbusfleet.com/news/719425/district-converts-school-bus-into-mobile-makerspace.
4 See https://www.fhsu.edu/smei/maker-van.

the dedicated space for making, but you can run vibrant making and programming by stashing supplies in a closet and bringing them out as needed. Because both Michigan Makers and Making in Michigan Libraries projects were organized by us but carried out in schools and libraries elsewhere, we have always organized activities around what fit in our cars. Therefore, we never acquired a laser cutter. Sure, our plastic tubs look pretty beat up (especially when winter comes!), but we've made it work. Your goal is design and organization—whether permanent or events-only—that inspires creative action and removes barriers to productivity. Here are some things to consider if you are trying to make space work for you.

The makerspace at the Zauel branch of the Public Libraries of Saginaw is in two adjoining closets.

Flexible and Varied Furniture

Many of us have libraries that still have heavy oak furniture, and moving it for events is a workout! Can you put furniture on wheels so it is easier to move by a single person? Also consider folding or banquet tables—these now come in a variety of sizes to fit your space and number of patrons. Chairs or stools that stack are efficient ways to save space when furniture is not in use. If you have the luxury of standalone space, you may discover that you need a standing tool bench for electronics; standard-height tables for painting, art, and sewing; ergonomic conditions for coding and laptop work; and/or rug space to gather youth makers. Also consider layout within the space—in an ideal setting, there might be spaces for public engagement, private conversation, solo work, energizing group work, and more. Keep in mind that many makers may be introverts who have a greater need for quiet and privacy. Many renovated makerspaces in libraries have glass walls, oversized windows, or doors with glass panels to welcome in potential makers' curiosity. If such space is not available, don't worry—makers are flexible folks by nature. After all, Hewlett-Packard was founded in a garage! Consider, too, that one of the magical things about makerspaces is what Dale Grover of MakerWorks calls "cross-pollination"—when tools and materials are mashed up together to make something new. Maybe your knitters will partner with your electronics buffs to make heatable socks. Or Dash and Dot robots will inspire youth to create their own LittleBits inventions!

Covering Existing Furniture and Flooring

You can also opt to cover what you already have. For example, Benzonia Public Library in northern Michigan keeps a stash of donated vinyl tablecloths for covering tables during events. Not only does it make clean-up quicker, but the tables remain pristine! Whenever we do something particularly messy, we cover the floor in oversized tarps. When we have not (the great Slime Mess of 2019), we've regretted it.

Lighting

Do you have adequate lighting to illuminate detail work such as hand-embroidery, painting of mini-figurines, and more? Niles District Library in southwest Michigan repurposed underutilized basement storage space as its creative space, but lighting for storage was not adequate for these tasks.

Inexpensive additional floor and task lighting from the local big-box store made a terrific difference!

Access to Water

Some projects—from magic beads to basket weaving, watercolor to glass etching—require water. If you have the funds, installation of a sink can come in handy. If not, consider water in lidded pitchers (or small bottles for little hands) to control the flow, as well as dish tubs and tarps.

Safety

Depending on the tools and materials you use, consider whether you need an eyewash station, fire extinguishers nearby, or even an extra smoke detector installed.

Tool Availability

Consider how makers will know which tools and materials are available to them. In permanent spaces, open shelving or pegboard can put everything on display. In other situations, signage can help makers feel safe knowing what they can and cannot do. (And in the case of one school librarian on the LM_NET listserv years ago, make it so that the dozen rolls of duct tape you have saved up for wallet-making doesn't accidentally get all used up on other things!) Clear plastic storage boxes with labels facilitate easy access. Because our makerspace has been on the move for nearly seven years, we endorse boxes with latches!

Electricity

Talk with your facilities manager about the types of tools and equipment you are considering and whether or not there is adequate power for them. Having spare extension cords and surge protectors on hand is always helpful, but you need to know just how many things you can plug in before the system is overwhelmed.

Ventilation

Some maker tools—like soldering irons, 3D printers, and adhesives—may give off unpleasant or unhealthy odors. In some cases, equipment such as laser cutters will require that you have dedicated ventilation hose to the building's exterior. Soldering iron ventilation kits aerate the space around the tool without requiring ventilation to the outside. Read equipment instructions carefully. For large purchases like laser cutters or CNC routers, sales staff can help you know what is needed before you buy.

Walls and Signage

A fresh coat of paint can do wonders for how people perceive your space. Even painting a single wall can go a long way to signal that something wonderful is happening in this space. Some school libraries and public library youth departments have installed LEGO walls where bricks can be added. (Keep in mind that gravity may limit how many bricks you can stack atop one another!) Searching Flickr or the web for other library-based makerspaces can give you lots of ideas. People, as a whole, want to do the right thing, so help them navigate the "rules" of your space by making them explicit. Where are use policies,

At the Chicago Public Library's signature maker lab at the Harold Washington location in 2013, we spied a space where the majority of walls were covered with whiteboard to record equipment settings, file types to use, and other policies and procedures.

safety procedures, and other information located? Having a whiteboard or bulletin board can create a powerful communal repository for information. From listing what file type you can import into Tinkercad to advice on loading your Silhouette Cameo, make it easy for people to do the right thing. We hear from some users that whiteboard paint, while tempting, can be hard to clean.

Bandwidth

Poor bandwidth can really hinder a makerspace. Some new 3D printers now allow print jobs to be sent via Wi-Fi. This is a great affordance for users, but it also adds one more device to your network. Gaming projects can also require more bandwidth. As you consider how your space will be used, take bandwidth into consideration and keep in mind that super-fast internet speeds might even become a selling point for your library!

Cleaning

While many artists, makers, and tinkerers are messier than the average person, having a space that can be cleaned easily is critical. Be sure to rope in your facilities manager as you envision new spaces. They can provide insights ranging from where the garbage cans should be located to how wide aisles can be. Remember that the Americans with Disabilities Act has guidelines for accessible spaces.

Maintenance and Inventory

Maker events can take a lot of energy to run, and proactive maintenance is easy to procrastinate! However, sewing machines run better with regular oiling, 3D printers need occasional realignment of their build plates, and Arduino kits benefit from occasional inventory of their many tiny parts. Try to schedule these activities into your typical workflow. MakerWorks in Ann Arbor uses Merlin Mann's 43 folders as a low-tech way to keep on top of daily, weekly, and monthly maintenance tasks.[5] Each day of the month gets its own folder (31 total), as does each month. Place recurring to-do items in the corresponding folder. Then, each day, staff opens the folder to be reminded of what needs to be cleaned, oiled, or checked. The paper-based method means that if you need to check the settings on a machine each month, you can just put the manual in the folder so it is there when you need it.

---

5   See http://www.43folders.com/.

In our project, where we would unpack the car, set up a space, then repack the car until the next week, we found that taking informal inventories as we packed up—with our Amazon app open to place new orders—helped us stay on top of supply needs. Our team was so busy with graduate school, other projects, and life that we would otherwise often forget. Additionally, despite our concerns about Amazon being a monopoly, the reality was that with all of us regularly working 12-hour days, it was much more feasible for us to order online than to drive to pick out items in person. Additionally, it freed up mileage costs and staff time (and costs) to have items brought to us. To keep track of our own to-dos, we used GQueues.com to organize to-do lists for ourselves, which integrates into Google Calendar.

And Is Your Library the Best Place, Anyway?

Take some quiet time to ask yourself if your space is the best space for making in your school or broader community. Is your library the most-suited place—and do you and/or other staff have the space, ventilation, expertise, capacity, funds, and stamina for the activities you envision? For example, 3D printers may be used in a more sophisticated way in shop or art classes, where there are more contact hours in which students can acquire skills. Similarly, a small-town library may be able to negotiate the use of an unoccupied storefront until a paid renter can be found. Just because someone else's library has a program doesn't mean you have to do it! In Michigan, many communities' school-age populations are shrinking. With less need for classroom space, there may be an unused room in the school building that a school librarian can adopt or that could benefit from being a school/library partnership. Sometimes, a computer lab is being closed because the building has adopted a 1:1 computing program instead. Art programs or shop class may be shuttered for lack of funds, opening up spaces that have already been designed for creative, hands-on use. In public libraries, observe how space is being used. For example, are kids no longer interacting with the play kitchen (perish the thought!), and its removal could free up space for a making table? If your library has an underutilized reference section or an oversized fiction section bulging with faded book spines, could a thorough weeding consolidate enough space for storage or the removal of a few sets of shelves?

TOOLS

Before purchasing any tool for the makerspace, important questions include, "What purpose does this tool serve? Who benefits from having this tool in this space? Are there enough potential users to merit the cost of purchasing this item?" Emily Thompson, a librarian formerly at the State University of New York at Oswego (now at the University of Tennessee–Chattanooga), has told us that she had a "three-department" rule. If she could foresee a particular purchase having value for at least three departments on campus, she would buy it. This resulted in the acquisition of a 3D printer that was used regularly. In your case, it could be an educational tool for children, a professional tool to help the members of your community make and sell their goods, or just a means of entertainment. A makerspace can support all or any of these types of activities, and ensuring that the tool fits within the makerspace's vision will help put it to good use.

Another factor to be considered while selecting a tool is the set of skills required to produce independent and creative work on a particular tool. For example, 3D printing and other digital equipment require a fair amount of 2D and 3D modeling skills and software to produce original work. It would be fine to 3D print models made by others to get familiar with the equipment. However, supporting original work and ramping up the skills to independently use the equipment should be given a higher priority lest the 3D printer become little more than a plastic vending machine. Digital fabrication work (the actual "printing" process) can be outsourced these days to services like Shapeways and Etsy. Thus, you can support your members in creating original work using cutting-edge equipment without actually investing in the equipment. (For more on this, see Chapter 8, "Should Your Makerspace Have a 3D Printer? Maybe.")

While selecting tools, it is important to have a good balance between tools that need training or supervision and tools that can be used independently. These decisions will be influenced by the number of staff members that the organization has and their availability.

STAFFING AND TIME

People who run a makerspace are just as important, if not more, as the people who use the makerspace. The availability of staff members and their attitudes toward the space will impact its growth. There are several ways to staff a makerspace. Before hiring, it is important to figure out hours of operation, tools that will be made available, and the type of activities that will be facilitated by looking at the needs of your community. There are also different models of access that you can provide to the members. Visits could be drop-in or scheduled. The makerspace could be open only for structured "maker time" or programs (a model that is commonly seen in schools). Or member access could be a combination of the above. Finding how many people you need at a given time and what their skill sets need to be can help you choose your staff accordingly.

If funds are available, hiring committed and passionate people who can be on staff all the time will give a consistent face to the makerspace. However, it is important to note that not every individual on the staff of a makerspace needs to be a tinkerer or a maker. There are several administrative tasks in the space where process-oriented people can help: ordering, inventory, scheduling, reminders, project management, and more. A mix of zealous individuals and people with strong administrative capabilities can ensure that all bases are covered.

Volunteers

In our experience, community members overwhelmingly support the *idea* of a makerspace, and even will say in advance that they will help support it. Our own work began with an all-volunteer team. Unfortunately, we have seen too many examples where that has not been proven to be the case. The idea that "if you build it, they will come" (to quote the movie *Field of Dreams*) has buoyed many early maker initiatives that have later fallen flat when those volunteers didn't pan out or had less commitment than anticipated. This can lead to facilitator burnout, frustration, or unmet goals. This is nobody's fault. The reality is that, well, reality sets in. Teachers who cheered on their librarian colleague when she proposed a makerspace in the library often become overwhelmed by the academic curriculum they must cover prior to testing and make fewer visits than anticipated. Volunteers may think they were signing up to be a helper at an event for youth, whereas you were envisioning they would volunteer as workshop leaders once a space for workshops was established. Volunteers' kids get sick and cancel, or they don't interface with your makers the way you'd like.

Does this mean you should avoid volunteers? Of course not—more hands are almost always more valuable, and more mentors means greater breadth of ideas and skills. Just be realistic as you design your program that you don't overdesign a program that is beyond what you have the in-house capacity (time, skills, proclivity) to carry out. Subliminally, volunteers assume that staff will just carry on without them. So be careful when a patron says that if you just bought a $15,000 laser cutter, she'd take full responsibility for learning how to use it and running programs. The desire and eagerness of every volunteer are real, but that's an awfully big investment to leave in the hands of a non-employee.

Hiring Experts

Taking a look at the tools that will be provided, experts can be hired to guide patrons through a makerspace. If this is not possible for all tools, inviting them for monthly workshops or on an hourly basis can help you get the staff and the members of a makerspace trained on a particular tool. If the onboarding process is streamlined with orientations and weekly/monthly classes, it will ensure that staff time is not consumed by fielding questions from the users. Documenting the steps to use tools that are not dangerous can also enable the members to learn and figure things out on their own with little to no help from the staff. For example, MakerWorks in Ann Arbor, Michigan, requires training on tools prior to their use and provides detailed standard operating procedures (SOPs) in binders that walk makers through every step of tool use. Developing a peer learning culture among the members also helps reduce the stress on the staff members. In the day to day running of the makerspace, staff members may burn out, graduate, or move on to different jobs. It is important to minimize the burnout by ensuring that the tasks are not repetitive and that there is a handover process put in place to transfer and retain the knowledge of an employee.

Any public maker event will involve a fair amount of logistics. You may not need this much help to run a makerspace each day. Asking your community members to volunteer for event setup and cleanup will be helpful for such days. And remember to recruit more volunteers than you think you need! FIRST Robotics programs for youth have a service component and can be found in many schools—your need might solve their challenge! Also consider professional or civic organizations that prioritize volunteerism (like the Society for Women Engineers, the Elks, or the ZONTA Club).

FUNDING

To ensure that a makerspace is sustainable, it is important to identify different sources of funds. A makerspace can budget up-front setup costs for tools and space and a steady expense each month for staffing and other resources. Let's take a look at the different sources of funds for both these costs.

Once a list of tools has been identified, setup costs can be estimated. Being a part of a school or a library means that you will have opportunities to look for funding within the organization itself. If you have identified the needs of a community and picked out tools to meet them, receiving federal or state grants will be a possible approach, though they are increasingly difficult to acquire given that so many new programs may have begun prior to yours. In our experience, local funding is the strongest bet at this point in the maker movement. Starting a campaign on Kickstarter or Donors Choose can help you crowdfund your program. If you live in Michigan, Indiana, or Massachusetts, you might consider working instead with Patronicity.com. Patronicity is a newer crowdsourcing platform that, in exchange for a slightly higher processing fee of all funds raised, will take a much more active role in helping you manage your campaign, providing templates, advice about promotions and timing, and more. Gaining a "team member" in this way can make the difference between being able to conduct a capital campaign and not. Be sure to work with your boss on differentiating between start-up costs (for once-only purchases like a sewing machine or Silhouette paper cutter) and ongoing expenses (for occasional purchases like cardboard, fabric, equipment repair, or 3D filament).

But before all this, look at how you can minimize these costs by asking for donations. You will be surprised at how much stuff resides in the garages, attics, and basements of your community. Being specific in what you ask for can help ensure you only receive what is useful. Look on Craigslist or in thrift stores for any items that can fit into your makerspace. Minimizing setup costs can help you get the makerspace off the ground quicker. Again, never be afraid to start small. Do not wait for the procurement of the entire list of tools. Start with what you have and add as you grow.

The next step is to identify a constant source for revenue for the makerspace to function on a day to day basis. If the makerspace is part of a school or a library, staffing, rent, and other costs will be assumed by the organization. If it is to be a standalone makerspace, which is increasingly rare given the difficulty of raising enough funds, or if the parent organization has an insufficient budget, there are several revenue models to ensure the makerspace stays running. Look at spending patterns of your community and their incomes, so that you can identify the best way to fund your program.

Charging for Maker Events

Libraries have been proud that patron activities are free. But this is tricky in the maker movement because what we can afford isn't always enough

A maker at Mitchell Elementary in Ann Arbor shows off his junk box creation: a "rope" that can sustain the weight of many marbles. Junk boxes are one low-budget way to encourage making in your school or library.

to make a finished project that looks cool. Many public libraries absorb the costs of running the 3D printer while charging patrons by the gram or by the minute for what is created. You might provide the button maker and a small number of test buttons, with the patron chipping in if they want more. You might thrift a bunch of knitting needles and give each patron a pair to keep while pointing them toward a donated basket of yarn. Those wanting fancier yarn can provide it themselves, while you provide the expertise. At Karen Klapperstuck's sewing events at the Monroe Township (NJ) Library, she selects and tests the monthly pattern, but patrons provide their own fabric. The library keeps a small stash of donated fabric for those who prefer a no-cost option. Some libraries charge a modest materials fee for larger, more ambitious projects and make scholarships available to those who need it.

DOTTING THE I'S: LEGAL AND PRACTICAL CONSIDERATIONS

Permission for Participation

If you are using anything that could cause harm, or if you want to be able to enforce behavioral expectations, you will want to consider a permission slip for participation. We've enclosed here some language we have used in the past, but we are not lawyers, so please consult with district administration or general counsel about what may be needed for your space. Keep in mind that as an after-school program, there were already school-level emergency procedures in place that we did not delineate here. We have had wonderful luck over the years with youth behavior, but the independence of our stations-based model was not right for all kids, so after the first year, we included language about behavior management.

SAMPLE RECRUITMENT TEXT: WHAT IS THE MICHIGAN MAKERS PROJECT?

Michigan Makers as Explained to Parents

We hear a lot these days about the importance of innovation for America's future. That takes practice! Kids need time to tinker, putter, design, and build stuff. The Michigan Makers project, a service learning activity sponsored by the University of Michigan School of Information (UMSI), is partnering with Mitchell Elementary School to make these activities available for your child.

On Tuesday afternoons this fall (11/15, 11/22, 11/29, 12/6, 12/13), the UMSI mentors bring a skill-building activity or a menu of activities from which your third-grade child can pick. From paper crafts to programming, computer animation to sewing, board game design to comics creation, your child will have many opportunities to explore new skill sets while practicing teamwork, perseverance, and creative thinking. The program is limited to 25 students on a first-come, first-served basis.

Note: Other professionals are really curious about what happens during Michigan Makers, so we often share our findings at conferences, in articles, and even in books for kids! Because of that, we'll ask you to sign a special permission slip in order for your child to participate.

Michigan Makers as Explained to Kids

Do you like tinkering and making stuff with computers, paper crafts, fabric, comics, or circuits? Is the process of making stuff more fun than the final product? If you're answering yes to either of those questions, then you might be a Michigan Maker. During Michigan Makers time on Tuesdays you'll work side-by-side with mentors from the University of Michigan School of Information. Each week, you'll get to pick from a bunch of choices to learn about: from game design to comics, Scratch and computer animation, electronics to sewing, plus more!

For More Information

- For an overview and blog of last year's Michigan Makers activities, visit http://michiganmakers.si.umich.edu.

- Check out photos of last year's Michigan Makers activities at http://www.flickr.com/photos/michiganmakers/sets/.

- Have more questions? Contact Kristin Fontichiaro at UMSI: font@umich.edu or 734.647.3593.

SAMPLE PERMISSION SLIP: MICHIGAN MAKERS

After-School Makerspace Project at Mitchell Elementary School

Parental Permission and Activity Release

I give my permission for _____ **to attend the weekly Michigan Makers meetings on Tuesdays after school until 5:15pm on 11/15, 11/22, 11/29, 12/6, and 12/13**. I understand that all activities will be supervised by a vetted adult and organized by students and faculty from the University of Michigan School of Information.

I understand that my student may be working with electronics equipment and that with that comes some inherent risk. **I give** _____ **permission to work with electronics (including soldering irons, manual tools, wiring, circuitry, LEDs, etc.) under adult supervision and with the proper training.** Neither the University of Michigan nor the Ann Arbor Public Schools nor its students or employees shall be held responsible for any accident.

This club is a collaborative effort involving a number of University of Michigan instructors and graduate students volunteering their time and resources. Making stuff is fun, and it is important that we maintain a productive, safe, collaborative learning environment. I agree that **if the student's behavior falls outside of these boundaries, s/he may be asked to step away from an individual activity or asked to leave Michigan Makers.**

As part of their ongoing professional growth, the University of Michigan team may discuss what they have learned in public blog posts, articles, face-to-face or virtual/online conference presentations, press coverage, and/or published books. They may survey my student or study his/her work. **I give permission for my child's photograph and work to appear in online, multimedia, and/or print products and publications and for my child to speak to the press according to existing District policies. I understand that there will be no remuneration for this and that, unless otherwise discussed with me, only my child's first name will be used.**

I understand that participation is limited to the first 25 third graders.

    Student Signature: _____
    Student Name (printed): _____
    Parent/Guardian Signature: _____
    Parent/Guardian Name (printed): _____
    Date: _____
    _____ I am interested in volunteering. Please contact me!

Licenses

You will want to work with your IT staff to make sure that you are up-to-date on any licenses for software or fabrication tools. This may include acquiring copies of open-source software, such as GIMP, an open-source variation of Photoshop, or Inkscape, or an open-source tool similar to Adobe Illustrator. Also keep in mind that with many pieces of software—such as the Adobe Creative Suite—moving to cloud-based versions, you may need to speak with the vendor about access options. Ask about educational discounts, too!

Warranties and Repair

Hold on to all equipment warranty information. Before hacking (customizing) equipment, you will want to know the circumstances under which the warranty will be voided. You may still decide to jailbreak that iPad, but you will do so knowing what the consequences may be. You may also be pleasantly surprised at the companies and vendors who have user-friendly repair and upkeep policies. For example, our first Silhouette Cameo jammed, and the company replaced it for free. LittleBits will replace broken "bits" at no charge. American Button Machines talked us through how to unjam our button maker, and StepCraft had multiple calls with our staff when missing parts and DIY assembly vexed us. Communal equipment takes a beating, so plan repair costs and time into your overall programmatic plans or purchase a support plan when you acquire new equipment.

Posting Photo/Video Permissions

As this book shows, we are evangelists for photo documentation in makerspaces. During a 2013 visit to the Chicago Public Library's Harold Washington branch, we noticed that they did the same—a digital camera was attached to the end of the front table with a lockable cable. But do people entering your space know their photo may be taken and how it might be used? You may wish to post a notice stating that photos may be taken as users engage with the space and ask patrons to let you know if they do not want their photo taken. We want to stop short of giving legal advice here, so school libraries should check on district media policy to see who can be photographed and how such images can be used. For public libraries, check the existing library policy.

We hope this chapter leaves you feeling informed and empowered to launch or refine your makerspace.

This chapter was written as a result of several interviews with Jeff Sturges, the founder and "conductor" of the Mt. Elliott Makerspace in Detroit, Michigan, now dormant, along with our own experiences. We thank him for his time and insight.

A toy takeapart workshop at the Niles District Library in Niles, Michigan. This library paid close attention to community needs when starting a makerspace, resulting in a unique Skill-Share program.

CHAPTER 4
"HELP! MY PRINCIPAL/DIRECTOR SAYS I NEED TO START A MAKERSPACE!"
Figuring Out What to Buy

Kristin Fontichiaro

I had already been leading professional development workshops on makerspaces for a few years when I sensed a significant shift in the tone of the room. Whereas earlier sessions had been populated by enthusiastic early adopters, the movement had grown so quickly that suddenly administrators were feeling the pressure to keep up with their colleagues. They, in turn, passed the anxiety onto their educators and librarians, who were showing up at workshops with this worry: "My principal says we have to do this—help!"

Being "assigned" maker education can be stressful, especially given that the movement is still relatively young and there are only a few years of research about the intellectual, academic, and social impacts of makerspaces. So how does one know what to do, what to buy, and how to implement things? If you picked up this book because you are a "volunteered" maker facilitator, let's take a look at some potential ways you could start one on a $500 budget.

STEP ONE: ASK THE RIGHT QUESTIONS

These will be familiar to you if you have already read the earlier chapters in this book, but I'll list them here again because they bear repeating:

1. What does a successful makerspace look like? Sound like?
2. What do you expect to see as outcomes? How will you know if I am being successful?
3. Is our goal attendance? Engagement? Changes in the culture of the library? New jobs? How will we document and measure success? How will you ensure I have time for that important work to happen?
4. For youth activities: does this project reinforce school curriculum by providing a new venue or hands-on way to explore what teachers are already responsible for? Or does this introduce new skills and needs?
5. How are you willing to support this initiative? Would you send me to _____ conference? Pay for some new books for kids about _____? What equipment are you willing to buy? How about ongoing materials? Is the expectation that I will transfer existing funds away from another initiative? Hold fundraisers? Write grants?
6. Should events be free or should we charge for materials? How do we handle this for our less-advantaged patrons?
7. Do you anticipate that these events will all be held in the library? In classrooms? In other buildings/organizations?
8. Is this a library-only initiative or are other classrooms/organizations/partners involved?

STEP TWO: PLUG INTO OTHERS' EFFORTS

The best way to get excited about an initiative is to align yourself with others who already are! Feed your RSS reader with these elementary-friendly school and library blogs and keep an eye on what others are doing. Consider these blogs:

- Andy Plemmons's Barrow Media Center blog: http://expectmiraculous.com

- Colleen Graves: http://colleengraves.org/
- Duxbury Free Library's Library as Makerspace blog: http://librarymakerspace.blogspot.com/
- Michigan Makers: http://michiganmakers.si.umich.edu
- Making in Michigan Libraries: http://makinglibraries.si.umich.edu
- Madison Bubbler: http://madisonbubbler.org/
- Laura Fleming's Worlds of Making: https://www.worldsofmaking.com/

And check out these organizations for planning and instructional ideas:
- Engineering Is Elementary: http://eie.org
- Maker Education Initiative: http://makered.org/makerspaces/

There are so many other resources out there, but I would recommend avoiding Pinterest boards at this stage. What you want to see when you're just getting started is not one-off projects but how a library or organization is organizing itself in general and what it has learned. We love Pinterest because it can inspire us, but it also showcases best possible outcomes. And if there's one thing you know about libraries, it's that anything can happen! You want to know what could go wrong, what you might need to wrestle with, and how that library or organization is organizing itself around big questions of making. How are they connecting concepts, ideas, and various age groups? What tricks and hacks have they used to make certain activities work better? And how are they managing to do it on a shoestring?

STEP THREE: SEEK MULTIPLE TOUCHPOINTS IN THE SPACE AT ONCE

One of the things I prioritize when planning for making is having a variety of entry points and options for students. In our elementary after-school programs, it is not unusual to have multiple activities going on in a space at the same time. Now there are definitely times when available funds, staff, or space mean you stick with a more traditional "here is the project we're doing today" approach, but remember that part of what makes making special is the ability to mash up ideas. As you develop your program, consider shifting from one activity at a time to having multiple materials and "genres" of making happening at once. This helps with cross-pollination of ideas and improves the odds that each child will find something appealing to work on. Thinking in *categories* of practice, not just in tools, can help you scale up in popular or well-used areas and keep your purchasing mission-aligned.

Figure 1 shows some common categories of maker activities found in youth maker corners. There are, of course, many others! (See Appendix A.) To minimize the coordination fatigue that can come from starting up too many activities at once, select between two and four categories with which to start your space. Remember that there is always a trade-off between depth and breadth. You don't want to overwhelm yourself by learning too many new things at once, and you want to have enough focus that you can be tracking the effectiveness and use of each category. Remember your "Why" as you choose categories.

FIGURE 1: SAMPLE MAKER CATEGORIES FOR CONSIDERATION IN AN ELEMENTARY LIBRARY

CRAFT	ENGINEERING	CODE	CIRCUITS	DIGITAL DESIGN	NEEDLE AND THREAD
Origami	Tinkertoys	**Robots:**	Paper circuits	Canva.com	Hand sewing
Modeling clay	LEGO	Dash and Dot	Snap Circuits	Picmonkey.com	Machine sewing
Wikki Stix	K'Nex	Sphero	LittleBits	Makebeliefcomix.com	Finger knitting
Recycled material challenges	Strawbees	Ozobot	K'Nex with electrical components	Pixton.com	Knitting
	"Junk box" of recycled materials	**Animation:**	LEGO WeDo or Mindstorm		Crochet
		Scratch			Fashion hacking
		Blockly	Circuit blocks		Embroidery
		Hour of Code			Cross-stitch
		Apps:			
		Hopscotch			
		Scratch Jr.			

If you need an even quicker path to starting a makerspace, Figure 2 shows how one might spend $500 on a starter set for an after-school and lunch-time tinkering program where the focus is on creativity, agency, and personal exploration.

FIGURE 2: SAMPLE PURCHASING LIST WITH A $500 BUDGET

CATEGORY	NON-CONSUMABLE ITEMS	RATIONALE	APPROXIMATE PRICE	CONSUMABLES TO BUDGET FOR LATER
Craft	Silhouette Portrait 2 electronic cutting machine	Kids can choose designs onscreen or create their own for bulletin boards, decorations, greeting cards, T-shirt stencils, or notebook stickers	$199	Specialty paper, cardstock, vinyl or self-adhesive papers (e.g., Con-Tact); replacement blades; replacement cutting mats. FableVision's MakerStudio software (https://www.fablevisionlearning.com/fabmakerstudio) may be a useful add-on purchase.
Engineering	Basic LEGO pieces (real or no-name brand)	Building pieces help students construct toys and prototypes. Basic pieces are more versatile than specialty kits.	$25	None. Some librarians are fond of vertical LEGO walls, tables with LEGO tops, or specialized border tape from which you can hang LEGO creations on the wall, which could be a future addition.
Code	Dash Robot (makewonder.com)	An anthropomorphic robot that can be controlled by remote app or with Blockly programming language. Dash scales up as kids age. Its "personality" makes it conducive to puppet shows and plays, which may increase usage with students who are otherwise not coders. Note: These are programmed or controlled by tablets, so check their site for compatibility	$149	A tablet or smartphone will also be needed to use the accompanying app.
Digital design	Picmonkey.com	Kids can learn to edit photos, create collages, or create simple designs without a log-in.	Free	Paper for printing out designs
Sewing	Basic sewing machine, fabric scissors, thread, needles	Ask for fabric donations! Sewing now appeals to all genders, not just girls! Easy starter projects include drawstring bags, pillowcases, bean bags, and flags	$125	Fabric, thread, needles, buttons, trims
TOTAL			$499	

STEP FOUR: ESTABLISH GUIDELINES AND THINK THROUGH CLASSROOM MANAGEMENT

Healthy maker culture encourages what I call PACE (for more on this model, please see Chapter 5):

- **P**rocess over product
- **A**gency—or student decision-making—over teacher-directed work
- **C**hoice over following directions
- **E**xperimental mindset over failing

If these are values you embrace, take time to think about what it will take in terms of classroom management to balance this new way of working at school with what students already know. Making often takes the training wheels off of students and has them ride solo for the first time. What scaffolds do your students need in place to thrive with reduced structure? How will you help them transition from formal instruction to informal exploration? What will you need to demonstrate or display to remind them of this new way of working? How will you gain their attention when they are engrossed in what they are doing? How should concepts of sharing and collaboration be balanced against the reality that a lot of innovation happens by one person being in the zone—by themselves? Establishing guidelines can help you make this transition easier.

CONCLUSION

Spending time planning before purchasing can feel like a drag. After all, it's much more fun to order equipment and play with it! But making is like any other part of the curriculum: it is in the vision and mental enactment of student activities that educators clarify their expectations and refine their purpose. As the carpenters say, "Measure twice, cut once!"

An earlier form of this article appeared as "Help! My Principal Says I Have to Start a Makerspace" in the October 2016 volume of Teacher Librarian. *Thank you to publisher Edward Kurdyla for granting permission for its inclusion here.*

When you focus on the "why" of a library maker activity, you'll find that specific materials become less important. One of our most engaging events was board game design, easy to do on a budget.

CHAPTER 5
MAKING AND LEARNING

Amber Lovett and Kristin Fontichiaro

MAKERSPACES AND LEARNING

In many ways, makerspaces demonstrate a departure from the realm of traditional teaching. Learning isn't always about sitting in a classroom, and often those who are most drawn to makerspaces may be those who have trouble excelling in school. Depending on the structure and focus of your makerspace, you may have little formal instruction time, although school makerspaces will likely devote more time to traditional instruction than community or private makerspaces. However, anyone who has spent time in a makerspace will tell you that these spaces are instructional in nature.

What makerspaces offer is an opportunity to develop a passion and to explore learning in a way that is personally meaningful. They are also unique because, in many ways, they redefine the roles of teacher and learner. In a makerspace, instruction might take the form of a formal teacher-led workshop. It could also happen on an *ad hoc*, one-on-one basis as makers look to their peers and staff for assistance. Self-directed learning is also an essential part of learning in makerspaces. At times, you might have an "expert" being taught a new technique by a novice. Watching these kinds of interactions happen is one of the most rewarding parts of creating a makerspace. However, while some of these interactions may happen organically, it is still vital for any makerspace leader to know what they want visitors in their space to learn, and how they will accomplish this.

WHAT WE TEACH

Often, makerspaces are talked about as spaces that create opportunities for learning specific skills and literacies, such as knowledge of electronics, sewing, or life skills such as how to mend a shirt or fix your bicycle. Makerspaces can also be constructed around specific in-school disciplines such as woodshop, home economics, the Scientific and Engineering Practices that are the backbone of the Next Generation Science Standards, and more, as discussed earlier.

But makerspaces also teach more intangible skills and qualities, which are harder to measure but which have the ability to profoundly impact a person's life. Some refer to these kinds of skills—such as how to collaborate or how to communicate one's ideas—as "soft" skills. These skills are often closely related to qualities or dispositions such as persistence, courage, and resourcefulness, and they can be difficult to teach in a traditional lecture environment. However, development of these dispositions, habits, and skills prepares people to be self-sufficient and to successfully meet challenges and opportunities in their future. Costa and Kallick (2008) refer to these softer skills as "Habits of Mind,"[1] and if you have observed people working in high-functioning design studios, makerspaces, or STEM labs, you may have seen these in action:

Persisting *and* Managing Impulsivity

Persistence manifests in many ways in high-functioning makerspaces, such as sticking with something even when it is difficult or frustrating or changing one's design to improve its function or aesthetics. Be mindful that persistence is a muscle that must be developed and tested over time. Many beginning makers need quick "wins," like science experiments that can be carried out in a single sitting. More experienced makers may enjoy a challenge and benefit from struggling with long-term skills development, like shifting from the visual programming language of Blockly into a professional, text-based language like Java. In order to be able to persist, we have to learn to manage our impulsive natures. A makerspace can stimulate our impulses. There is so much to look at, so many tools and materials to explore, moving purposefully and deliberately through the space and getting focused can be difficult, particularly for young makers. This is part of why we believe in bringing back past activities and materials over and over: once the novelty wears off, it can be easier for makers to "sink into" the work.

---

1 You can read more about these Habits of Mind via a free chapter preview at http://www.ascd.org/publications/books/108008/chapters/describing-the-habits-of-mind.aspx.

Listening with Understanding and Empathy

Listening is a composite of many skills: being in the moment as someone speaks, trying to hear others' perspectives and points of view, and listening for subtext. The "Empathize" stage of the Design Thinking framework is a wonderful chance to practice this habit because empathy for others' needs is explicitly outlined in the model.

Thinking Flexibly

Examples of flexible thinking include making alternate choices when a preferred tool or material is not available or shifting from following one's own preferences to designing for others. Because Design Thinking promotes prototyping and iterative (repeating) rounds of design, it naturally develops this habit of mind.

When making is both personal and aesthetic, taking time to listen with empathy is even more important. Photo taken at Senior Summer Camp at the Ypsilanti District Library's Michigan Avenue Branch.

Thinking about Thinking (Metacognition)

If you are a school librarian or classroom teacher, then you are already familiar with the value of stopping and having students reflect on process, product, and working relationships with peers. In a makerspace, it can be just as important to save time to reflect. Especially when students are at awkward growth points, stopping to see how far one has come is particularly important. This is another reason why we love to bring back the same activities and materials—students can see how their skills have grown with experience.

Striving for Accuracy *and* Taking Responsible Risks

While we support open-ended exploration in makerspaces, accuracy matters. When it comes to lighting up your LED ("light-emitting diode," a kind of light bulb with two "leads," or "legs"), one lead must connect to the positive side of the battery or circuit, or the project stays dark. Using a soldering iron requires safe tools like Helping Hands,[2] a heavy tabletop base with alligator clips to hold your work so your hands don't come in contact with the soldering iron. A game piece made from Shrinky Dinks needs the proper temperature to work its magic. Responsible risks also mean facilitators consider in advance which tools can be used without training or supervision (e.g., K'Nex and LEGO) and which may need oversight or support (e.g., power tools and chemicals).

Questioning and Posing Problems *and* Gathering Data through All Senses

We want students to ask questions and explore the world. Makerspace *culture* is important here: establishing an environment in which questions are welcomed, explorations are encouraged, and room is made for, "Let's try it." In a well-functioning makerspace, we see makers who are more attuned to the materials, textures, and details of the world around them. Think about the five senses: touch, smell, taste, hearing, and seeing. We see makers who stroke fabrics, run their fingers through Mardi Gras beads donated to the Junk Box, or are keenly aware of the sounds (and smells!) of a 3D printer as it runs. This sensory input can provoke new ideas and tickle makers' imaginations.

Applying Past Knowledge to New Situations *and* Remaining Open to Continuous Learning

In creating makerspaces for learning, we want to create an environment in which there is opportunity for progression over time. A paper circuits project

---

2 See, for example, https://www.harborfreight.com/helping-hands-60501.html.

A participant at Senior Summer Camp at Ypsilanti District Library's Michigan Avenue Branch saw a 3D printer in action, then went home to tinker with Tinkercad.com's online 3D modeling software. The result? These bling-y gold initials representing the names of the maker and her husband.

(see Part II of this book) may introduce makers to the concepts of circuitry, but over time, the makerspace, program, or events available should give students the opportunity to expand that knowledge into new and more complex explorations of circuits. We want to keep the horizon wide and to encourage students to see errors as part of the growth process.

Creating, Imagining, Innovating

A learning-centered makerspace is not merely full of activity or "hands-on" experiences. It's "minds-on" as well. Makers should be striving to do more than follow the directions and replicate the work of the facilitator. In 3D printing, for example, it does take some practice to learn how to import a file into the 3D printing software, to determine whether or not the object needs a "raft" (a disposable printed base onto which the desired object is printed) or supports (temporary stalagmite-like columns that "hold up" cantilevered parts while they print), and to get a sense of how size and scale translate from screen to printer. It makes sense to use a file from a free 3D models site like Thingiverse.com or MyMiniFactory.com while you master the mechanics. But is that creating, imagining, or innovating? No! That is merely the 21st-century version of learning to make a Xerox copy. The real creativity comes in learning how to 3D model, how to adapt existing models so they are fit to purpose, and how to use the resulting printed objects to solve problems or bring aesthetic joy. Remember: learning the mechanics is easy; *applying* the mechanics is where the learning happens.

Responding with Wonderment and Awe, Thinking Interdependently, *and* Finding Humor

Our work has always been driven by three words we learned from Dale Grover, co-owner of MakerWorks, a for-profit makerspace here in Ann Arbor: "Tools + Support + Community." Makerspaces should have *tools*, of course. It should have *support*: peers, mentors, and others who can help you when a machine breaks, you realize you don't know how a parallel circuit works or why you need one, or the Snap Circuits fan flies off the base and behind the library's bookshelf. But it also should have *community*: the people who help you celebrate a new step, a new project, or a new idea. Your community is made up of the people who laugh and hand you a seam ripper when you've sewn your finger puppet to your pants. Again. In a high-functioning makerspace, care is taken to appreciate the impact of one's decisions on the group, to make a positive addition to the group's goal, and to think of *we* over *me*.

As has been said throughout this book, there are many "right ways" to have a makerspace as long as the mission is clear and agreed upon by all stakeholders. Kristin knows of a high school in a Western state where the goal was to have a safe, warm place to keep high schoolers occupied before school started. That goal—not STEM learning, Design Thinking, or any other learning goal—was embraced by building administration and staff alike. Our Michigan Makers work has always leaned toward creating a safe, loving place where mentors share their interests and where kids are free to explore, knowing that help is there when they need it. Many schools are creating new STEM curricula, with Hour of Code, LittleBits, and programmable robots at the core of the work. Ultimately, we see makerspaces as a place where youth and adults can become more well-rounded, self-sufficient, and equipped to engage meaningfully in their world, rather than acting as passive consumers.

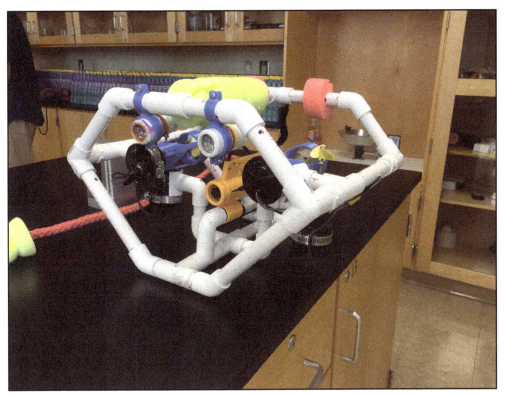

Students at Frankenmuth (MI) High School build and compete with underwater remote-controlled cameras.

LEARNING HOW TO LEARN

Another way to think about making and learning is this: makerspaces teach people how to learn. The self-reliance, problem-solving strategies, and attitudes which can be cultivated in makerspace environments can be transferred to new situations. And in terms of versatility, learning how to figure things out is more valuable than knowing a single skill or having deep content knowledge in one area. So, while every user of your makerspace might not end up using their newfound soldering skills in their daily life, they may well remember the confidence and self-sufficiency they felt, or the way they overcame their anxiety or fear of failure. Maybe they won't remember very much about how electricity works, but they'll leave feeling confident that they could find the answers they need to troubleshoot their personal electronics and knowing how to ask for help when things go wrong. As a maker facilitator, you establish the *culture* of your space: you signal—explicitly or implicitly—what and who is valued. Amber likes to consider these "It's OK" principles:

1. It's OK to fail. Learn from it and keep trying!
2. It's OK to be afraid—but don't let that fear stop you from doing something!
3. It's OK to get inspiration from others.
4. It's OK to ask for help!
5. It's OK to help others and share what you have learned.

HOW WE TEACH

We believe there is a reason that we have seen transformative learning take place in makerspaces. As shown in the Habits of Mind exploration above, we see support for the idea of makerspaces in many educational models and theories, and have found it tremendously valuable to reflect on how these ideas can inform how we teach in maker environments. This section will give you an overview of some of these ideas, and specific strategies on how to integrate effective instruction in your makerspace.

Connected Learning

One of the models which has been popular in education recently is Connected Learning[3]. This approach combines many of the ideas of other learning theories into one model, and we find that makerspaces fit naturally within it. The basic idea behind the original Connected Learning model is that peer culture, individual interests, and academics are all interconnected and all influence student learning. Students learn from peers, at home, and in other contexts, not just in school. And this learning is most powerful when it is personally relevant and interesting to students. Learning in formal academic contexts can support and further the learning that takes place outside of school, while drawing on students' knowledge from other contexts to develop deeper understanding. This may sound like old news to educators, and in many ways it is built upon well-known research and established theories. What makes Connected Learning a little bit different is that it also emphasizes hands-on production of products, cross-generational learning, and the linking of distinct learning environments in what it calls an "open network." Makerspaces are a perfect way to support all three of these unique features. Not only do makerspaces incorporate hands-on learning and creation, but they can do so by harnessing the skills of experts in a social learning environment that allows exploration of personal interests.

---

3 https://clalliance.org/about-connected-learning/.

Multiple Intelligences

Another way of looking at the value of makerspaces is through Howard Gardner's famous theory of multiple intelligences and learning styles. Gardner proposes that each one of us possesses some degree of intelligence in eight key areas (verbal, logical, spatial, kinesthetic, musical, interpersonal, intrapersonal, and naturalistic), though we may excel more at one than others. There is not one best learning style, and each individual is capable of learning in many different ways. However, makerspaces are uniquely suited to teaching using kinesthetic and spatial means, which can be a way to reach out to learners who struggle with traditional modalities of text or lecture and watch them shine!

THE ROLE OF THE INSTRUCTOR

The traditional model of education involves a teacher who is the "expert" and who is imparting knowledge that they have to students, often through

Michigan Makers mentor Kelsey Forester works with a student at East Middle School in Plymouth, Michigan, to hack PowerPoint into a stop-motion animation tool.

lecture or other means. This is often referred to as the "Sage on the Stage" method of teaching. This is a method which may be used in makerspaces in situations like a one-off workshop which teaches a specific skill that all participants need.

However, most often the "teacher" in a makerspace is more of a facilitator: someone who creates a space conducive to learning and equipped with the tools and resources necessary for learning a given concept or skill. Instruction in this kind of environment is more likely to be aligned to the "Guide on the Side" model, in which the instructor might demonstrate, provide context, and otherwise guide learners as necessary.

Some question whether even a facilitator is needed—why not set makers loose to explore on their own? We believe that there are numerous reasons why facilitation helps. First, it keeps the space emotionally and physically safe for learners. Secondly, we do not believe that STEM kits or other maker tools substitute for teachers (see "Beware the Magical Object" elsewhere in this volume). Left to their own devices, most youth makers would be happy to "drive" a robot around the room via remote control. Yes, the kids who already like coding might open the programming app, but they are already advantaged. Facilitation helps us have confidence that most, if not all, students in a learning-focused makerspace are, indeed, learning. Consider Toy Takeapart (see Part II of this volume). Taking apart toys is a fun act of deconstruction. Add a facilitator who can point out various components, discuss how the toy works, and help connect the dots between the toy's exterior switch and the interior circuit board, and it becomes a lesson on circuit boards that paves the way for learning about Arduino microcontrollers.

Another way to think about facilitators is by thinking of yourself—and hopefully additional staff or volunteers—as a *mentor*. Our project, Michigan Makers, has always run on the mentor model. A faculty member serves as project director, but event activities are designed and led collaboratively with graduate students from the University of Michigan School of Information. While we have some activities that we run repeatedly with youth (such as Toy Takeapart, making paper flashlights as an introduction to circuits—an idea we borrowed from Baltimore's Digital Harbor Foundation—and hand sewing finger puppets to quickly build sewing confidence), we flex our offerings to mirror the graduate students' hobbies and interests.

Early mentor Kelsey Forester was curious about how she could repurpose Microsoft Office tools to serve more creative purposes and tried out

PowerPoint-based stop-motion animation. When Sarah Cramer joined our school from a children's literature program, she organized a small group of writers to create a Choose Your Own Adventure–style story. Rachel Moir loved photography and comics, so she taught kids to edit photos with Pixlr and to create one-page comics (using the same page layout described in the Zines chapter later in this book), culminating in a ComicCon, where comics creators swapped copies with their "fans." Tori Culler's knitting hobby led to multiple nights of finger knitting. Sandy Ng wanted to re-create the wonder of the egg drop she remembered from competing in Science Olympiad. Mayank Khanna asked his mother back in India to send wooden stamps to apply to fabric. It bears repeating that we had this flexibility because we have worked as an after-school program in elementary and middle schools and with family programming in public libraries. If we were in a school library or a discipline-specific middle school classroom, we might choose different activities.

Your community is full of people with unusual and intriguing hobbies. Bringing in mentors can be a great way to raise the expertise in the room—and remember that not all mentors are adults! In the early days of Minecraft, a graduate student was the teaching assistant for a middle schooler, not the other way around. A mentor model also reduces overreliance on any one

Mentor Tori Culler (left) works alongside two makers at the Ypsilanti (MI) District Library.

exuberant facilitator who, if she changes schools or moves to another library branch, takes all the in-house expertise with her.

Who makes for a good mentor? Amber suggests you look for people with these traits:

- **Charisma** to engage and inspire action through excitement
- **Humor** to keep things light and fun, even when there's learning going on
- **Patience** to issue challenges, and help work through resistance and apathy
- **Love** to show that you care, and that you are invested in their engagement and success (Love doesn't mean letting makers take the easy way out—it means knowing how to gently push them to do a little bit better each time.)

On a more pragmatic level, be sure to consult with your school district, church leadership, or library administration about how to onboard volunteers. Increasingly, institutions are asking for background checks or requiring training of volunteers before they can work with youth.

LEARNING ENVIRONMENT AND VALUES

Think critically about how the values and vision for your makerspace are reflected in the learning environment you create for students. Everything from the messages you write on the board to the level of free access to tools and materials send implicit or explicit messages about the expectations and values for your space. Having a clear vision and expectations is essential to creating a successful learning environment.

Setting Expectations

Consider the following questions as you develop your expectations:

- What behavior is appropriate or inappropriate in this space?
- How are learners and teachers expected to behave?
- What snacks are allowed?
- What items can be taken home? What stays?

- What counts as making? Where are the boundaries between making and messing around?
- Who cleans up? When does clean up happen?
- What are the consequences of inappropriate behavior?

Michigan Makers mentor Rachel Moir modeled comic storytelling at Mitchell Elementary School in Ann Arbor, Michigan.

- How do we treat each other?
- What kind of language do we use?
- When is it OK to ask for help?
- When is it OK to abandon a project?
- What are the expectations for adults versus children?

These expectations should be explicit and evident in your space. Parents, mentors, and other adults should be aware of and expected to uphold them as an example to children and youth. When we were traveling the state of Michigan holding MakerFest events (our name for Maker Faire–style events) in various small and rural communities, we realized that some parents seemed to be overly directing their children's open-ended experience. Of course they were—we hadn't given them any guidance about how we hoped they would engage with their children! In response, we came up with a half-page flyer shown on page 97. When we passed out the flyer, we instantly saw parent behavior change: they stepped back to allow their children to learn through exploration. Like people say, when we know better, we do better. And we all want to do better!

INSTRUCTIONAL STRATEGIES

Throughout this chapter, we have emphasized facilitation over more didactic forms of teaching. Here are some strategies you may find useful:

Use a "Morning Message"

When we first partnered with Mitchell Elementary School in Ann Arbor, principal Kevin Karr asked us to write an after-school version of the Morning Message his teachers were adopting from the Responsive Classroom model discussed in the book *The Morning Meeting* (Kriete and Davis, 2014). To minimize student cries as they enter the room saying, "What are we doing today?" (which can be an anxious moment for learners and an annoying one for facilitators), a Morning Message—written on a class whiteboard, on flip chart paper, or simply on a piece of paper next to a sign-in sheet at a public library event, is a letter from the facilitator(s) to the makers. Our Michigan Makers after-school "morning message" was usually two columns: a letter from us to the makers and a list of the activities available that day.

Work at It, Ask a Friend, Ask Three before Me, Ask Google, Collaborate!

We cannot possibly offer one-on-one assistance to all makers all the time, yet many makers—not just youth!—frequently request assistance or individual attention. While this is at times appropriate, we have found that most of the

Welcome to MakerFest!

We're from the Michigan Makers program at the University of Michigan School of Information. We've organized this event in partnership with your local library to bring an evening of open-ended learning and exploration to your area.

Our goal is to facilitate learning through doing. That means we may be a little bit more hands-off than what you're familiar with to allow kids to figure things out on their own. This approach also lets kids create or experiment using their own creativity, without feeling pressure to do the "right" thing.

We emphasize
Creativity

Open-endedness

Improvement; learning through mistakes

Productive fun

Doing our best work

Being kind with our words to ourselves and others, offering positive feedback or constructive criticism when asked for

Resourcefulness and problem-solving

Asking for help when stumped

We avoid
Everyone making the same thing

Telling people what to make

Perfection

Reckless or destructive play

Working as quickly as possible or making the most things

Negative talk about our own work or unsolicited criticism of others' work

Giving up easily or having someone do it for us

Relying on others to prompt us forward

SCHOOL OF INFORMATION
UNIVERSITY OF MICHIGAN

INSTITUTE of Museum and Library SERVICES

This project is made possible in part by the Institute of Museum and Library Services RE-05-0021-15.

A flyer distributed to parents at public events during the Making in Michigan Libraries project.

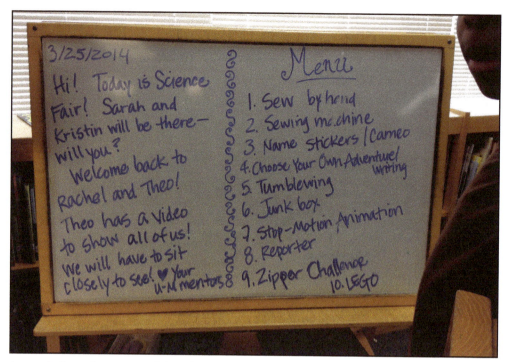

A sample "morning message" for Michigan Makers at Mitchell Elementary School in Ann Arbor, Michigan.

time makers are simply bypassing hard work by asking for help. Nudging them to put forth the appropriate effort to resolve their challenge often does the trick. If not, we ask them to try to solve problems as we often would—by searching online or talking to a trusted colleague. "Ask Three before Me" is often used by primary grade teachers to titrate the deluge of questions: students should be encouraged to seek help from one another prior to asking the teacher. This helps the teacher have the time and bandwidth to focus on the big challenges, as the little ones generally can be resolved with peers.

Train the Trainers

The roles of teacher and learner are fluid in makerspaces. Particularly in community and private makerspaces, it is unlikely that the instructor will be a trained educator. Young children might teach their peers something which they have been taught previously by you. The next minute, they might be teaching their parents or another adult the same thing. Your goal is not to be the sole expert in the room (from an organizational perspective, healthy institutions do not rely on a single expert if they want long-term sustainability), but to develop the *overall capacity* of the program or space.

Teaching with Your Hands behind Your Back

Children and youth in particular can sometimes struggle with the idea of demonstrating and instructing rather than taking over. Teaching with hands behind your back is an easy rule to implement that helps everyone in your space remember that teaching someone requires you to allow them to do the work for themselves. A variant for peer makers sharing a computer is for one person to be the "driver" (who types on the keyboard and uses the mouse) and the other to be the "navigator" (who decides what should be clicked on next).

Each One, Teach One

If you learn it, you must teach it! Establish expectations for everyone involved in a makerspace that they must share their knowledge with—i.e., teach—each other. This helps to build a culture of knowledge, idea exchange, and peer mentorship which builds a sense of power and responsibility among youth. It also lessens the load on formal teachers.

Professor Charles Severance, who has had millions of students enroll in his online MOOC courses about Python programming, had never used the beginner's programming language Scratch. He learned from a Michigan Maker tween at East Middle School in Plymouth, Michigan.

One-on-One Meetings

Meet with makers individually whenever possible to better understand their personality and interests. This will help you assess your offerings so you can better engage makers and meet them at their center of gravity. These personal relationships will also help you know who has particular skills and interests so you can match makers with mentors. As you adjust your offerings to match the makers in your space, you will also help to ensure that you stay relevant and that makers keep coming back.

Providing Context and Examples

Before beginning a project in which you are teaching, be sure to provide an overview of what participants will learn, what they will create as a part of that process, and how they will know when they get there. This is a very valuable strategy for a group and can help preemptively answer questions in addition to inspiring interest and sparking creativity. Throughout the process of instruction, showing examples is a valuable way to make sure that everyone knows if they are on the right track.

Challenging the Status Quo

One strategy which can be used to stretch understanding or redirect energy is by adding a constraint question to your maker feedback. This can be a tool to encourage youth to try something more difficult, and it also helps them to refocus if they have wandered off-task. Some ideas for challenge phrases:

- Can you do it without the help of _____?
- What if you did it _____ way?
- What would happen if you changed _____?
- Do you think you could make it out of _____? How would that change _____?

Short- vs. Long-Term Projects

Depending on the structure of your makerspace program, it can sometimes be difficult to plan longer-term projects. Particularly if you are a community-based makerspace with variable attendance, planning projects which can help scale understanding over time is a challenge. One strategy is to consider building pathways of iterative projects. Think about the kinds of projects you can do within 5, 10, 15, 30, and 60 minutes. Projects of variable length that explore similar materials or concepts and can build into multiday projects require a lot of thought and planning, but they are essential in order to build transformative learning.

Consider a "Reporter" Role

Sometimes, a makerspace which offers complete open-endedness can be overwhelming, particularly for children who are used to more structured environments. If a child is struggling to find something to do in your makerspace, consider adding an option for them to be the reporter for the day. They can take pictures and videos and observe others' activities. We found that after about 15 minutes of watching, our reporters usually figured out what they wanted to do.

Determine What Really Matters

Our after-school Michigan Makers work has been guided by what we call the PACE model:

- **Process over Product.** We try as much as possible to allow children to work through the process on their own. Direct instruction is minimized except when needed to impart specific skills (e.g., how to solder, how to link to CSS) or when safety is at risk. Instead, we focus more on providing pathfinders, mentors, marination or thinking time, and nudges.

- **Agency over Teacher-Directed Work.** Who's supposed to be learning, anyway? Whose job is it to untangle the complicated stuff and figure it out? We believe that it's the kids who should be tackling these problems as much as possible. Similarly, we believe that kits can build skills but that they are not a substitute for open-ended thinking and synthesis.

- **Choice over Following Directions.** We strive to give students options within reasonable limits, though the age of the makers will impact the range of choices. We also differentiate between what we believe everybody needs to know from interest-driven possibilities.

- **Experimentation over Failure.** Making is an iterative design, and that means rapid failure is a part of the process. Creating stuff that matters often takes more than one try. Think of all the attempts it took Michigander Thomas Edison before he had a functional light bulb or audio recording device, or the number of vacuum cleaner prototypes James Dyson tinkered with before settling on his revolutionary model. Inventors know that it takes experimentation over time to lead to something great. However, many of the children you teach have been taught over time not to persevere beyond their first attempt. After all, it's contradictory to tell students that everything is a prototype and not a failure when this is not true in their classrooms. To combat the fear of failure, we need to build mental muscles for this new flexible way of working. Makerspaces are safe places to stretch those muscles through experimentation and iteration.

With guiding principles like these, it becomes easier to evaluate potential tools and activities. Ask yourself questions like, "Given what I/the school/the library/the community wants this makerspace to be like, is this a fit?"

In the next chapter, we'll delve further into how we can keep makerspaces' special learning culture when reality creeps in and we need to measure what has been learned.

REFERENCES

Costa, Art, and Bena Kallick. 2008. *Learning and Leading with Habits of Mind: 16 Essential Characteristics for Success.* Arlington, VA: ASCD.

Kriete, Rozanne, and Carol Davis. 2014. *The Morning Meeting Book.* Turner Falls, MA: Center for Responsive Schools, Inc.

Is this an intentional design or merely whimsical? Combining open exploration with easily-implemented assessment strategies can help you find out.

CHAPTER 6
MEASURING LEARNING

Kristin Fontichiaro and Amber Lovett

At this point, if you are a makerspace educator working in a school, you may be wondering how exactly you are supposed to grade the kind of open-ended work that happens in makerspaces. And even if you are a private or community organization which is not subject to the same standards of student accountability as a school, you may still wonder how to measure if your makers are learning something. In schools, we often hear, "What's measured, matters," and we believe it's only a matter of time before makerspaces start showing evidence of growth lest they lose viability.

There is no doubt that assessment is difficult in makerspaces. Providing a rubric for open-ended work is not only challenging, but it also limits creativity and can result in children creating a bunch of similar projects which check all your boxes but demonstrate little original thought. Our strategies for assessment in makerspaces center around assessing the *thought* behind a project rather than the product itself.

MEASUREMENT STRATEGIES

So, how do we assess makers' thinking? Here are some specific strategies which we believe are realistic and easy to implement in both school and public library makerspaces. If your maker work is in informal settings like scout troops or public libraries, you can still use these techniques without the measurement. They often bring a lovely completion to an event.

Title:Subtitle

One of the simplest strategies we have for getting students to express their thinking behind a project is what we call "Title:Subtitle," which asks students to name their own project after they have completed it. Here, the "title" is something creative, artistic, or otherwise attention-grabbing. The subtitle includes the more straightforward and detailed explanation. A well-crafted Title:Subtitle is engaging and exploratory in equal parts. Without having to ask students to write more than a sentence, you get an idea of their vision of the project.

You might be wondering why we don't just ask students to title their work and save the effort of coming up with a subtitle as well. Consider this example:

In a workshop hosted at the University of Michigan School of Information for classroom teachers and librarians, participants used Title:Subtitle to describe their invention for helping new kids navigate school on their first day.

At an independent school conference several years ago, mentor Alex Quay and Kristin challenged the teachers in attendance to solve a back-to-school challenge using only recyclable/disposable materials they had found in their hotel room. (No Gideon Bibles were destroyed during this activity!) One group made a complex and fascinating robot and, when asked to title it, gave it a title written in binary code (a series of 0s and 1s). Kristin pushed back, saying the title didn't reveal insight about why they made the invention they did. Needless to say, the teachers thought Kristin was a real stick in the mud. They wanted to be witty and fun; we wanted insight. The compromise was Title:Subtitle. You can thank those teachers for this.

Examples:

- Taking Flight: Paper Airplane
- MonkeyMatic: A New Toy Using Centrifugal Force
- Origami Leia: A New Star Wars Toy

Process Journals

Process journals are a more traditional way of getting at the thought process, ideas, and inspiration behind a project. They are meant to capture thoughts, ideas, and goals at the daily level. Rather than waiting until the end of the project to reflect, as is typical in school, process journals capture learning as it happens. For many years, teachers used student blogging sites for work like this, but you can use any number of options. Kristin sometimes has students keep a Google Doc where, each day, they put that day's reflection *on top* of previously written content, creating a reverse timeline. This way, she's only tracking one document per student (not one per student per day), and she can easily scroll down to answer questions like, "Just how long has he been doing 'research' for his project?" or "How has this project evolved over its existence?" Social media offers great possibilities for process journals, in the form of Instagram posts, private Twitter and Facebook posts, short videos, and more. (Check your organization's guidelines as well as site requirements that may limit youth participation to those over age 13 in the U.S.). Process journals document the project as it develops through stages, and they are a great tool to use to showcase to stakeholders how your makerspace is creating meaningful learning. They also preserve the messiness inherent in making, which is often glossed over in a product-focused environment.

Stand-Up Meetings

Haven't we all been in one of those meetings that never ends, and yet also never accomplishes anything? Stand-up meetings are a strategy that businesses use to make meetings less terrible—and you can use them, too! The goal is to keep the meeting short—and by standing through the entire meeting, people's tiring bodies remind them to keep the agenda succinct. We usually hold stand-up meetings in the last few minutes of the day, when everyone is packed up and ready-to-go, or to reconvene after we've sent a group off for a challenge. Near the end of your makerspace, ask the makers to share their favorite part or something that they learned. You can try implementing constraints, like limited time or number of sentences, so that only the most important points are shared. Stand-up meetings' efficiency means you can hear from many work groups or individuals in a very short amount of time—no paperwork to keep track of, either!

Artist Statements

Professional artists use artist statements as a means of conveying the purpose or intent of their work. Artist statements can also include information on the process of how a work was created and the inspiration behind the work. Simply put, they unpack the thinking behind a piece in order to make it easier or clearer for an audience to understand their creation. Think about a contemporary art piece hanging in a gallery: often, these works are extremely subjective and abstract. If an artist statement is provided, the audience viewing the work has greater context and a framework to guide their thinking on the piece.[1]

While traditional artist statements tend to be a paragraph or longer, you can consider using shorter, simplified versions depending on where your makers are in the process. For a short project or one which is still in process, you might consider assigning artist statements as a "ticket out the door." They can be just a few sentences written on an index card. You can also provide sentence starters as a framework to guide student thinking. For example, "The visuals I chose are meant to _____" or "I chose this medium because _____." Longer, multiparagraph artist statements are great to use for completed projects, especially long-term ones. Longer artist statements should include more developed thoughts and reflection on the product and process.

---

[1] For a great guide on what to include in artist statements, check out http://www.artbusiness.com/artstate.html.

Gallery Walking

Gallery Walking gives makers a chance to see each other's work. When we do Gallery Walking, we split the room and have half of the room present their work, and the other half be the audience. Then, we switch. You can combine Gallery Walking with other assessment strategies like artist statements or Title:Subtitle. Consider having makers use table tents along with their object. These table tents can have a Title:Subtitle, a prompt regarding what the creator wants the viewer to focus on, an explanation of what the object is, or something that the creator is particularly proud of. Gallery Walking can be used after projects are finished, but it's also a great tool for projects that are still in process. When we Gallery Walk, we always remind our makers of the expectations we have for viewers:

- Lend support, not critique
- Ask questions
- Listen intently
- Give advice only if asked for it

Having explicit guidelines like this helps to ensure that Gallery Walking is a supportive and encouraging experience for makers to showcase what they are working on.

Pitches

If you have activities in which students create or invent, then pitches are your friend! Pitches are short speeches (like an elevator speech) which are designed to be captivating and persuasive. Pretend everyone in the room is an investor with $100 to spend. Why should they invest it in your project? Pitches are strongest when they define a specific problem—or "pain point" in the words of our colleague Chuck Severance—and then explain succinctly how their solution will solve this problem, alleviate an inconvenience, save time, etc. A good pitch is concise, clear, and creative. It captures the audience's attention and gets them on your side. This means that despite its short length, a good pitch still requires thoughtfulness and well-executed delivery.

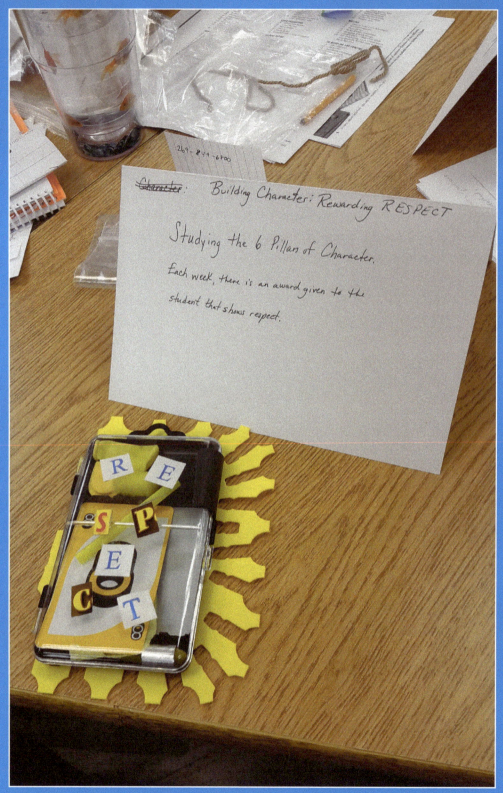

Without a table tent of explanation, this creation, at a workshop at Benton Harbor (MI) Public Library, could be easily misinterpreted or misunderstood.

Portfolios

Portfolios are tools that have been in many educators' belts for years. Portfolios are really a showcase of student work, and they can be presented through both digital and physical means. The important thing to remember when using portfolios as an assessment tool is that portfolios are a curated selection of work. Not every single project belongs in the portfolio. Makers should have a rationale behind including each piece. One project might be the one which they are most proud of, one might be the most successful, and another might be a failed project that they learned the most from. To guide makers' thinking, you could consider having them write artist statements for key pieces in their portfolio, or display their portfolio in a Gallery Walk or more formal exhibition of work.

CONCLUSION

Although not everyone running a makerspace might consider themselves to be an educator, learning is one of the quintessential by-products of a successful makerspace. Offering thoughtful, well-developed learning opportunities to your makers will help to ensure that your makerspace is accomplishing its goals as an educational space in your community. And assessing what your makers are learning will help you to provide stakeholders with proof of the value of your makerspace, as well as providing students with an opportunity to reflect on their own work.

Are robots toys or tools? It depends on how their use is mediated by adults.

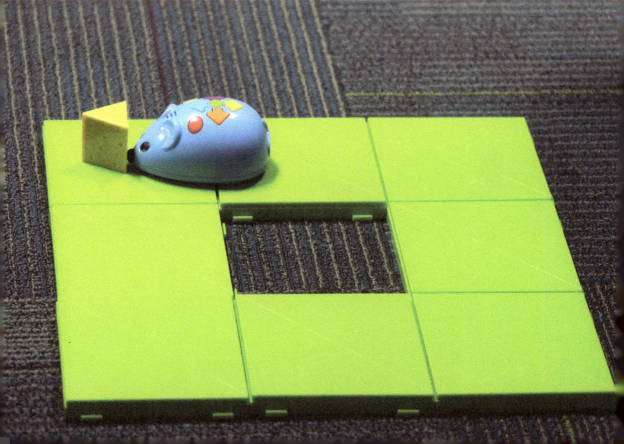

CHAPTER 7

BEWARE THE MAGICAL OBJECT
Don't Expect Tools to Be Teachers

Kristin Fontichiaro

If you have ever attended a webinar or conference session on makerspaces, you've heard the inevitable question: "But what should we buy?" Far too often, we feel an urgency to keep abreast of the newest, most popular, or most viral tools. The result is that we value objects over needs and learning objectives. If it's on Pinterest or Instagram, we must have it, because surely we want nothing but the best for our students.

But let's back up a bit. Certainly, as librarians, we are predisposed to consider acquisitions and collections first when it comes to any new educational trend. However, when we allow the marketplace to decide what is urgent for the students in our care, we are letting strangers determine the educational priorities. When we let social media—which often shows us the first time kids have used a tool, not mature or time-tested lesson plans—drive the decision-making, we may be prioritizing what's cool over what works.

Most importantly, when we thrust kits and supplies into students' orbit without fully understanding them or how they integrate into larger curricular, social, or intellectual goals, we give away some of our own educator credibility. When a "Perfect for STEM!" sticker on a box determines whether we purchase something, we abandon some of our librarian professionalism as well. And when we rely on objects as being magically capable of transferring meaningful learning from the thing to the learner, we set up a system in which the motivated continue to succeed and thrive and the strugglers merely play with a toy. In other words, beware the magical object.

MAGICAL OBJECT SYNDROME

Are you or others in your building suffering from any of these symptoms?

- "I'm going to need you to set up a makerspace. Othertown School has one, and it's awesome."
- "Just set some Makey Makeys out on a table for children to explore."
- "I'm just doing this because my principal told me to."
- "I don't get it, but everybody else in the department seems so enthusiastic."
- "I guess it's just playing."
- "If you put things out, children will learn—just get out of their way!"

If any of these ring true to you, then let me diagnose you: you have magical object syndrome (MOS). MOS occurs when we *assume* that objects, in and of themselves, create learning opportunities for students.

Consider, for example, the Dash Robot by Wonder Workshop. If we leave this chatty blue robot out with the apps pre-installed on a corresponding iPad, students will undoubtedly be curious about it. Dash's coos, cheeky language, smooth movements, and witty animations are appealing. But consider what many students, lacking any further intervention or guidance from an educator, will do with Dash. They will likely use the iPad as a remote control, zooming it around on the floor while flashing its light and making sounds. That's an easy and fun activity, but how many students will choose to move away from the remote control app and explore coding, which Wonder Workshop does in an effective way? Of these, how many will persevere when early coding efforts don't yield cool or anticipated results? That's a much smaller number. So who benefits from this laissez-faire, hands-off approach? Those who are already self-motivated. How, then, can makerspaces achieve their goal of all students achieving more?

We fall victim to MOS when we assume that different devices will *de facto* produce different solutions. A school district that brags that their younger elementary children use Ozobot and their secondary students Dash, for example, may be overlooking that both devices use the same programming language to navigate a path. The goals and objectives are virtually identical. Does changing from a small translucent robot to a rotund one magically improve coding ability? Unlikely. Similarly, construction materials like Strawbees, Tinkertoys, or LEGO, each outstanding in their own right, essentially support the development of highly similar building skills.

Without careful planning, we might catch MOS with tools like Snap Circuits, time-tested kits in which kids "snap" various components onto a wired board to create electrified inventions. With guided facilitation, students realize that circuits have certain components, inputs, and outputs that help them understand how electricity and the inventions around them work. If, instead, we treat them as a magical object that will mystically transmit principles of electricity without our guidance, things may fall short (especially given that Snap Circuits and LittleBits often obscure the circular nature of circuits).

Perhaps you're wondering, "Wait, should I put those kits away?" Of course not. What makes an object truly stellar is *you*; you building a bridge, by using an activity, toy, kit, or experiment to connect students' current knowledge and growth capacity.

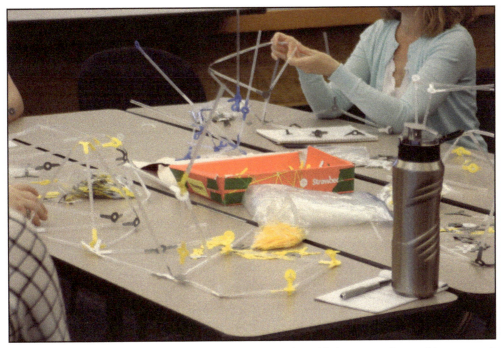

Strawbees, die-cut connectors that integrate with store-bought straws, can be used to communicate sophisticated ideas.

ALTERNATIVES

If you're suffering from MOS, don't fear. It's human. You likely have dozens of competing concerns, priorities, and building needs that you're juggling at any one time. And if you are anything like the majority of K-12 librarians, you don't come from a science background. It's much easier to lay stuff out than it is to spend time studying how objects work. That being said, if you don't understand the science underlying STEM kits, how will students? Take these curatives for a test drive:

Know *why* before you buy. Don't buy something until you can clearly articulate what students learn from engaging with it *and* how it distinguishes itself from similar tools. Unless you are running an out-of-school program, you have an obligation to design learning experiences for students that lead to greater capacity, understanding, or comprehension. If you cannot articulate this, or if you find yourself defending your purchases as "highly reviewed" instead of highly impactful, then step back. Seek out a manual, product review video, or product website that articulates the learning objectives behind the item. In some cases, product producers will create clear links between their products and the Next Generation Science Standards, for example. This is not new territory for librarians—we have always relied on reviews and external support in our collection development.

Reconnect to standards. As librarians, you're spanning a variety of ages, grades, and subject areas, so this can feel overwhelming, but one easy way, especially if you are in a state that has adopted the Next Generation Science Standards of 2013, is to revisit the eight Scientific and Engineering Practices discussed on pages 41 and 42. With these practices as a decision-making lens, you will shift from, "What do I buy?" to "How does this kit help my kids grow in *x*?"

Seek on-ramps. If your space has a variety of stations, it's hard to facilitate many places around the room at once. Often, we lack the budget for each child or team to have access to their own kit, so there are many potential kinds of facilitation needed. A whole-class demonstration may not suffice. In that case, consider "on-ramp" tools that help build the bridge between the child's prior knowledge and the materials before him or her. You might create web pages with video links or put out information sheets with labels of parts, safety sequences, or challenges on them.

Challenge them! One way of getting students to engage deeply with materials and their functions is with challenges. Challenges such as "Design something for a ninja to sleep on" not only call on skills with materials but also problem-solving and the creative imagination. There are plenty of Design Challenges available out there. The company behind Strawbees makes Design Challenge cards that work with their pieces but also with other construction materials like Tinkertoys, LEGO, Lincoln Logs, and more. For free challenge cards, visit http://makinglibraries.si.umich.edu/handbook.

CONCLUSION

You can eradicate MOS in your school. Apply your existing collection-development skills, sharpen your goals, and bring in some problem-solving activities that maximize open-ended exploration, and you're on the way to a MOS-free future. Remember, in your library makerspace, the real magical object is you.

An earlier version of this chapter appeared as "Beware the Magical Object: Stop Expecting Tools to Be Teachers" in the December 2018 "Makerspaces" column of Teacher Librarian. *Special thanks to Edward Kurdyla for permission to reprint it here.*

REFERENCES

National Research Council. 2012. *A Framework for K-12 Science Education: Practices, Crosscutting Concepts, and Core Ideas.* Washington, DC: National Academies Press.

Next Generation Science Standards (NGSS). 2013. "Read the Standards." Retrieved November 11, 2018, from https://www.nextgenscience.org/search-standards.

Ricky Cichewicz, a 3D printing enthusiast, loaned his translucent items for display at the Senior Summer Camp, a partnership with the Ypsilanti District Library's Senior Summer Camp in 2019.

CHAPTER 8
SHOULD YOUR MAKERSPACE HAVE A 3D PRINTER? MAYBE

Kristin Fontichiaro

In March of 2016, I was in the midst of planning a large summer road tour to bring professional development about maker mindset, maker culture, and makerspaces to rural and underserved communities throughout Michigan.

As I talked with librarians in communities throughout the state, the topic inevitably turned to 3D printing. What role, if any, should 3D printing play in their libraries and communities? Are 3D printers a symbol of progressive librarianship, so libraries should have them to look hip, sacrificing other purchases to get one? Or are they a sign of responsiveness to local needs? The answer isn't always clear.

A week later, I was at the SXSWedu conference on a panel discussing a National Maker Plan. My portion of the panel was a discussion of the importance of knowing one's community's needs, then using that information to inform a purpose statement, charter, or manifest for one's makerspace. As an example, I quoted one of the librarians to whom I had spoken. In her small rural town, there is a DIY group that teaches anything from how to make fishing flies to how to taxidermy a fish. Then I wondered aloud: in a community where fish taxidermy is valued, is a 3D printer necessary?

Someone responded on Twitter that a better answer would be to make a 3D scan of the fish, a file that could later be used to 3D print fish, compare them in size, and measure them. Then it hit me: the whole reason fish get preserved and mounted is because they are a souvenir of a great day of fishing. They are talismans that signal a fisherwoman's success (after all, they don't call them "fish stories" for nothing!). It's seeing the actual fish that validates and authenticates the experience. A 3D replica onscreen or printed in plastic is an abstraction, a step back from the authentic experience.

In other words, scanning the fish sounds cool but actually adds little intellectual or personal value. This example raised critical questions for me, reminding me of how tangled up our thinking is about 3D printers in libraries. To put it bluntly, do libraries need 3D printers or just want them? In acquiring these near-magical tools, are we solving an authentic problem? Or are we trying to show how cutting edge we are? What are libraries' 3D printers for, and do you need one?

3D printers have a natural place in engineering or shop courses, where students can develop skills in 3D modeling over time, with extensive guided

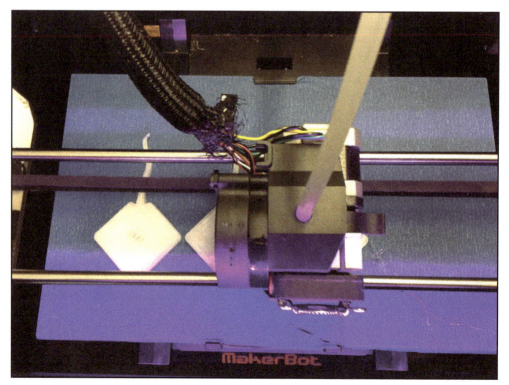

We used our 3D printer to print some stingrays, which would become skittering robots with a motor and CR-2032 battery attached. Could you use your 3D printer to support other library programs?

practice. Additionally, 3D printers can help art and jewelry makers explore their craft in new ways. For example, jewelry makers, once confined to costly metals, can now experiment with using resin to create either one-of-a-kind designs or easily replicated multiples.

Does your library need a 3D printer? Try using these questions to help you decide.

What is your vision for your maker program? If your program's goal is to develop entrepreneurial skills (and you have a strong indication that you have entrepreneurs interested in this kind of industry), then a 3D printer can be a great way to produce custom objects that students can prototype, market, and sell. If, instead, your goal is to have a drop-in activity between classes, then a 3D printer wouldn't likely be able to print quickly enough to meet that timeline. Hand manipulatives (e.g., LEGO, LittleBits, or Snap Circuits) might be a better fit.

Why do you want a 3D printer? If your answer is something like, "Because So-and-so has one," or, "Because I'm scared my job is going to be on the line if I don't keep up with the latest tools," think again. If, instead, you recognize that there is an aesthetic, curricular, entrepreneurial, or constructivist purpose, then this might be a good tool for you. If you cannot articulate a solid rationale, hold off until you can.

Is the library the best place for the 3D printer? If an art, engineering, or shop program has a regular, ongoing need for the 3D printer, it may be most efficient to place 3D printers in the corresponding classrooms, not with you.

Do you have the budget to purchase one? 3D printers have come down significantly in price in the past 24 months. You can now buy a MakerBot for under $1,000 or a highly-rated LulzBot Mini for $1,250. Programs like DonorsChoose.org, Patronicity.com (in selected states), bake sales, and PTA donations can often make the initial purpose possible. Securing funding for purchase may be one of the easier steps.

Do you have the budget to purchase filament both now and in the future? Filament is the industry term for the spools of plastic that feed through the printer and, once melted and extruded into threads, "draw" each layer of a 3D print. As the number of filament manufacturers goes up, a resulting price decline has occurred. Be sure to price out the cost of replacement spools when you are comparing printer models (know if the printers you are considering require ABS or PLA filament—most printers take only one of the two kinds). Some libraries offset the cost of filament by charging a token amount per minute or size of print, but for school libraries charged with serving all students, this option may not be available to you.

Do you or someone on your team have the time to run the machine? In a real-world makerspace, individuals would schedule time on the 3D printer and monitor it while it works. In a school setting, students may have to dash off to another class or activity. Do you or a member of your staff have time to queue, monitor, and quality-check 3D prints during library hours? Who would be in charge of this step? I hear sometimes about public library patrons—particularly youth—selecting a design from a free online repository and then leaving the file with the library for printing. I can't shake the idea that this feels like library-as-gumball-machine. We weren't in the business of provisioning toys for youth before 3D printing—how has this become a library priority? As a library science educator, I have to ask if the community benefit is valuable enough to merit using a professional's time in such a way. (Don't get me wrong—we use our 3D printer, but not nearly as much as other tools!)

Can the printer accommodate the number of print jobs it would take for an entire class to print something? While the print speed of 3D printers has accelerated greatly in recent years, most consumer-grade printers were designed for individual, not group, use. Imagine that a Consumer Education course assigns all 60 students (30 in each of two sections) to create and print a smartphone case. (If you're a public library, reframe this as, say, two Girl Scout troops.) At a conservative estimation of 45 minutes each, it would take 45 hours—more than a week's worth of school—to print out everyone's project. Is that doable? Now let's imagine that the librarian makes $40,000 a year for 50 weeks of work. That's $800/week. So that means about $800 worth of labor to print out those cases. Whether or not that's a good investment will depend on your local priorities and values—but it should give us something to think about.

Do you or someone on your team have the expertise to run the machine? Do you know rafts from supports and slices? Rafts are removable, 3D-printed "floors" underneath your print that can help tall and narrow objects stay upright and immobile. They are removed after the print job is complete. Supports are temporary scaffolds—akin to stalagmites—that provide support for cantilevered areas of the object. You might need supports if you are printing a dog because the head sticks out beyond the base created by the torso and legs. Slices are the individual "rows" into

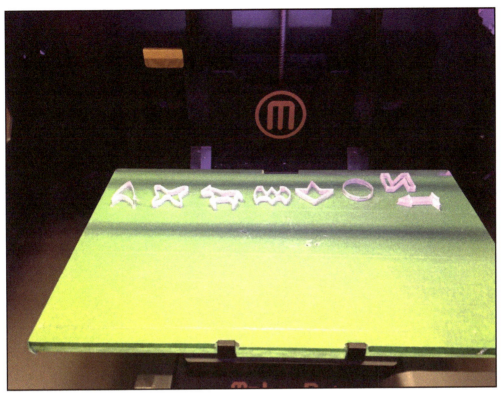

Scaling down these cookie cutters made with CookieCaster.com made them print much faster, so we were able to print several at a time.

which every 3D print is split. Similarly, do you know how to transfer a file from 3D modeling software to the software that controls the 3D printer? Do you have time and energy to learn?

Do you or someone on your team have the expertise to repair the machine? Even the best 3D printers can stop working right. Extruder nozzles (where filament is heated and then pushed out in tiny strands) can clog and circuit boards can need replacement. Who will wield the screwdriver?

Who has the CAD or 3D modeling experience? Technology has become so good that it's almost as easy to send a 3D file to print as it is to send an email. The real effort comes in being able to create 3D models so your patrons can solve real problems. Do you or someone on your team feel comfortable with 3D modeling software? Most 3D modeling software is difficult enough to be covered in college courses. Certainly, it's fun to find someone else's work on Thingiverse.com or a 3D fossil file site and download and print it. But ideally, a 3D printer is the final step in a student's design process. Are you aware of and comfortable with 3D modeling software that can help your student create something that merits printing? Free software includes Tinkercad.com, Sketchup.com, and AutoDesk 123D.

How does 3D printing fit with your school's existing environmental and recycling plan? Sometimes, it takes more than one try to get a 3D print that has the desired functionality, size, and appearance. Can misprints be recycled? If not, what will you do with bad print jobs?

Do you, your administrator, and your classroom colleagues have a clearly defined metric for success and plan to collect data to support that metric? What will successful 3D printer implementation look like? How will you and others know that it has been successful: By the number of prints? Projects? Instructors? Squeals of excitement? How will you gather data as evidence of that success?

There is a reason that many 3D printers sit broken or underutilized. By asking yourself some tough questions before purchasing, you and your colleagues will be able to make a well-informed decision.

An earlier version of this chapter appeared as "Should You Buy a 3D Printer?" in the April 2016 "Makerspaces" column of Teacher Librarian. *Special thanks to Edward Kurdyla for permission to reprint it here.*

Researching your community's demographics can help you make a compelling case for funding. Photo from a Making in Michigan Libraries workshop at Niles (MI) District Library.

CHAPTER 9
GRANTWRITING

Kristin Fontichiaro

When we travel and do professional development around makerspaces and maker culture, one of the most common questions we are asked is, "Where do you get funding?" There are certainly local, state, and federal funding opportunities, but to create a winning proposal, it's useful to keep some ideas in mind. In this chapter, we'll sharpen your grantwriting focus to maximize your chances that your students will gain access to the dream maker materials you envision for them.

BEFORE A GRANTS PROGRAM IS ANNOUNCED

Grants can be announced on short notice, so the best time to get ready for grants is before they are announced. Create a paper or digital folder to stash relevant information, past proposals, and background information.

To begin, create a wish list: What would you purchase if you had the funds? Include a list of desired items, quantity, a URL or phone number where you would place the order, and a dollar amount. Now, if a new grant pops up on the horizon, you can quickly compare what you want to the grant criteria to see if you have a match. And if your principal or director suddenly announces that she has $1,000 that must be spent or lost by 5pm, you'll be able to quickly skim the list of items, confirm current pricing, and place the order.

Next, you will undoubtedly need some demographic information. Many grant proposals ask that you show a specific need, and statistics from trusted organizations are persuasive tools. Often, you will be asked to demonstrate financial need, but sometimes you can make a case for other reasons. For example, perhaps there is a growing immigrant population, indicating a need for more bilingual materials. Perhaps you are in a sparsely populated area with limited after-school public transportation, meaning that any activities might need to be held right on site at school—that's a need, too.

The free version of ESRI Tapestry (http://www.esri.com/data/esri_data/ziptapestry) lets you search by individual zip code to discover the kinds of personas (aggregate consumer "personalities") in your area, as well as comparing your zip code's median age, income, and population density to the county, state, and national averages. That comparison data can help you make a compelling case. Of course, if your school or library straddles multiple zip codes, you may need to cobble data together. The subscription Business-Decision database provides more granular customer data mashed up with employment, education, census, and lifestyle data. Also consider the U.S. Census Bureau's American FactFinder (http://factfinder.census.gov), which allows you to search via census tract, political district, and more. Check out the school data tools at https://ies.ed.gov/data.asp; search your school district and discover its student to teacher ratio, special education population, and more. Some states also provide state-level statistics.

It may take some searching to find useful information for your community, but it's a good rainy-day activity. When a grant opportunity arises, you want to be focused on building your team and your idea, not on looking for background information.

A CALL FOR PROPOSALS IS ANNOUNCED

Many newsletters and listservs publicize calls for educational grants. When one comes out, read and highlight a print or digital copy. Watch for who is eligible, what kind of spending is permitted (smaller grants, for example, may pay for supplies and equipment but not salaries), what specific populations are identified, and the types of items that can be purchased. Listen for the language they use—those vocabulary terms should be echoed in your proposal. Look at the deadline, date, time of day, and time zone. For mailed proposals, do they need to be *received* or *postmarked* by the deadline? Look at the scoring rubric or guidelines, if available, and make sure to check your work against them. The rubric and instructions can also help you know the order in which the proposal should be written. Make it easy for people to give your proposal a good score! Look back at your wish list and demographics—which items and ideas would be the best fit? It's tempting to shoehorn your idea into a call for proposals that isn't really a fit, but the reality is that grant reviewers almost always have less money than proposals. If it's not a fit, your time may be better spent on another proposal, rather than trying to put your round peg in their square hole.

FIRST STEPS

Practice talking about your big idea until you can explain it to someone in an "elevator pitch" of a few words. Then go to your principal or director and ask for permission. Point out any parts of the proposal for which you will need her help. There may be federal identification numbers, letters of permission, or other components you will need from her. Recruit faculty or community partners to work with you and divide up what needs to be done. You don't want to win a grant for a 3D printer if no one in your building has time to teach 3D modeling, for example. That's a waste of time. Once you have approval, create a proposal timeline. Work backward and divide up the work to be done into smaller deadlines, so it's less overwhelming. At the University of Michigan School of Information, our crackerjack Research Office manages many proposals at once. I've adopted their strategy of creating a checklist that sets intermediate deadlines and reminds me of what is yet to be done. When I read proposals, it's often obvious that it has been rushed and put off until the last minute. Numbers don't quite match up, the narrative doesn't hang well together, documents are in incorrect order, and more. Give yourself a 48-hour cushion so you don't panic.

Look in the guidelines for a program officer or contact person assigned to the grant. If there is, contact him or her. Program officers want to fund great projects; most of them will happily give you 30–60 minutes of time and advice. As excited as you are about pitching your proposal, listen carefully; they often know the tics and preferences of reviewers and can give you valuable advice about the kinds of projects that will likely appeal. Once you get off the call, you can re-evaluate whether your initial idea is a match. Remember, your time is limited, so if they don't sound interested, decide whether you have the spare time to "prove them wrong" because it may not work.

WRITE IT

It can take many tries to write a successful proposal. Word limits and formatting rules can limit the space in which you can express yourself, so save time to write and re-write. Remember that your goal is to create a compelling story: Our patrons have needs, we believe that *x* equipment and *y* programs will solve those needs, and we're successful when *z*. Work diligently to answer exactly what is asked. Use bold, underlined, or italicized words when possible to make key ideas jump out. Follow the rules closely! Dozens of proposals to renew Upward Bound funding from the U.S. Department of Education were summarily denied because applicants did not follow a rule requiring double-spacing. They double-spaced the *narrative* but did not double-space the *tables* and were deemed ineligible (Blumenstyk, 2017). Ouch! Hours of work can go to waste because of silly mistakes. You may be asked for ancillary documents or materials, such as a budget or list of equipment. Make sure the budget tells the same "story" as the written narrative.

BEFORE YOU SUBMIT

Have everyone on the team read and edit the proposal. This helps to minimize errors and gets everyone on the same page about expected contributions. Have a few people outside of the project pretend to be reviewers and provide honest feedback. Getting criticism now is better than finding out later that you've made a mistake! Try to submit the day before the deadline. You never know when an internet outage might happen.

WHAT IF WE'RE NOT FUNDED?

At the end of the day, remember that no matter how good your proposal is, there's still an unpredictable human factor—perhaps reviewers had a bad day or a bad experience with a program such as the one you proposed, or they simply don't find your idea compelling for some reason. Keep in mind that a good "hit rate" for an organization—meaning the percentage of proposed grants that are funded—is never 100%. In fact, success might be more like 40%. So if funding doesn't work out, be sure to call the program officer (if one was made available to you) to get some feedback. Then stash that feedback and your proposal back in your folder and get ready for the next opportunity.

IF YOU ARE FUNDED

Congratulations! Be sure to write any deadlines, reports, or deliverables in your calendar so you're a good steward of the funding. (After all, you'd love to be funded next time, so keep your reputation sterling!) Then roll up your sleeves and get started. Keep documentation showing progress in the form of photos, checklists, student responses, and more. Enjoy the fruits of your labor!

NEED MORE?

Check out our free online course, Grantwriting and Crowdfunding for Public Libraries, at https://www.edx.org/course/grant-writing-crowdfunding-public-michiganx-publib607x.

An earlier version of this chapter appeared as "Need Maker Equipment? Write a Compelling Grant" in the June 2017 "Makerspaces" column of Teacher Librarian. *Special thanks to Edward Kurdyla for permission to reprint it here.*

REFERENCES

Blumenstyk, Goldie. 2017. "Dozens of Colleges' Upward Bound Applications Are Denied for Failing to Dot Every I." Chronicle of Higher Education, April 26. Retrieved March 31, 2020, from https://www.chronicle.com/article/Dozens-of-Colleges-Upward/239895.

Students at Scarlett Middle School in Ann Arbor document their own work with photography.

CHAPTER 10
VISUAL DOCUMENTATION IN MAKERSPACES

Kristin Fontichiaro

Makerspaces in schools and libraries can provide rich and dynamic learning opportunities. A tinkering mindset allows us to relax into the serendipity of discovery, experimentation, iteration, and alteration. STEM activities can take abstract, textbook concepts and make them tangible. Small invention and entrepreneurship activities can open up new career possibilities and illuminate financial realities. A warm and nurturing maker culture even makes room for some daydreaming as our brains work through possibilities and our hands engage in repetitive actions like stacking LEGO or making stitches.

However, to the uninitiated observer, many of these activities can look like play, unfocused puttering, or even time-wasting. How can we convince stakeholders to invest in the long-term skill development of makerspaces? In other words, in an age of metrics and data, how do we know that these activities are leading toward something meaningful?

One way we can sharpen our focus is by being more intentional about documenting what is happening in our spaces via photos, videos, journaling, exit slips, and more. In this chapter, we'll examine how photography and videography can help you capture learning as it happens, as well as what to consider as you periodically review the collected images and videos. Consider the ideas below as a jumping-off point for what might be effective for your workflow, program, and students.

CAVEATS

Before posting any student photos or videos online, check with your building or district administration about media policies to which you must adhere. You may be asked to photograph students from the back, to capture their hands but not their faces, or to avoid photographing particular students. If you are participating in a community makerspace or after-school project, you can make media permissions part of the participation permission slip, as we do with the after-school Michigan Makers project. Additionally, while in general we endorse Creative Commons licensing and the corresponding sharing of resources to promote sharing and information reuse,[1] we do not assign Creative Commons licenses to images of children. If you assign a Creative Commons license to a photo of a student, you give permission for others to use that student's image in their own work, which can make some families and administrators understandably uncomfortable.

PHOTOGRAPHY

Whether you use your smartphone, tablet, or high-quality DSLR camera, photographs help you show what is happening while triggering an emotional response when you view them. We use Flickr.com,[2] because each of us can quickly upload groups of photos and we can access it from any device. Some educators and librarians find Instagram, Twitter, or Facebook to be better integrated with how they already communicate with families. Whatever platform you decide to use, you will want to vary the kinds of images you shoot. For example:

- **Birds' eye or distance shots** help viewers see the totality of a space. This is advantageous for showing diversity of projects or for keeping a record of the layout of a space. However, these shots are less emotionally impactful because we cannot see any particular face or project clearly.

- **Hands-only images** focus on the tool and what is being made. The presence of hands can signal the age of the makers, the scale of what is being made, or even the diversity of the makers. These images are good for schools with stricter social media policies or to describe the universal nature of an experience.

---

1 See https://creativecommons.org/licenses/.
2 See https://flickr.com/michiganmakers.

- **Close-ups of groups** can show the community and collaborative dynamics of the maker movement. Good close-ups often show students focused collectively on a single object or project, and body language—huddled together or separated—can signal the unity (or discord) of the group.

- **Close-up photos of individuals** are good for capturing emotions like pride, frustration, concentration, or enjoyment. We can sometimes be tempted to avoid photos of intense process work in lieu of smiling children holding up finished projects. I'd encourage you to consider that it is in the grimaces that we often see the spark of new learning.

Be selective about the images you upload. A hundred photos of Squishy Circuits can easily clog your feed or photo album and appear needlessly repetitive to other viewers. Aim for photos that are emotionally evocative in some way or that capture an anecdote or episode that you will remember when you see the photo next (even if it's an object lesson on what *not* to do next time!). But, as you edit, keep an eye out that you do not accidentally omit critical narratives. For example, if all the photos in your album feature girls at a sewing machine, but you know it's popular with all genders, your photos are misleading. Whenever possible, caption and tag your images—they make your images more findable and, in the case of spaces where there are multiple staffers, help with institutional memory.

For more photography tips, see the chapter on photography in Part II of this book.

VIDEOS

Capturing short videos can be useful when motion, responsiveness, or extended documentation are needed. Try to keep most videos under 30 seconds to save storage space on your devices and keep the interest of viewers. Videos can be preferable to photos in such cases as the following:

- **Capturing cause and effect** (a finger presses an Arduino button, and the light illuminates; a marble is released into a maze and emerges at the other side)

- **Demonstrating how a skill is executed** (e.g., how to bend Strawbees or bore a hole with a Makedo tool)

Photographer Jeff Smith shows Benzonia Public Library patrons how to take better photos. This was also valuable information for the library staff, who post photos of library events on Facebook.

- **Panning the room to show overall activity, noise level, and/or furniture arrangement**
- **Capturing student product pitches, advertisements, peer feedback, and other public sharing moments**

Don't overlook podcasting as an option. Sometimes removing the stress of peering into a camera opens up richer conversations with shy or reluctant students and patrons. Most smartphones have—or can download—an app like Apple's Voice Memo for quick recordings.

Another video option we have used is a time-lapse video. This helps us get a bird's-eye view of how a space gets used over time. For an example, see https://www.flickr.com/photos/michiganmakers/11429374316/ for a Project Runway fashion hacking challenge with students from Ypsilanti (MI) Community Middle School several years ago.

MAKER REPORTER

You may find that you have students who would rather watch than initiate maker play and interactivity. Rather than sideline such students or force them to "be creative," empower them to play reporter instead. Give them a tablet, phone, or digital camera and invite them to take photos of work in action, in which they unobtrusively capture work in progress or photograph students posing with their creations. Here are some photo challenges you can give to reluctant photographers:

- Show someone's project from **beginning to end**.
- Use a particular **photographic frame** (e.g., hands only, wide shot only) to shoot all photos that day.
- Use a **specialty setting** (e.g., black-and-white only).
- Showcase the **widest variety** of activities you see.
- Take photos that **demonstrate** teamwork or another soft skill.

You can even create a checklist where students have to take at least one of each kind of image.

Alternatively, invite them to use video. A selfie stick or tripod makes it easy for them to be in the shot alongside their classmates, should reporters enjoy that option. Here are some options they could deploy:

- Record some **"live on the scene"** narrations describing what is happening in a space.
- Conduct short video **interviews with makers**. Some questions to consider include:
    - "What are you working on today?"
    - "What have you learned today?"
    - "What would you want other makers to know about this?"
    - "What was your biggest challenge?"
    - "What would you make if money wasn't a concern?"
    - "For whom are you making this project?"
- Film **tutorials and demonstrations** in which makers provide orientation to a particular tool or process.

- Set up a **reality TV confessional corner**. Ask the reporter to come up with a reflective, open-ended question and tape it to a tripod. Then get the reporter to recruit one student at a time to respond to the prompt.

In our after-school maker work, we repeatedly observe the Reporter Phenomenon. After about 20 minutes with the lens as a safe intermediary, the reporter gives up her camera, because she has found something more interesting to engage in. Problem solved: you've got photo and video data, and the student is now engaged!

Maker Reporter is most effective with elementary or early middle school makers. That being said, we occasionally have reluctant participants in our educator workshops who come alive when they can use their observation skills.

REVIEWING VISUAL DOCUMENTATION

Find time to review the images and footage that have been filmed. With the assistance of these visual memory aids, you may be able to see details and patterns that you may not have noticed in the flurry of real-time activity. You can use these insights to modify the tools you put out, the assistance you provide, the ways in which you structure independent and interdependent work, the students or patrons you nudge, and more. Here are some questions to consider as you review:

- Do you see any patterns in **who** gravitates to which tool?
- Is someone **repeatedly sticking with the same materials**, and is that productive (e.g., advancing in complexity) or a sign that a maker is stuck in a no-growth period?
- Do you notice that a maker is often **on the sidelines** week after week, observing but not participating?
- What do student-collected visual **artifacts** show you that you might not have noticed?
- Are certain students repeatedly working together to the **exclusion** of others?
- Who **works alone**, and is that productive (e.g., easier for him to focus) or an impediment (signaling loneliness)?

- Whose work **grows** every week?
- What **gender-specific patterns** do you notice? For example, in reviewing photos of 3D printing in our program, I discovered that we only had photos with boys in them. They had been first to gravitate to the printer, but we now knew we needed to make a bigger effort to connect female makers.

CONCLUSION

By gathering and then reviewing visual documentation, you can gain additional insight about how your makerspace is working, give administration and families a chance to see what is happening in your space, and reflect on current and needed practices.

An earlier version of this chapter appeared as "Visual Documentation in Makerspaces" in the December 2017 "Makerspaces" column of Teacher Librarian. *Special thanks to Edward Kurdyla for permission to reprint it here.*

Questions. 10/16/12

What have you taken away from MM so far?
   I have learned how hard it is to come up with a creative video game without the software to create it, and that it can be complex to do the simplest task.

What do you hope to learn in the future?
   I hope to learn how to program a watch, and how electricity flows through different substances, and much more.

A student journal from Michigan Makers' first year at East Middle School in Plymouth, Michigan.

CHAPTER 11
WRITTEN DOCUMENTATION IN MAKERSPACES

Kristin Fontichiaro

Alongside our graduate students, I've been running the Michigan Makers project since 2012.

Sometimes I pause and think, "Ahhh, it's working." But articulating what success looked and felt like to my less-experienced students was, in early years, a bit of a struggle. "I know it when I see it" is unconvincing at best and alienating at worst. Learning how to describe the growth, engagement, and synergies I saw was critical to my maturation as a facilitator of creative, fruitful maker activities and helped to sharpen my practice. Now, on days when I struggle to communicate successes, it's far more likely that the successes were not there that day, not that I cannot describe them.

It's tough to articulate what is happening in a makerspace, in part because there is such variety in answering what a makerspace is, what it accomplishes, and what the larger benefits are. Consider that the maker movement began as a kind of rebellious collective, then moved into the White House with language like, "Today's D.I.Y. is tomorrow's 'Made in America'" (Obama 2014). Today, many school makerspaces are organizing themselves around STEM (science, technology, engineering, and math). Silicon Valley has hyped the need for more coders, launching code-friendly plug-and-play toys, robots, and free curriculum. Meanwhile, public libraries are seeing growth in traditional handcrafting activities like knitting or quilting.

So which type matches your maker initiative, how do you know it is working, and how do you gather the artifacts and observations that support your stance when you communicate with outcomes-oriented administrators and decision makers? It starts with documentation.

In the previous chapter, I discussed how photos and videos can be powerful tools for recording what is happening in spaces and how we can use those multimedia files to reflect and share. In this chapter, I turn my attention to documentation methods that feature text, including journals, exit slips and Google Forms, blogs and portfolios, Maker Reporter, and lesson plan books.

JOURNALS

In our Michigan Makers program after school, we have had mixed success issuing each student a composition notebook. If your school already practices science notebooking to document one's scientific thinking throughout the planning, execution, and analysis of student-designed experiments, or writer's workshop, which encourages short writing bursts, you know this can be an effective way of getting students to document their planning and thinking over time. In a middle school with high academic achievement and several student makers of above-average motivation, this was a successful strategy. Students used their notebooks to store their digital badge stickers, sketch prototypes, and document the day's learning and reflection.

On the other hand, we had minimal success with journals and underachieving after-school elementary kids, who told us they loved Michigan Makers but hated writing. These students, we discovered, were being rightly pushed hard during the academic day and, like any kid, craved time to make their own decisions and exercise agency. Anything related to writing felt like more school. (The academic push was worth it—they have since abandoned their status as the lowest-achieving school and are now so in-demand as an International Baccalaureate school that they have built an addition!) Here, we learned that students were much more open to photographing their work or participating in video interviews.

If you choose journals, it can be helpful to have a prompt to which students can respond quickly, as you won't want your students' making,

WRITTEN DOCUMENTATION IN MAKERSPACES 143

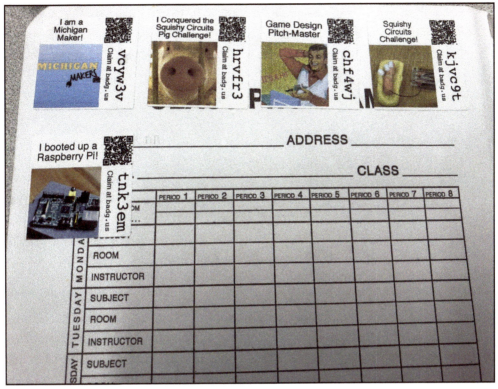

Inside of a maker's notebook at East Middle School in Plymouth, Michigan, during the project's first year.

experimentation, and prototyping time interrupted significantly by this reflective practice. Here are some prompts that you may find helpful:

- What do you know today that you didn't know yesterday?
- If a new student joined your group tomorrow, what would you tell him or her to explain what you've been working on this week?
- What questions do you still have?
- What "aha" moments have you had?
- What are you trying to learn? How close to your goal are you?
- What do you understand about engineering/coding/knitting that you didn't know before?
- Describe the progress you made today.
- What did you learn today?
- Where are you in the Design Thinking process?

- Do you have the information you need to move forward? What's missing? What might be getting in the way of clarity in moving forward?
- How would you pitch this product to customers? Investors?

EXIT SLIPS AND GOOGLE FORMS

Exit slips can be a quick alternative to long-form writing. Whether you ask students to fill an index card with ideas or hand out a photocopied prompt from above, remember to ask for the student's name and the date so you can sequence these slips over time and look for lulls in energy, fixating on the same tools repeatedly without making progress, and other signs that instructional, entrepreneurial, personal, or interpersonal interventions are needed.

A method that can make data collection and sorting even easier is to repeatedly use the same Google Form for each class. I learned this strategy from Amanda Nichols Hess, now at Oakland University Libraries in Rochester, Michigan. A form with a reflective prompt can make it easy for you to keep track of student reflections over time because you can sort the results in a spreadsheet by student name and quickly see the longitudinal trajectory of student thinking. Alternatively, searching entries by date allows you to see the class response on a particular date.

BLOGS, PORTFOLIOS, AND INSTAGRAM

These tools can help track process and/or product and create a central repository for student work, which assists with their ability to see their growth over time. The trick to these is not just to use them as places to document everything, but in setting aside time for students to do what Niguidula (2010) describes as the "collect, select, reflect" process. Students can certainly collect a wide variety of process documents and artifacts but should then gain experience selecting items that convey a cohesive narrative and reflecting on the reasons each item was chosen (e.g., to demonstrate a soft skill like teamwork or a thematic skill like electricity). In the case of an individual WordPress blog, for example, regular updates on process and product might be created using posts, with standalone pages set aside for thematic portfolios. The popularity of the online portfolio tool Seesaw, used often by classroom teachers, can be an easy and fluid way to engage in this process. A blog that you and/or a small team of students write can be an excellent reflective practice for you while also documenting activities. Instagram accounts (if your makers are over 13) are fast and easy ways to record daily progress; images can later be pasted into a portfolio page as needed. Reviewing the posts over time can help you see patterns and sharpen your focus moving forward. As I review our Michigan Makers and Making in Michigan Libraries blogs[1], I'm reminded of past projects and tools, now-graduated mentors and the unique skills they brought to the table, and days when we just didn't seem to hit the mark.

MAKER REPORTER

This is a role well suited to someone who takes more time to get settled into creative acts. You can designate a reporter (try a "Reporter" lanyard for elementary makers) and invite them to make notes, blog, create a news feature, or design a poster about what they are observing. In the previous chapter, I mentioned that some Maker Reporters abandon their task 20 minutes in, once they find something that interests them (and this is a good thing!); still, their perspective can reveal insights and details that you may have overlooked from your bird's-eye perspective. Alternatively, this can be a rotating role for one student daily.

LESSON PLAN BOOKS

A long-ago classroom colleague gave me great advice about lesson planning. The trick, she said, was to go back at the end of the day and write what you actually accomplished. This not only creates a more accurate record but also provides a road map for what to do next year. Whether you work in a school or public library, consider the same as you keep your plan books—are there tools or materials you wished had been on hand? Extension activities you thought of after the fact? Supplies you'll need to restock before attempting this next time?

REVIEWING WRITTEN DOCUMENTATION

Just as with portfolios, move from collection to reflection. Find time to review the paperwork or digital artifacts you are collecting. Ask yourself questions like, "What do I see here? How do I know X is happening? Which of these anecdotes will best resonate with various stakeholders and decision makers?"

---

1 See http://michiganmakers.si.umich.edu and http://makinglibraries.si.umich.edu.

CONCLUSION

Asking students to document their thoughts and progress, as well as documenting your own observations and insights, can seem tedious or even counterintuitive to the serendipities you want to seed in your space. But it is by this evidence that we gain the ability to see where we are: our ruts, our blind spots, and our opportunities for renewal and growth.

REFERENCES

Niguidula, David. 2010. "Digital Portfolios and Curriculum Maps: Linking Teacher and Student Work." In *Curriculum 21: Essential Education for a Changing World*, edited by Heidi Hayes Jacobs.

Obama, Barack. 2014. "Remarks by the President at the White House Maker Faire." Retrieved December 30, 2017, from https://obamawhitehouse.archives.gov/thepress-office/2014/06/18/remarks-president-white-house-maker-faire.

An earlier version of this chapter appeared as "Written Documentation in Makerspaces" in the February 2018 "Makerspaces" column of Teacher Librarian. *Special thanks to Edward Kurdyla for permission to reprint it here.*

Community maker events like this one in Frankenmuth, MI, can help you sustain support for your makerspace in the community.

CHAPTER 12
SUSTAINING A MAKERSPACE

Kristin Fontichiaro

Have you ever run out of maker materials before the activity even began? Exhausted yourself because you took on too much? Panicked because your students are blowing through the semester's new tools and toys . . . and it's only February?

If that's the case, then you might be facing a sustainability problem. Thinking differently about makerspace sustainability—about the long-term vision, budget, activities, human power, and goals of the program—can help in making more robust choices, conserving energy and budget, and forging valuable partnerships. In this chapter, we look at strategies to help you create sustainable maker culture and projects.

PLAN YOUR WORK AND WORK YOUR PLAN

Earlier in this book, you read about the importance of purposeful planning to aid both in cohesive planning and in communicating your goals with others. Once you have a vision, it becomes much easier to think about policies and purchases.

CHOOSE REUSABLE, EXTENSIBLE EQUIPMENT THAT SCALES

The maker movement did not begin in schools or libraries. It bubbled from the ground up, maker by maker, with makers paying from their own pockets. Many of the cool and exciting kits out there are designed and priced for individuals, not groups. Not all of them scale well for schools and libraries, where materials are usually provided at no cost to makers. For example, consider Drawdio, a nifty tool from the maker movement's early years that electrifies your pencil and lets you make electronic sound with pencil lead. Cool . . . but at $17 per kit, it can only be constructed once and is outside the budget of many groups. By comparison, consider a $50 box of LEGO—endlessly reusable and flexible, whether your students are creating new worlds, responding to Design Challenges, or prototyping ideas for inventions.

Similarly, think carefully before purchasing tools that can only be used by a single person at a time. 3D printers are hypnotizingly cool, and they often signal, "We're a makerspace!," but they print slowly. A Snickers-sized job can take an hour or more. Sometimes only one project can print at once. Multiply that by 20 students, and suddenly you're on non-stop print-monitoring duty. Additionally, given that some 3D projects take multiple tries before they print accurately, how is it that the librarian went from being the head of the recycling committee to throwing bad plastic prints in the trash?

Consider balancing single-use or single-user wonders against flexible, reusable tools such as LEGO, Tinkertoys, Lincoln Logs, K'Nex, programming languages, Snap Circuits, and Arduino microcontrollers with breadboards. These tools aren't just reusable; they're extensible, or "extendable," too. They offer features, challenges, or options that grow as patrons or patrons do. Students remain interested in them for longer periods, revisiting them repeatedly as they ramp up their skills. From a long-term financial position, that means that your single purchase has a stronger return on investment, and from an energy standpoint, you aren't panicking each week wondering what new gizmo to buy next. Besides the tools listed above, others that grow alongside students include sewing machines, LEGO Mindstorm robotics kits, and Dash and Dot robots that preschoolers can control with the remote control app and with which middle schoolers can program in challenges. Writers of code, poetry, comics, and prose need only screens or paper to make their work, so once the initial investments are made, they grow for free. At every conference you'll see the temptations of wondrous, new STEM toys for your library. Ask yourself, how flexible is this tool? Will my students use it once and abandon it? Or can this intrigue and occupy their thinking over weeks and months?

When hosting make-and-take events, set a per-participant budget limit. We have public library colleagues who budget $2 per person per event, just enough for a few LED bulbs, a battery, and a handful of wires and components. That amount is also enough to cover a half-yard of low-price fabric, a handful of balloons and straws to make balloon-driven cars, some basic cooking ingredients or knitting supplies, Shrinky Dinks film, and much more. Some public libraries budget for 50 cents' worth of supplies per participant. Remember: a junk box is free!

ASK FOR DONATIONS OF TIME, EXPERTISE, AND MATERIALS SO YOU CAN DIVERSIFY

Donations provide an easy way to shore up and extend your program's viability. Many crafters hold on to a far larger stash of fabric and materials than they will ever use. They are often willing to part with supplies if they know students can use them creatively. Put the word out in newsletters and list the kinds of things you are looking for. Michigan Makers happily accepts old cameras, desktop computers' CPUs, and VHS players because all are interesting things for a takeapart or appliance autopsy activity. (We decline computer monitors because they contain potentially dangerous chemicals.) We are still using up the fabric, yarn, and thread donated two years ago, and it's no longer unusual for me to find a bag of fleece, old T-shirts, or a discarded video game console outside my office door.

Behind every successful makerspace is a network of relationships. Consider reaching out to local makerspaces and hackerspaces; local unions for plumbers, electricians, carpenters, and stage employees; members of the parent community; student groups at local universities from a variety of departments; public library colleagues; the local Maker Faire™ or Mini Maker Faire™; and other community creativity groups like potters' guilds, quilting groups, woodworking groups, and coding clubs. Many people passionate about their own creativity are willing to contribute a few hours' time to support you and your students, so ask for a few volunteer sessions instead of a long-term commitment up front. Some districts do require background checks for volunteers, so check district policy. Put a call out for those with these and other skills, and you might find that you can double the number of adults in the room . . . and the number of activities! Keep in mind that today's generation of volunteers tends to prefer to volunteer for one or two finite events rather than an extended series of activities.

More donations and more hands mean that you can expand your offerings. If your initiative is only reaching a niche segment of your population, then it may fall short of inspiring and developing the skills of a wider swath of students. To increase impact, consider diversifying beyond these engineering or circuit tools. One of the ways Michigan Makers has diversified beyond STEM has been to introduce needle activities. A sewing machine can be bought for as little as $100 and yield dozens of potential projects, from pillows to puppets to Halloween costumes (and, remember, these extra activities can often be accomplished with donated materials). The Michigan Makers team watches for local thrift store sales and picks up denim jackets, button-downs, T-shirts, and fleece for $1 or less apiece. These can be cut up, refashioned, painted with stencils printed on our Silhouette Cameo and Portrait machines, and otherwise customized. Donated yarn plus low-cost knitting or crochet needles, coupled with a passionate mentor, once turned reluctant urban boys into enthusiastic crochet artists. Whereas an earlier generation might have said fashion was for girls and electronics for boys, we don't find this in our work today. And who knows? Maybe today's tailor, working with today's circuit enthusiast, will create the next generation of smart wearables! For ideas, browse Appendix A.

DEVELOP AN IN-SYSTEM ROTATING COLLECTION

One cost-effective way to get district- or system-wide making off the ground is to pool finances and materials. Assemble a team of fellow librarians to brainstorm a list of common starter activities and the per-library budget. Each library chooses one item off the list to purchase. Each month, the libraries send the kit they have been using on to the next library on the list. By the end of the year, the library has exposed students to 8 to 10 new tools, has built some buzz, and has a better sense of the kinds of tools and activities that are just right for their library and can make better purchases next year.

Imagine, for example, that each of eight elementary libraries were to invest $150. That is enough to buy one Dash robot (if you already have a newer model Android or iPad, which you need to run Dash), a healthy batch of LEGO and other construction kits, a new sewing machine (or a few second-hand ones), six kits of Tech Box Tricks starter microcontrollers, three Ozobot robots, a LittleBits kit, several Snap Circuits kits, or an on-sale Silhouette Portrait digital cutting tool. That's a big return on investment! Partner your rotating tool of the month with freebie activities like Scratch programming (http://scratch.mit.edu), origami made of discarded newspapers or phone books, and a junk box whose contents can be repurposed into fanciful original creations, and you're well on your way to having a robust, interesting exploration. Of course, keep your mission in mind!

DOCUMENT SUCCESS . . . YOU'LL NEED IT TO SEEK FURTHER FUNDING

When you have figured out your purpose, tools, goals, and budget, things can really take off. Now the time comes to document success. Keep your smartphone handy to capture videos of your students' catapults, audio recordings of their prototype pitches, and photos showing your mission in action. See if a maker or volunteer can help you share these accomplishments (with parent permission) via a blog, Flickr, Instagram, or Twitter. Capturing this learning-in-progress will give you data, insights, and images to communicate needs and successes to parents, administrators, and future funders. Reviewing documentation over time helps you reflect on next steps.

CONCLUSION

Taking time to think and plan can help you create a makerspace that is inclusive, set up for long-term success, embraced by the community and funders, and captivating to makers without maxing out your energy or budget. As the saying goes, "To go quickly, go alone. To go far, go together."

An earlier version of this chapter appeared as "Sustaining a Makerspace" in the February 2016 "Makerspaces" column of Teacher Librarian. *Special thanks to Edward Kurdyla for permission to reprint it here.*

At a maker idea swap, maker facilitators trade ideas while trying a new activity.

CHAPTER 13
LEARNING FROM PEERS
Maker Idea Swap

Ben Rearick

After our first summer of travel for the Making in Michigan Libraries project, a short survey given to all participants in our three-day workshops revealed that the most-requested workshop for the next summer would be an opportunity to hear about low-cost maker ideas. There's been a large adoption of maker culture over the past few years, as well as STEM education, so there are plenty of books, blogs, and listicles on maker ideas using any number of materials. The focus on technology and new gadgets, however, could lead to some librarians being overwhelmed—who starts off as an engineer and winds up as a librarian?

Again, the number of books and support for training in these gadgets is high, but there's also something to be said for the desire to hear from others in-person. Follow-up questions are easy to ask, and themes can easily be established, helping even the shyest librarians to open up and everyone to learn at least something.

A maker idea swap, as we've termed this exchange of ideas, is all in who attends. If people don't come with ideas or don't know that they are primary contributors to the swap, the leader can feel overwhelmed by carrying the discussion. We learn from every library we visit. Staff are eager to tell their

Because toy takeapart is a tried-and-true Michigan Makers activity, we used it as our focus activity during Maker Idea Swap. Taking apart a toy—like this electronic Snoopy doghouse—brings out people's sense of whimsy and discovery. Photo by Kristin Fontichiaro during a toy takeapart workshop at the Madison-Oneida (New York) Board of Cooperative Educational Services.

successful projects. Setting up an an informal environment can help each participant feel excited about imagining future programs. Some people are natural brainstormers and program coordinators, while others are more focused on results and will do whatever works. It's good to make space for every type of librarian at a maker idea swap, but also let them know who the core audience is likely to be.

The leader of the swap should feel confident in the number of ideas they can contribute. Should the worst happen and no one else was to contribute a single idea (can you imagine!), there could still be a discussion around aspects of the programs the leader suggested. The leader doesn't need to be the most innovative librarian on the planet: they simply need to be able to explain the materials used and the results of ideas. Come prepared with about five specific programs that you have witnessed or hosted, and five more that you are interested in, gives you enough fodder for an hour-long discussion. Participants can ask about specifics and follow-ups. The leader can also prod the participants for ways in which their own community might interpret the event in a different way, or what community resources could be used to hold the event. As the planner of the event, the leader can ask people to submit one or more of their ideas when registering for the event. This way, the leader can call on people to share ideas of a particular stripe.

On the day of the swap, it can be extremely useful to demonstrate an idea and have the participants be able to do something with their hands. This can be an idea that the leader has done multiple times, a tried and true idea the leader knows inside and out. We used toy takeapart (see Chapter 17).

Discussion can be had about mistakes made early on and how they were overcome. Participants can feel what it's like to be a patron and give feedback. In this way, the ideas of the participants get flowing and sparks start going off. If the hands-on project only lasts 30 minutes or so, multiple smaller projects can be used to supplement this initial hands-on idea. Don't skip this step, unless you know you have a few great brainstormers out there, as it can be essential in keeping conversation moving when participants run out of things to say on different topics.

Whether you're a librarian or not, it can be extremely helpful to catalog the ideas or potential ideas into different categories. Again, this can help spark different ideas from participants. Some categories we've found helpful are listed on the following page:

- General Resources
- Building and Engineering
- 3D Modeling/Printing
- Circuits and Microcontrollers
- Coding and Programmable Objects
- Design Thinking
- Paper and Recycled Materials
- Fabric, Sewing, Knitting, Crochet, Other Needlework

An important category is also resources, as more novice participants can be at a loss for where to obtain materials. These resources can also be places to get ideas, like the aforementioned books and blogs, but it can be overwhelming if this is the focus. Remember: it's about the people!

Sharing ideas can be harder for some people, so you might experiment with different ways of sharing. You could have participants write down their ideas, giving each an index card or sticky note that can later be collected and posted into an idea collage on the wall. You could have people get into smaller groups to brainstorm and share ideas based on categories. You could have a list of materials and have participants come up with multiple program ideas based around a certain number of them. All of these different ways of sharing can help jump-start a conversation and after that, the leader can help direct it.

Finally, and most importantly, you must have someone take notes at the event. ***Idea swaps can't be where ideas stop.*** These notes must be shared with the participants, and it takes the burden off of the swappers. If a projector is available, it can even help participants continue to share as they see the list growing longer. When participants have a connection with—or a phone number of—a fellow librarian who they know they can contact to ask for clarification or advice on a particular event, they can more easily return to the list and try events that they remember hearing about.

For ideas from the Maker Idea Swap we held in 2018 at the Frankenmuth James E. Wickson Public Library in mid-Michigan, please see our project's free eBook at https://www.smashwords.com/books/view/731191.

Cover for the eBook we published at https://www.smashwords.com/books/view/731191 with the ideas we heard at the Frankenmuth James E. Wickson Public Library in mid-Michigan.

Michigan Makers mentor Sarah Cramer works with Mitchell Elementary School students in Ann Arbor, Michigan, to map out a Choose Your Own Adventure story.

CHAPTER 14
MAKERSPACE TUNE-UP

Kristin Fontichiaro

From time to time—whether it's the launching of summer reading, the start of a new school year, or just the feeling that the energy has dipped in your makerspace—it's useful to step back and take an informal assessment on where you are, what you've accomplished, and where you see your maker program going in the coming year.

Is your mission the same as it was last year? Is your equipment in good order? Have any materials worn out or lost their luster? Are you ready to jump when new grant opportunities are announced? Can you afford to keep current programs, tools, and materials functioning even if one-time grants or special funding dry up as the movement matures?

By completing the checklist questionnaire below, you'll have the opportunity to reflect on what's working, what needs repair, and where you might go next.

Mission and Purpose

1. Why do you have a makerspace in your library? Choose all that apply:
    - ☐ To provide a safe place for stressed-out students or patrons to relax, regroup, and self-soothe

- ☐ To provide a safe place where kids can go in lieu of after-school care, dangerous neighborhoods, or low-stimulation home lives
- ☐ To introduce schoolchildren or adults to STEM concepts that are not currently in the curriculum
- ☐ To enhance current STEM or design activities already within the school curriculum
- ☐ To prepare kids for science competitions
- ☐ To prepare patrons to think in new ways using Design Thinking
- ☐ Because Mr. X or Ms. Y has one (Hint: Bad answer!)
- ☐ Because it's fun (Hint: Bad answer!)
- ☐ Other: _____

2. What programs, events, tools, and materials directly contribute to that mission?

3. What evidence do you collect to showcase how the maker program is contributing to the mission outlined in #1?
   - ☐ Photographs
   - ☐ Process journals written by makers
   - ☐ Observation logs or checklists completed by you
   - ☐ Social media or course management accounts (Twitter, blogs, Facebook, Blackboard, Moodle, Google Classroom) kept by makers
   - ☐ Social media or course management accounts kept by you
   - ☐ Exit slips
   - ☐ Video or audio interviews
   - ☐ Reports shared with administrators
   - ☐ Bulletin boards
   - ☐ Nothing. I know learning when I see it, and my principal/director should, too. (Hint: Bad answer!)
   - ☐ Nothing. We're just having fun. (Hint: Bad answer!)
   - ☐ Other: _____

4. Quick! The principal/director just entered your library, accompanied by the mayor and a TV crew from the local news station. They ask you to tell the others about your makerspace project. What's your pitch? How are you using the funds you steward to promote concrete deliverables? (Keep your audience's bottom lines—financial, marketing, and curricular—in mind!)

Service Population and Cost

5. Approximately how many students or patrons used those tools and materials during the past year?

6. Approximately how much money did you spend on maker activities and projects last year?

7. How much of that money came out of your regular budget?

8. How much from nonrenewable (or one-time) grants?

9. How much from PTO, PTA, or Friends of the Library groups?

10. How much from special budgets, such as an administrator's discretionary budget?

11. Divide your answer to #6 by the number of patrons in #5. The resulting number is your per-participant cost. Fill it in here: _____.

12. How does that per-participant cost compare to your organization's per-participant cost for other activities? For library book budgeting? Does it seem too high? Too low? Is it sustainable even if outside funding dries up? (As the novelty of makerspaces wears off, external funding for maker materials and tools likely will tighten up as well.)

Measuring Success

13. How do you measure success in your space?

    ☐ Noting increased numbers of kids being in the library

    ☐ Recording number of attempted and/or completed projects

    ☐ Assessing STEM competencies

    ☐ Comparing standardized test scores to years prior to the makerspace being implemented

    ☐ Counting the number of patrons who decide to go to college

- ☐ Recording the number of patrons, especially women and minorities, who now plan to attend college or vocational school in a STEM field

- ☐ Noticing how happy the kids look (Hint: you probably need an answer in addition to this one!)

- ☐ Other: _____

Curriculum Alignment (for School Libraries and Classrooms)

14. Unless your maker program is a standalone course, long-term sustainability may require that your program aligns with curriculum priorities. With which of these curriculum priorities does your library maker program align?

    - ☐ Next Generation Science Standards or your state's science curriculum
    - ☐ Common Core State Standards in Math or your state's math curriculum
    - ☐ Common Core State Standards in English Language Arts (ELA) or your state's ELA curriculum
    - ☐ International Baccalaureate
    - ☐ American Association of School Librarians
    - ☐ ISTE standards
    - ☐ We just do it for fun (Hint: This one probably isn't sustainable in the long term.)
    - ☐ Other: _____

15. Based on your answer for #14, identify at least one specific standard for each grade level that uses your makerspace.

Taking the Temperature of Your Maker Program

16. What is working really well in your maker program?

    - ☐ Developing socioemotional skills, including _____
    - ☐ Increasing appreciation for STEM, including _____
    - ☐ Impacting traditional academic achievement, including _____

- ☐ Deepening maker skills, such as _____
- ☐ Developing agency or executive function in participants, including _____
- ☐ Increasing personal responsibility in participants, including _____
- ☐ Increasing attendance, such as _____
- ☐ Organization of materials, such as _____
- ☐ Storage, such as _____
- ☐ Scheduling, such as _____
- ☐ Curricular integration, such as _____
- ☐ Administrative support, such as _____
- ☐ Other: _____

17. Where might your makerspace need further improvement?
    - ☐ Developing facilitators' skills
    - ☐ Developing socioemotional skills, including _____
    - ☐ Increasing appreciation for STEM, including _____
    - ☐ Impacting traditional academic achievement, including _____
    - ☐ Deepening maker skills, such as _____
    - ☐ Developing agency or executive function, including _____
    - ☐ Increasing personal responsibility, including _____
    - ☐ Increasing attendance, such as _____
    - ☐ Organization of materials, such as _____
    - ☐ Storage, such as _____
    - ☐ Scheduling, such as _____
    - ☐ Curricular integration, such as _____
    - ☐ Administrative support, such as _____
    - ☐ Other: _____

Strategic Planning

18. Find your school, library, and/or district's strategic plan. Identify at least one strategy that your maker work supports. (Hint: If you cannot find one, ask yourself what you could change about your library maker program to make it more aligned with the organization's priorities.)

19. Who is helping with this initiative and could take it over if you were transferred or changed jobs? Or does success rely solely on your shoulders?

20. Who in the community could become a mentor for your program, so the program can grow without you giving up other responsibilities, tasks, or projects?

21. What tools, materials, or projects are ready to be retired?

22. What tools, materials, or projects do you need to stock up on?

23. What new challenges are your space and makers ready to tackle?

24. What new skill-building activities, tools, or materials are your accomplished makers ready to handle?

25. Have you started a grantwriting folder containing previous proposals, demographic data, and other materials, so that you are prepared when a grant opportunity arises?

Safety

26. Do you have or need the following?

    - ☐ Permission slip
    - ☐ First aid kit
    - ☐ Burn cream if working with high-temperature tools like soldering irons
    - ☐ Emergency eyewash if working with chemicals
    - ☐ Eye goggles or safety glasses
    - ☐ Safety guards
    - ☐ Chemical-safe gloves if working with chemicals
    - ☐ Medical gloves to protect hands from paints

- ☐ Work gloves
- ☐ Other: _____

27. Do you have a training or orientation system in place that participants must engage in prior to being able to use specialty tools and materials? List the tools and required skills.

Storage

28. What storage needs do you have?
    - ☐ Shelves or space to stack boxes
    - ☐ Lockable storage for expensive or dangerous equipment
    - ☐ Leakproof storage for paints, etching cream, and chemicals
    - ☐ Wheeled carts to move materials from space to space
    - ☐ Charging stations for robots, tablets, etc.
    - ☐ Other: _____

Technology

29. Are the online tools, tutorials, and sharing sites you wish to use available and unfiltered?

30. Have tablets and other devices been updated with the newest versions of apps and operating systems?

Miscellaneous

31. Do you need any of the following?
    - ☐ Tarps or drop cloths for painting
    - ☐ Tablecloths
    - ☐ Surge protectors
    - ☐ Extension cords
    - ☐ Batteries
    - ☐ Power cords
    - ☐ USB cables
    - ☐ Flash drives

- ☐ Cloud-based storage
- ☐ Subscription services
- ☐ Other: _____

CONCLUSION

Taking a moment to step back to consider how your maker activities are working and where you can make improvements is one way to continually keep your maker pedagogy fresh and relevant.

An earlier version of this chapter appeared as "Makerspace Tune-Up" in the October 2017 "Makerspaces" column of Teacher Librarian. *Special thanks to Edward Kurdyla for permission to reprint it here.*

Are these still the tools you need? It pays off when you schedule time to reflect on project priorities.

CHAPTER 15
MAKERSPACE TUNE-UP 2.0 FOR SCHOOLS

Kristin Fontichiaro

The previous "Makerspace Tune-Up" was designed as a checklist to help you think through your makerspace needs and goals prior to the start of the school year. Now, we return to the "tune-up" theme with some future-focused big questions to consider. While maker activities are still new to some, the movement overall is maturing. It is a good time to reflect and ask, "What are we doing that is showing concrete benefits to learners and school culture?"

"SO I PUT OUT A LOT OF STUFF AND KIDS PLAYED WITH IT . . . SO WHAT?"

What is the "So what?" of your makerspace? The impact of your maker efforts? Are you seeing tangible changes? In all students? Most? In the students who were already showing interest in computing, LEGO, sewing, and more before you started your initiative? How do you know that change is occurring? How are you verbalizing that change in your discussions with colleagues, social media, reports, administrator walkthroughs, and more? If you are stumped (or your administrator seems unsatisfied), this could be a powerful activity.

Try this now: Add at least a paragraph to your annual report, website, or employee review about your maker activities like this: "This year, we set out to accomplish _____ in our makerspace. We did this to align with district curriculum / strategic plan / Next Generation Science Standards / AASL Framework / other. We worked toward this by _____. We saw these results _____. Next year, we plan to focus on / modify / address a new issue by _____."

Try this next year: Try setting a SMART goal (specific, measurable, achievable, relevant, and time bound) for your makerspace. What are the curricular, social, "soft skill," or other goals that you have? Name them and start setting concrete action steps in motion. Remember that there are ways to nudge students toward explorations that don't involve you dictating all of the steps on the inquiry journey; instead of dictating process, try deploying what Stanford University's Bing Preschool calls "provocations." Doorley (2014, p. 16) describes provocations as "creative invitations" that invite children to engage with intriguing materials. By being intentional about the materials you set out, the processes and procedures, and a way of establishing student accountability for one's time, you can keep the learning open-ended but still nudge students toward being able to demonstrate and articulate new learning.

ARE WE OFFERING STARS OR CONSTELLATIONS?

I've used this metaphor before to describe scattershot versus cohesive actions (e.g., Fontichiaro 2013). When we do one-off activities that don't synergize with other activities, we create a "star" skill, isolated from others. Makerspaces are wonderful opportunities for cross-pollination of skills, so consider how you can strengthen connections between the "stars" to create constellations of learning instead. For sake of argument, let's imagine a middle school library with these stations: **computers** for coding (e.g., Hour of Code / Codecademy / Scratch / MOOCs from Coursera or EdX); a **sewing machine**; a **circuitry** station with paper circuits, Snap Circuits, Squishy Circuits, LittleBits, and robots (e.g., Ozobot, Dash/Cue, and MeeperBOT). Can you identify how students move through any of those stations? How the stations may be connected? Do activities naturally scale in complexity as students attain skills, or are we offering a lot of introductory activities that allow students to discover new tools and materials . . . but never go very deep with them? Are your activities more like stars, or do they work together to create constellations of deeper knowledge?

Try this now: Choose one of your maker stations. List all the activities kids do (or could do) at that station. Then draw lines connecting related activities. For example, when we do sewing in our extracurricular program, we start by sewing hand puppets. We do this because the project does not require a lot of stamina, has creative play attached to it, and because it teaches a lesson that if you make just a few huge stitches, your finger will poke out of the puppet between the stitches! From there, we spend a few weeks exploring how to customize fleece scarves with cutting and hand-stitching. From there, we transition to a sewing machine, sewing simple bean bags, exposing raw pinked edges as we sew, again a low-stamina, play-oriented result. As you can see in Figure 1, we indicate sequence by placing a circle at the earlier, easier activity's end of the line and an arrow toward the more complex one.

If the two activities have similar complexity, then put a circle at each end. For example, MeeperBOT and Dash/Cue both have a remote control program and a Blockly-based program. Does changing the robot type represent a skill rise? Are you finding that your activities are variations on a theme (e.g., Ozobot, MeeperBOT, and Dash/Cue) and that your program delivery accidentally reinforcing existing skills (e.g., many robots, all teaching Blockly-like programming) instead of building in complexity? Is that a fruitful decision or one to reconsider? Are there items in your station that do not connect to anything else?

Try this next year: Extend your mapping exercise by seeing how each station relates to one another. Flag equipment that is not currently working, needs repair, or is no longer impactful on students.

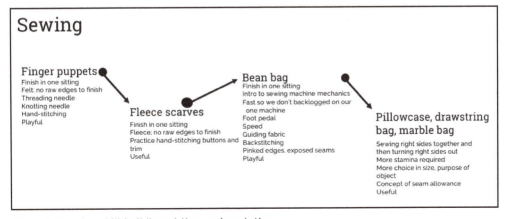

Figure 1: Mapping skill-building at the sewing station.

"SHOULD EVERYONE IN OUR DISTRICT BE LEARNING TO NAVIGATE A SPHERO THROUGH A MAZE?"

Some of us have been librarians for long enough to remember the Web 2.0, when suddenly students of all ages were engaged in wikis, blogging, or podcasting activities. I clearly remember going from our upper elementary podcasting club to teaching podcasting to graduate students at night. "Everybody learning the same thing at the same time" is a predictable cycle when new learning priorities arise, but now that the maker movement is maturing, we may need to step back and consider which skills and experiences belong best in which grades. Tasks that are easily mastered by elementary students need not repeat in upper grades if our goal is student impact. A school or district may do well to compare activities across grades and even individual classrooms to minimize unnecessary overlap and maximize new skills and challenges for students.

Try this now: Using your information from Figure 1, create Table 1 and populate it with your school's grade levels and areas of making. (High school librarians may find it easier to sort by course, not grade.) Don't stress if you are leaving boxes blank—just try to capture a bird's-eye view of what has happened in your space and that of your classroom colleagues to date. What you're doing is an informal vertical alignment that captures where you are—while also challenging yourself to discover places where you can challenge students further.

MAKERSPACE ENGAGEMENT AT ANYTOWN ELEMENTARY

ACTIVITY	K	1	2	3	4	5
Robots/ robotics / coding	Robot Mouse, Codeapillar	Ozobot and drawn paths	Ozoblockly, transition to Scratch	Scratch 3 – basics (plus Hour of Code in Mr. F's class)	Scratch 3 - intermediate	Scratch 3 + LEGO Mindstorms (for sensors)
Circuits	Squishy Circuits – open exploration	Electric jewelry and flashlights (fundamentals of circuits)	Snap Circuits, paper circuits	Lego WeDo	(none – focus on Scratch)	LEGO Mindstorms
Sewing	Hand sewing with embroidery floss/felt	Hand sewing with needle and thread	Basic sewing machine	(machine available for practice)	(machine available for practice)	Working with patterns
Stories and Writing	(open drawing)	(open drawing)	Zines about personal interests	Poems for your Pocket	Existing *Writing to Explore* adventure unit	Comic zines & ComicCon
Design Thinking	(none)	Design thinking game + paper	Design thinking game + LEGO	Design thinking: Create a better object	Design thinking: Create a better game	Design thinking: Create a better service

Table 1: A table like this can be completed quickly and exposes potential repetition or gaps.

Try this next year: In staff or department meetings, compare tables with others. Try comparing elementary, middle, and high school activities in a combined table. Where is there a repetition? Is the repetition necessary because it awakens prior knowledge before embarking on new challenges? Or is it unnecessary duplication? It feels inevitable that making will eventually be codified as a curriculum if it is to survive in K-12. So while giving up favorite activities can be difficult, you can steer the process proactively to best fit your campus and pedagogical priorities.

AS STUDENTS' SKILLS GROW, WHO IS BEST EQUIPPED TO SUPPORT THAT GROWTH?

You may have been the first to claim the STEM or maker mantle in your school. Now that your program is maturing, are you the best to take students beyond introductory-level activities? For example, you may have been the first to have a 3D printer in the high school, but now the art department has a formal 3D modeling curriculum. Should you phase out of being the 3D guru and tackle new challenges? If the library is the sole hub of maker activities, are there community mentors who have more experience or expertise to help get kids to the next level? If not, are there summer courses, workshops, books, or tutorials that can help you skill up?

Try this now: List the moments where you have felt underprepared or overwhelmed this past year. Create a reading/viewing list that can help you deepen your skills and set aside a few hours a week over the summer to complete them. For example, if your students are outgrowing block-based coding and ready for Python, check out the Coursera.com Programming for Everybody MOOCs.

Try this next year: Find local or online peers and challenge one another to learn new skills together for an hour or two a month over the course of the year.

Maker activities, clean-up, and inventory can preoccupy us during the year. Take advantage of this time to reflect on what has unfolded. You'll enjoy how it recharges you!

REFERENCES

Doorley, Rachelle. 2014. *Tinkerlab: A Hands-On Guide for Little Inventors*. Boston: Roost Books.

Fontichiaro, Kristin. 2013. "Metaphors for Badging." *Active Learning Blog*, April 2. Retrieved May 8, 2019, from http://www.fontichiaro.com/activelearning/2013/04/02/metaphors-for-badging/.

An earlier version of this chapter appeared as "Makerspace Tune-up 2.0: Looking Into the Future" in the June 2019 "Makerspaces" column of Teacher Librarian. *Special thanks to Edward Kurdyla for permission to reprint it here.*

PART II
PROJECTS AND PROGRAMS

Making headbands and jewelry out of the junk box at Mitchell Elementary in Ann Arbor, Michigan.

CHAPTER 16
JUNK BOX PROVOCATIONS

Kristin Fontichiaro

For years, celebrities have been asked, "If you were bound for a desert island and could take only one thing with you, what or who would it be?" It's a fun exercise to narrow down to a singular object.

If you asked me, "If you were making a makerspace on a desert island, what is the one thing you would take?" I would have no hesitation in saying, "A junk box."

WHAT KIND OF JUNK?

The easiest and cheapest way to start is to place a shoe box atop your refrigerator and another next to your desk. Each time you are about to put something in your recycling or trash bin—that frozen food box, a rinsed yogurt cup, a bottle cap, scrap pieces of wrapping paper and ribbon, a paper towel tube—put it in the shoe box instead. Leftover puzzle pieces? Scraps of sponge? Extra paper plates from the last birthday party? It's all fodder for the box—and for your creativity.

As you place each item into the box, turn it around in your hand. Let your inner child's imagination loose as you study it from all angles. Could your yogurt cup become a basket for a hot air balloon? A golf cup? Half of a Russian nesting doll? A nose on a funky animal mask? If you teach tweens or teens, how could they use the cup's curved edges to prototype something, say, a new kind of smartphone speaker?

Don't overlook pantry staples: toss expired noodles into a ziplock bag and into the box they go.

When the shoe box becomes full, empty it into a large, lidded plastic box with a latch. You may wish to sort your junk treasures into gallon-sized ziplock bags: one for beads, another for fabric scraps, a third for cardstock, and more.

What you are doing is collecting *provocations*, a term borrowed from the Stanford Bing Nursery School (Doorley, p. 186) or the Reggio Emilia preschool movement in Italy.

Provocations are items whose texture, size, material, shape, color, or sparkle inspire your students' imaginations. Intriguing materials will inspire intriguing prototypes. In our Michigan Makers program, junk box provocations have inspired athletic challenges, board games, birthday gifts, cards, dollhouse furniture, vehicles, edifices, paper airplanes, flying creatures, and more.

INCLUDE NATURE

Long before there were Styrofoam trays and plastic cups, preschool teachers relied on natural materials to spark students' creativity, such as rocks with interesting shapes or colors, branches, dried flowers, pine cones, acorns, shelled nuts, and leaves. In today's world of Xboxes, earbuds, and iPhones, many of today's children have never built a stick fence for fairies or a pine cone porcupine. Building with natural materials may have been de rigueur to the Boxcar Children yet downright exotic for your students.

SEEK PROVOCATIONS

You may also wish to supplement these found items with small, inexpensive trinkets from a thrift store. If you are near a Goodwill Outlet, a last-resort warehouse where unsold Goodwill donations get one final chance for acquisition, stop by to stock up on loose game pieces, jewelry, Mardi Gras beads, feathers, toys, and more. Wind-up toys can be hacked into crazy new movable creations. Spools of velvety holiday ribbon or crepe paper can inspire future ribbon dances. Leis can be deconstructed and, with the addition of a wire from an old speaker, converted into floral bouquets. Electronic toys can be taken apart and harvested for their switches, buttons, wire, wheels, axles, and circuit boards. As always, test objects against your own imagination. If it sparks multiple ideas for you, it will likely do so for your students. Goodwill Outlet—a unique warehouse-style thrift store, not a typical Goodwill storefront—sells items by the pound, a bonanza for educators. You can find a location near you at https://www.gwoutletstorelocator.com/.

Not a fan of thrifting? Ask your local fast food restaurant if they have surplus kids' meal toys or unused food containers they can donate, an idea we learned from Pam Williams at the Frankenmuth James E. Wickson District Library in Michigan. Dollar and big box stores can yield inexpensive jewels, party decorations, marbles, small plastic animals, paper plates and cups, inexpensive batteries, and paper.

At hardware stores, look for interesting washers, nuts and bolts, tapes, scraps of wood, and more. At floral shops, seek out plastic cellophane sheets. Office supply stores are great sources of cardboard delivery boxes, index cards, and stickers. Ask colleagues or parents for contributions of unused craft supplies, yarn, fabric scraps, twist ties, toothpicks, bottle caps, gift boxes, and more. Can't decide? Ask kids to help you brainstorm!

Spend as little as possible—the most provocative items will go fast, and if you are mentally adding up the cost of each item in a student's creation, it will add a layer of are-we-going-to-run-out anxiety that is completely preventable.

ADD ACCESSORIES

In Michigan Makers, we generally bring one junk box at a time to our site, though we often have a few spare boxes waiting to go. Inside our large box, we place a smaller plastic, lidded shoe box we call the accessories box that contains glue, tape (washi, cellophane, masking, duct, or gaffer's), scissors, and staplers. While we have some child-sized scissors, we find that students aged nine and up can handle full-length shears we buy for about $1 at dollar or fabric stores. Longer blades can cut thicker materials and make neater cuts. Kitchen shears have good torque while still fitting comfortably in children's hands.

SETTING THE TABLE FOR MAKING

When it's time to make at Michigan Makers, we occupy borrowed space, and tables are limited. We stick the junk box in the middle of the table, set the accessories box next to it, and the kids make an enormous mess right there, with inventory and their works-in-progress intermingling. Sometimes, it seems like there is as much junk on the floor as there is on the table or in the box!

When we travel and have the luxury of more space, we can unpack the box, making piles of like items (or laying them out in bins or clear plastic bags), so that the entire table becomes shopping space. Makers approach the table, can easily survey the materials, get what they need, and move to a separate table for making. This is ideal because gathering materials up front and cleaning up at the end are so much quicker!

FREE RANGE JUNK BOXING

Most weeks, the junk box is the kids' domain. The kids we work with, primarily in grades three to five, tend to be bubbling over with ideas. They are industrious and don't need us to monitor or inspire them. Therefore, the junk box is a station to which we don't assign an adult mentor (except at clean-up time). As many as 10 kids can work productively without adult intervention, which frees us up to work with smaller groups in developing new skills with other tools or materials.

GUIDED JUNK BOX CHALLENGES

At certain times, or with particular students, mentor-initiated challenges can be a better fit. In this case, you might post a challenge designed to inspire a variety of possible solutions. Here are some that former mentor Alex Quay or I have used:

Prototyping: Talk with your group about what an ideal library, classroom, village, smartphone, or homework machine might look like. Create a prototype using items from the junk box. Be ready to give a 30-second pitch that highlights the great features of your creation.

Maze: Use the junk box to create a maze for a marble to pass through. Whose marble can last longest in the maze? What would you need to do to make yours last longest?

Chain Challenge: Using only the materials in the box, create the strongest chain you can. When everyone has created one, hang a cup from each chain. Slowly add bolts, pennies, marbles, or other weights to the cup, one at a time. Whose chain can hold the most?

Metaphorical Sculpture: Create a junk sculpture that represents a key theme or belief of the last book you read or historical era you studied. Be ready to explain it when we Gallery Walk as a class. During a Gallery Walk, half the class stays with its creations, and the other half visits each creation to ask questions. Gallery Walking can be a great way for students to see a diverse collection of potential solutions. It also exerts a gentle peer pressure that nudges students into constructing stronger explanations.

Rube Goldberg Machine: Use the junk box to create a Rube Goldberg machine that has the most triggers or the longest trajectory (by time or linear feet) from start to finish. You can even use the junk box with the Design Thinking Game found elsewhere in this book.

Biographical Sculpture: In lieu of take-home book report crafts, spend a day in class with students creating junk box memorial sculptures in honor of a biographical figure. Then discuss with students how to create an artist statement (see http://www.artbusiness.com/artstate.html for advice) that unpacks the choices made in creating the sculpture. Grade the artist statement, not the sculpture.

For more ideas, see http://sciencespot.net/pages/junkboxprojects.html.

For only a few dollars, a junk box is a K-12 maker program's best investment, an everlasting spring of creativity. Best of all, any student can re-create it at home, regardless of household income, making it a medium that transcends the school day. That's why it's my desert island maker tool of choice. After all, surely I could make a canoe and a paddle out of one and get home that way!

An earlier version of this chapter appeared as "Junk Box Provocations" in the June 2016 "Makerspaces" column of Teacher Librarian. *Special thanks to Edward Kurdyla for permission to reprint it here.*

REFERENCES

Doorley, Rachelle. 2014. *Tinkerlab: A Hands-On Guide for Little Inventors*. Boston, MA: Roost Books.
Fontichiaro, Kristin. 2014. "Provocations." MakerBridge blog. Accessed May 12, 2016, from http://makerbridge.si.umich.edu.proxy.lib.umich.edu/2014/11/provocations/.

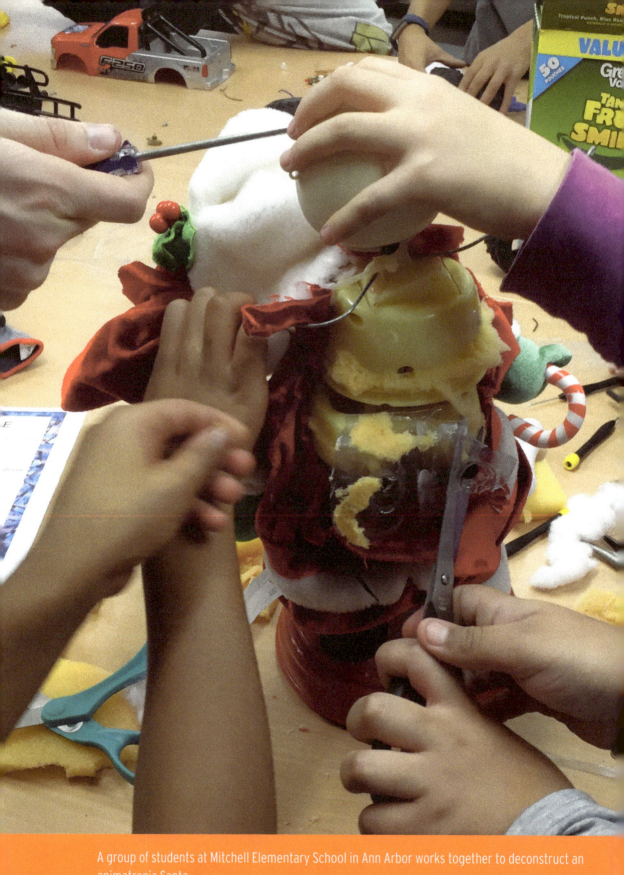

A group of students at Mitchell Elementary School in Ann Arbor works together to deconstruct an animatronic Santa.

CHAPTER 17
TOY TAKEAPART

Kristin Fontichiaro

There are so many products one can buy to let kids experiment with circuits and, by extension, inventions. LittleBits, Arduino microcontrollers, and Snap Circuits come to mind. Each offers affordances to those who use them. But ask yourself: Can your students construct a functioning circuit after engaging with those materials? Do these tools help them see that circuits are circles of energy that flow from wall outlets or battery packs to various components and back to the energy source? That can be a lot trickier. Can we help them see how the components they see in a kit—like speakers and lights—look in the real world? You bet.

INTRODUCING TOY TAKEAPART

An answer may lie in your donation pile: unwanted battery-operated toys. In toy takeapart (also known as wreck lab), unscrew some screws, pry off the back, and you and your students will be engaged in a fascinating journey through how toys are made and molded; how batteries connect to components; how pieces are stacked and fitted together in a compressed space; how circuit boards, resistors, and capacitors are used; and how a toy's exterior buttons, switches, and levers translate into circuits on the other side of the plastic. Best of all, when you're done, you've got more components that

WHAT'S INSIDE YOUR TOYS?

1. Take out the batteries.

2. Put on goggles.

3. Unscrew any visible screws. Choose a screwdriver that is not too big and not too small!

4. Use scissors or pliers to snip off wires or other components.

5. You can take home anything you take apart!

WHICH OF THESE ARE INSIDE YOUR TOY?

SPEAKERS make sound. Magnetic!

LEDs light up. May be different colors.

CAPACITORS store electricity temporarily.

RESISTORS reduce the amount of energy flow. The stripes are a code to tell how much energy they absorb.

Created by the Making in Michigan Libraries project, of the University of Michigan School of Information, made possible in part by the Institute of Museum and Library Services RE-05-15-0021-15. Download additional copies: http://makinglibraries.si.umich.edu/handbook .

Images: Wikipedia & Wikimedia Commons

 SCHOOL OF INFORMATION UNIVERSITY OF MICHIGAN   INSTITUTE of Museum and Library SERVICES

We leave this page out at takeapart events so children and families can make meaning of what they find. Available for download from http://makinglibraries.si.umich.edu/handbook.

you can add to your existing inventory of supplies. Why buy speakers or battery packs when you can harvest them yourselves?

A quick note before moving forward: A variation on toy takeapart and wreck lab is appliance autopsy (hat tip to Sean Elliott in Melbourne), where kids can take apart household items like fans, VCRs, old VHS-sized video cameras, or PC towers. These all make great takeaparts. Just keep in mind that these plug in, which means they can handle 120 volts of energy. By comparison, a toy with four AA batteries provides only 6 volts of energy. If you want to take apart anything with a plug, keep it unplugged for about a week before deconstructing it. This is because many appliances have capacitors in them, which are components (often shaped like short cylinders or orange ibuprofen tablets) that store energy for later use. Allow time for those capacitors to drain their energy so that your students can work without fear of electric shock.

FINDING TOYS

The easiest way to acquire toys is to ask for donations. Some parents are eager for an excuse to shed toys that sing, chirp, or move. As Michigan Makers mentor Nicole Sype points out, donating unwanted toys also offers the opportunity for families to discuss the importance of donating, repurposing, or recycling things they no longer need. Otherwise, look at thrift stores. We frequent the Goodwill Outlet. This isn't your typical Goodwill; instead, an outlet is where items that did not sell at Goodwill stores get one final shot to be sold before being disposed of. Items are sold by weight, not by item. Each Goodwill Outlet has its own culture and pricing system, but you can pretty much count on finding an incredible number of toys on any given day that are priced around $1.20 per pound. Most Goodwill Outlets roll out enormous carts of merchandise every hour or so, with the old carts whisked off and discarded. I like knowing that I'm getting toys that would otherwise be dumpster-bound and that I'm not robbing needy kids from the only toys they can afford, something worth considering if you work in a low-income neighborhood. Look for toys with a battery pack on the bottom. If your makers struggle with impulse control, you may wish to skip toys or appliances that have screens, as they may be tempted to crack them and let out unknown chemicals. Speaking of chemicals, mentor Tori Culler reminds facilitators to remove batteries in advance or, if you prefer children learn to do that first, that you at least inspect the batteries for leakage prior to distributing toys to kids. Don't overlook the possibility of

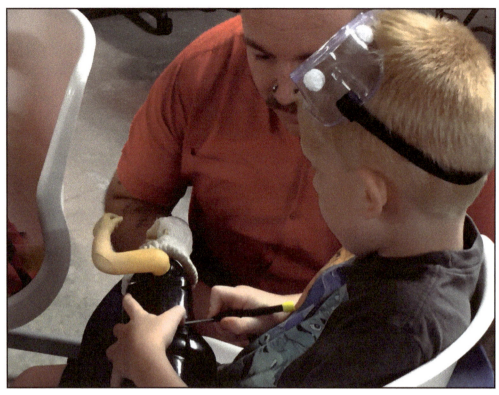

Making in Michigan Libraries graduate student research assistant Jean Hardy helps a patron at the Niles (Michigan) District Library who is disassembling an animated Santa.

animated stuffed animals—sometimes, these are priced even lower. Keep your eyes open for animated Coca-Cola bears, Santas, or snowmen—they are fascinating to deconstruct!

GATHERING TAKEAPART EQUIPMENT

You'll need some tools and safety supplies as well. We store the following in a lidded plastic tote:

- Safety glasses or goggles
- Thin gloves to protect hands when prying components apart
- Precision screwdrivers (the tiny screwdriver kits that have screwdrivers small enough to adjust an eyeglass screw)
- #1-sized standard screwdrivers, ideally with a magnetized head (also known as Phillips head screwdrivers)
- Pliers (needle- or long-nosed and slip-joint)

- Slotted screwdrivers (also known as flat head), mostly used to pry apart layers
- A handout to help students identify parts (find ours at http://bit.ly/toytakeapart)
- A junk box into which students put unwanted parts
- Bowls into which students can place loose screws and batteries
- A garbage can or recycling bin into which unwanted, deconstructed parts can be placed
- A small box or bin in which students can place old batteries, because these will need to be specially recycled

A few shopping tips: it can be tempting to buy a screwdriver set that lets you switch out the tips, but avoid these, as their shaft is wider and may not be

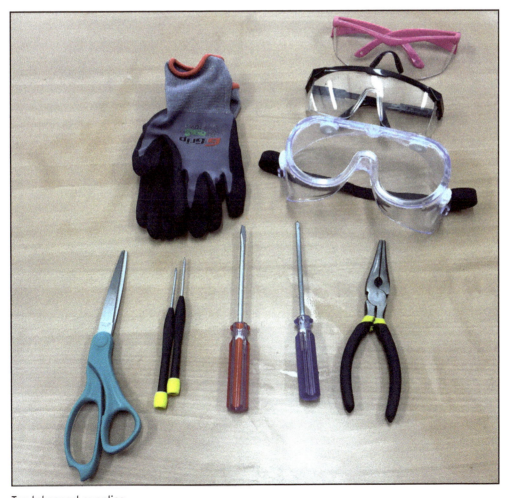

Toy takeapart supplies.

LET'S HACK SOME TOYS!

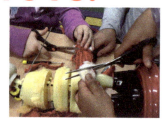

Thursday, August 23, 1-3pm
Niles District Library Skillshare Space

Have you ever wondered what's inside your toys? Let's take them apart and see what makes them move, light up, make music, and more. We'll provide the toys, the tools, and the safety equipment. Do you prefer to make your own games and toys? Glue toy parts together to make a new invention, or make a bean bag! **And did we mention free pizza?**

Meet us in the new basement Skillshare space, where you can get tools and help to make your DIY projects come to life. Whether coming to a class or checking out games, tools, and equipment from the Library of Things, Skillshare wants to help make your life better! Ages 5 to 105 welcome.

This event will be filmed by the University of Michigan. This event is part of the Making in Michigan Libraries project of the U-M School of Michigan and is made possible in part by the Institute of Museum and Library Services RE-05-15-0021-15

Marketing matters! This poster, made for free with Canva.com, was used to explain toy takeapart to families at a Making in Michigan Libraries event at Niles District Library in southwest Michigan.

narrow enough to reach recessed screws. Also, screwdrivers are available in either metric (millimeters) or standard (inches); buy standard, even though most toys are made abroad. Finally, while almost everything on this list can be purchased at a dollar store, "bargain" tools are often made of soft metal that does not stand up to repeated use.

GET KIDS STARTED

We ask students to work in teams of two. This is important for a few reasons. Firstly, sometimes you need one kid to hold on to a toy while the other unscrews it, especially when using tools for the first time. Secondly, it supports the community approach to hands-on work that we value. Finally, four hands work faster than two, meaning that a toy will likely be fully deconstructed at the end of a work period. If kids work alone, you can end up storing an enormous number of half-deconstructed toys that no one wants to explore the following week.

Here are a few tips:

1. Safety first! Take out batteries, put on safety goggles, and wear gloves. Remember: goggles are meant to protect your eyes, not your forehead.
2. "Lefty loosey, righty tighty." Push down while turning the screwdriver to the left. (Some kids actually double up on the screwdriver, with one kid pushing and the other turning, until they get the knack.)
3. Anything you take apart can go home with you.
4. Pick a screwdriver that is the right size for the screws you are working on. (Students are often first drawn to the tiny precision screwdrivers when the external screws usually need the standard/Phillips head screwdriver.)
5. If you can't get a part of your toy to come off, find the hidden screws that are holding it in place or move on and loosen some other screws and components first.
6. Put loose screws in the bowl.
7. Keep taking apart until there is nothing left to take apart.
8. Save unwanted circuit boards, buttons, switches, and components for future projects.

Questions to Consider while Taking Apart

1. Follow the wires to and from the battery pack. Where does the energy go?
2. How does this toy work? How do buttons and switches on the outside make things change on the inside?
3. Does the toy have solder or hot glue holding components together?
4. Can you name the components based on the handout?
5. What kinds of skills would a worker need to assemble these quickly?
6. Compare different toys and identify similar parts. (Toys that look very different on the outside may share many of the same components.)

For additional activities related to takeapart, such as looking up the patent for the toy, calculating labor prices, and considering economic factors, please view the worksheet that follows this essay.

Even a simple baby monitor speaker can reveal complex electronics!

RESPONDING TO WHAT'S INSIDE

We find that children of different ages respond differently to what they find inside. K-3 students tend to find screwdriver use fascinating, enjoy seeing what's inside, like knowing what buttons and levers look like on the outside, think the magnetic quality of speakers is cool (speaker, meet screws!), and particularly relish cutting apart the wires. They seem less interested in following the circuit around the toy and seeing where things travel. Middle-grade students become more interested in the circuitry itself, identifying parts from the handout. High school students and adults may act like they're too cool to take things apart, but when you're not looking, they'll admit that it's pretty fascinating that a lever outside a Fisher-Price toy actually rubs along an electronic circuit board on the inside!

WHAT COMES NEXT?

As a follow-up to a toy takeapart session, students could:

1. Reassemble their toy.
2. Use the components to make a new toy.
3. Draw the circuits they found in the toy.
4. Put leftover pieces in the junk box for future low-tech inventions.
5. Make circuit board jewelry.
6. Play with Squishy Circuits (squishycircuits.com), which uses playdough instead of solder to connect components, or explore purchased or homemade circuit blocks (cippgh.org/circuit-blocks/).
7. Ask students how many kinds of each item they saw, such as screws and capacitors. Ask how long they think it would take to install each part. How much would they want to be paid for each installed part? How much does that add up to, and how much did the toy cost? What does that translate to in terms of wages?
8. Figure out where the toy was manufactured and use a globe to compare that location to where students are now.

The worksheet that follows this essay has even more ideas.

A young patron at the Niles (Michigan) District Library gathered discarded toy parts from other makers and hot-glued them into a new wall hanging.

CONCLUSION

Toy takeapart is infectious—we love taking things apart as much as kids do. It creates a sense of wonder and gives new life to cast-off items. Sometimes the value of the batteries and other parts harvested from a toy outweigh the purchase price, so it can pay for itself! Most importantly, it helps students see circuits in the things they play with every day.

An earlier version of this chapter appeared as "Toy Take-Apart: Mass Destruction for a Purpose" in the February 2017 "Makerspaces" column of Teacher Librarian. *Special thanks to Edward Kurdyla for permission to reprint it here.*

NAMES _____

TOY TAKEAPART WORKSHEET

PART I: BEFORE YOU TAKE ANYTHING APART

Look under your toy or near the battery pack to find information. You may not find every answer there, but answer what you can!

1. Before you start, take a photograph of your toy.

2. What is the name of this toy? If no name is present, describe it here.

3. What does it look like this toy does? Make noise? Light up? Move? What else?

4. Who manufactured this toy (e.g., Mattel, VTECH, Fisher-Price)?

5. What is the trademark date stamped on the toy?

6. In what country was this toy manufactured?

7. Is there a patent number on the toy? If so, write it down here.

8. Set up a cup to collect your screws. You will need them later!

PART II: MID-DECONSTRUCTION

1. Have each team member time the other. How long does it take Person A to completely **screw in** one screw? _____
How about Person B? _____

2. Grab scrap paper or some sticky notes and use them to create annotations around your partially-deconstructed toy. Consider **cool things you have noticed, questions you have,** or **aha moments**.

3. When you are done, take a photo of your annotated work-in-progress.

PART III: AFTER TAKING A TOY APART

1. Do another round of annotation, labeling the parts you recognize.

2. Snap a photo and email it to toytakeapart@umich.edu.

3. Did you have time to remove all screws? YES / NO

4. In total, how many screws did you remove? _____

PART IV: ANALYSIS AND REFLECTION

1. What did you learn from taking this toy apart?

2. What will you do with the pieces you have taken apart?

3. Look for the recycling symbol on the plastic parts of toys. Can you find it? What does that mean for the life cycle of the toy after you are done with it today?

4. If you know the name of your product, search a big store website like Target.com, Walmart.com, or Amazon.com. If the product is still being sold, write the price here. If it is *not* being sold, use the description you created in Part I to search for a similar product. Write the retail price here: _____

Let's calculate how long it would take someone just to screw this toy together. Multiply the number of seconds from each person in Part II by the total number of screws from Part III.

Total seconds required for Person A: _____

How many minutes is that? _____
(total number of seconds divided by 60)

How many hours is that? _____
(total minutes divided by 60)

Total seconds required for Person B: _____

How many minutes is that? _____
(total number of seconds divided by 60)

How many hours is that? _____
(total minutes divided by 60)

5. Look up the hourly minimum wage for your state. How much would you have earned to make this toy? Multiply your total hours from above by the minimum wage per hour.

   a. Wages for Person A: _____
   b. Wages for Person B: _____

6. Retail prices are usually half (50%) of sales prices. Divide the retail (selling) price in two to determine how much the factory received for manufacturing the toy (the wholesale price). Write it here _____.

7. Compare the wholesale price to the wages. Do you think this toy could be manufactured in your state if the total cost of components was $3? $5? $10? Explain why or why not.

8. Consider that there is a trade war brewing between the U.S. and China that could raise the price of products brought over from China. Toys are not currently on the list for consideration. Think about these statistics:

   a. The U.S. imports over $20 billion worth of toys from China annually.
   b. According to the U.S. Commerce Department, almost 91% of toys sold in the U.S. are made in China.
   c. The toy company Hasbro is already planning to move some toy production out of China to hedge against these potential tariffs.

If the proposed tariffs were to include Chinese toys, what might the impact be on your household? On businesses and entrepreneurs in your region? What recommendations would you make to your political leaders? Would you have a different opinion if you lived in Michigan, where American Plastic Toys has its headquarters?

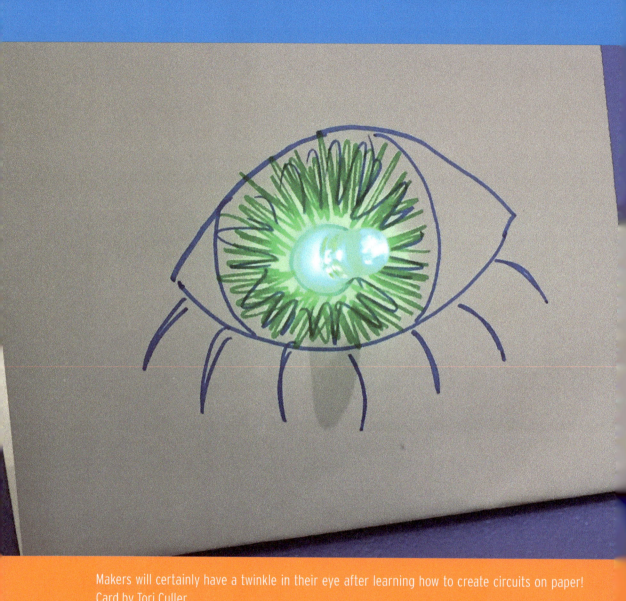

Makers will certainly have a twinkle in their eye after learning how to create circuits on paper! Card by Tori Culler.

CHAPTER 18
PAPER CIRCUITS

Tori Culler and Caroline Wack

If you've never done anything involving electricity or circuitry, the idea of incorporating it into your makerspace can be daunting. Luckily, there are many different kinds of circuitry activities that are safe and enjoyable for makers from all levels to engage with. You may be familiar with other entry-level circuit activities such as Snap Circuits, LittleBits, and play dough–based Squishy Circuits, but perhaps less known is paper circuitry. Paper circuitry is a great introduction for makers who are new to working with electricity and/or those who want to work up to larger projects using electricity but need a simple place to begin learning the basics.

GETTING STARTED

What also makes paper circuitry such a great activity is that it only requires a few affordable materials that are easily obtainable online:

- Conductive copper tape
- LED light bulbs
- 3-volt coin cell batteries (the CR 2032 size is useful because it has a flat profile)
- 9-volt alkaline batteries

- Resistors
- Clear tape
- Markers
- Paper
- Binder clips

You can view our Amazon shopping list for recommended materials at http://bit.ly/michigan-makers-paper-circuitry.

HOW TO LEARN

Paper circuitry is easier than you think. At the beginning, it is best if you and your makers garner an understanding of how the materials you will be using work. A circuit is a complete path through which electricity can flow. Complete circuits consist of a power source, a light source, and some sort of conduit that allows the electricity to travel between these components. For our purposes here in paper circuitry, the coin cell battery is the power source, and the copper tape that connects the LED bulb to the battery is our conduit, channeling the electricity that makes it light up. A few video resources are listed below that explain each of these materials in more detail:

- **Copper Tape**—http://bit.ly/copper-tape-basics
- **LED Bulbs**—http://bit.ly/led-bulb-basics
- **Batteries**—http://bit.ly/battery-basics

Once you have an understanding of these materials, you are ready to dive in and create a simple circuit. A simple circuit is the easiest kind to make, and involves connecting only one LED to a battery via a single, unbroken line of copper tape. You can see one in action here: http://bit.ly/simple-circuit-example.

The projects that can be made using a simple circuit alone are numerous, and could include greeting cards, masks, and storybooks. But for makers who would like to use more than one LED at a time by playing around with series and parallel circuits using resistors, mastering Ohm's law is the next step. Ohm's law does require a basic understanding of algebra, and so may work best with makers who have reached that point in their education.

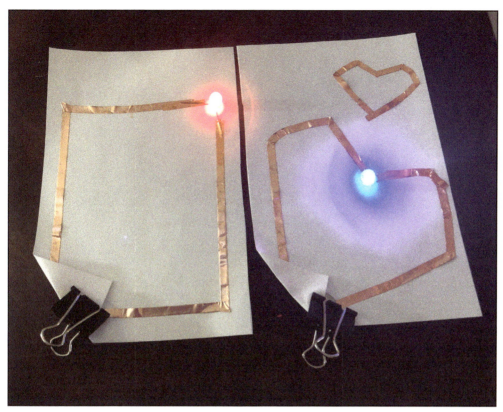

Simple circuits can be straightforward or decorative and artistic. Encourage makers to get creative!

Ohm's law describes the relationship between voltage, current, and resistance. Voltage refers to the amount of potential energy in a circuit. You can think of this as why a shock from a 9-volt battery would sting just a bit more than a shock from a 3-volt battery: it has more potential energy! Current refers to the flow of electrons in a circuit, and resistance is a measure of the amount of force in a circuit working against the flow of electricity.

Ohm's law is a formula written as:

$$V = IR$$

Where V = Voltage, I = Current, and R = Resistance.

To better understand how to apply Ohm's law in creating circuitry projects, these short tutorials can help to get you started:

- http://bit.ly/calculating-resistance
- http://bit.ly/ohms-law-and-resistance

In this context, understanding Ohm's law helps to incorporate resistance into circuits and keep our LED lights from burning out by accidentally feeding them too much electricity. By doing so, you can incorporate more LEDs into your projects in more interesting arrangements. Learning how to calculate resistance in circuits allows makers to go beyond the simple circuit to series and parallel circuits.

It is worth noting here that while all of this may seem complicated, this is an activity that can be adapted to the levels and needs of your maker community. Younger makers, for example, can still engage with paper-based circuitry activities without needing to incorporate resistors or even copper tape! A few of the projects listed below, such as the paper flashlights and the LED greeting cards, require nothing more than a coin cell battery and an LED bulb to create a functioning circuit that will introduce makers to the foundations of creating with electricity.

PROJECTS

A recommended way to introduce circuitry to your makers is by presenting them with circuit templates as a guide. Such templates are available many places online for free. Check out Chibitronics[1] for some examples, or simply draw your own as we've done below!

A template can help makers become comfortable internalizing the concept of circuitry and laying down continuous strips of foil and bending them to turn corners. It takes some practice to lay down continuous pieces of foil tape, but bending instead of breaking the tape creates a stronger conduit for electricity. Once this has been mastered, there are many opportunities for variation.

In terms of specific projects, makers can generally incorporate paper circuitry into any paper-based project they wish, leaving lots of room for creativity and experimentation. Using LEDs in greeting cards is one way to make something that can be shared with others. To make a greeting card, simply have makers fold a page of cardstock in half. They can draw a design on the front and incorporate LEDs in any number of arrangements. On the inside of the card, they can then draw a simple, series, or parallel circuit out of copper tape to bring their creation to life. Design choices can include whether or not to keep the circuit exposed or hidden or even whether to include a switch to turn the light on and off. Many great tutorials in that vein can be found online, such as this one detailing how to make a cupcake- and a robot-based card: http://bit.ly/circuitry-greeting-cards.

---

[1] See https://chibitronics.com/templates/.

PAPER CIRCUITS 207

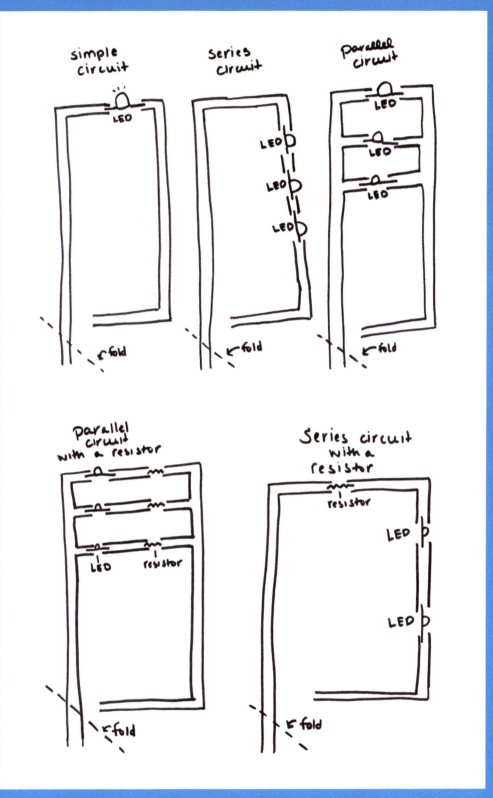

Instead of photocopying templates for makers, have them draw their own as we've done here. This saves you prep time while also giving makers experience in creating schematics!

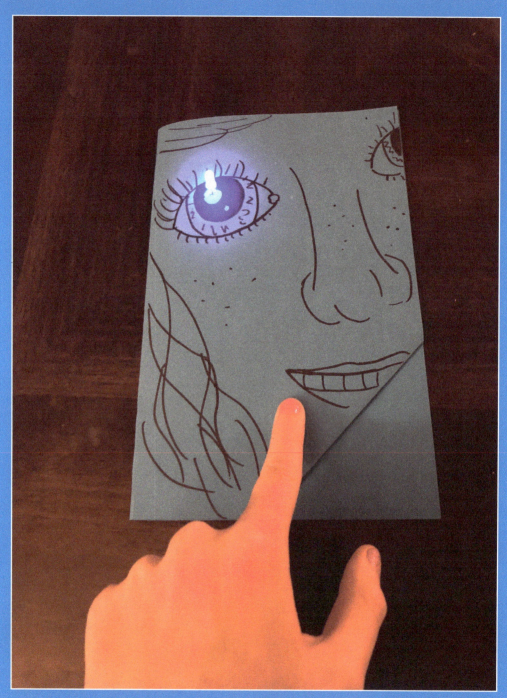
Example of a greeting card which uses a push-button switch to light up the LED.

PAPER CIRCUITS 209

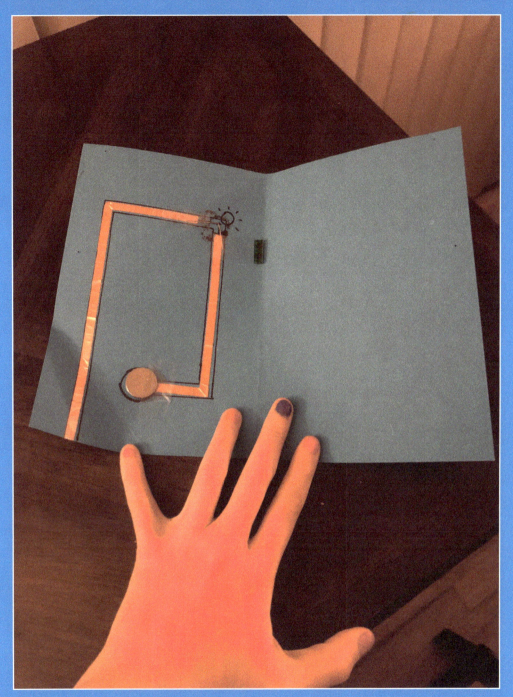

The inside of the card features a simple circuit created using a quickly drawn template similar to those provided above. In the top right corner of the circuit pictured here you can see the legs of the LED which have been poked through the paper and folded down to make contact with the copper tape (the bulb is on the front of the card). The switch was created by folding the bottom corner so that when pressed it connects with the battery and completes the circuit, thus lighting the LED!

Circuitry for Beginners: Simplified Greeting Cards

Does the use of copper tape to create circuits within greeting cards sound like it may be outside the scope of your makerspace? If so, consider beginning with the simplified version of this activity, which is especially well-received by younger makers.

The setup of this activity is the same as described above: Have makers fold a piece of cardstock or construction paper in half and draw their design on the front, accounting for where they would like their LED bulb to be incorporated. Next, poke the leads of the LEDs through the designated spots. Instead of fussing with copper tape, the beginner version of this activity simply has makers place their coin cell battery between the leads of the LED to get it to light up. Make sure the positive side and negative sides of the battery are touching the positive and negative sides of the LED lead, respectively. You can tell which is which on the bulb by remembering that the longer lead is the positive one. Once the LED is lit, makers can secure the connection by applying electrical tape, tightly securing the LED's

Examples of greeting cards created by makers at Ypsilanti District Library utilizing the simplified version of this activity.

leads ("legs") to the battery. The leads of the LED can then be bent and affixed to the back of the card so that it stays secure. See the photos below for reference.

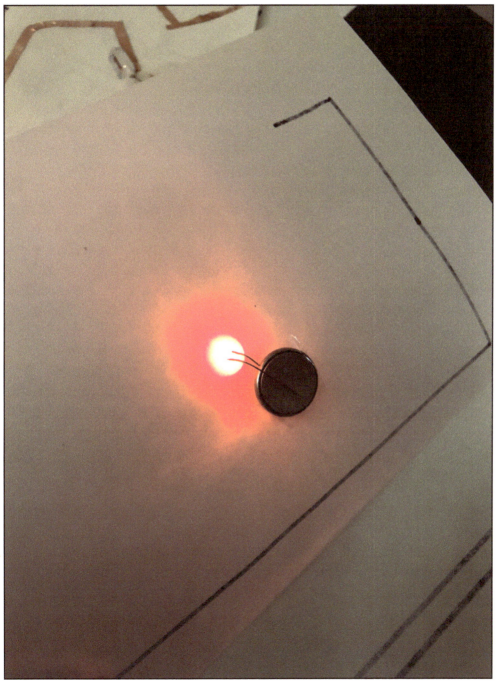

In the low-tech version of this activity you don't have to fuss with any copper tape—simply use a piece of tape to affix the coin cell battery directly to the LED!

Circuitry for Beginners: Flashlights

Flashlights are a slightly more complicated project for when makers have mastered LED greeting cards. Begin with a paper template like the ones on page 214 (cut along the solid lines to produce the template). You should end up with rectangular pieces of paper with a tab sticking out the top. With younger makers, we also use a scissors blade to score along the bold line where the tab meets the main flashlight pattern. Fold in the sides along the dotted line, then fold up the bottom half and fold down the tab on the top. Pre-creasing before you've added any batteries or tape will make the final folding easier.

Now poke an LED through the paper on the top edge, right on the dotted line between the tab and the main body of the template. The light should be on the outside of the paper template, while the leads are on the inside.

Bend the longer (positive) LED lead down so that it lies flat on the paper. Place a piece of double-sided foam tape on the inside of the template, underneath where you just bent the positive lead down, so that the lead now sticks to the tape. Now place a coin cell battery on top. Remember to make sure that the flat, or positive, side of the battery is down, so that it matches up with the LED lead!

If we taped the other LED lead to the battery now, we'd have a flashlight that was always on, and where's the fun in that? Instead, cut out two small pieces of double-sided foam tape and stick them to the top and bottom of the battery, leaving a gap in the middle where the battery is exposed. Lay the LED lead on top of the tape. When constructed properly, the lead will not touch the battery normally, but when someone pushes on it, it will make contact, lighting up the LED until pressure is removed.

Now that your flashlight is constructed, re-fold it to hide the battery and tape. Fold in the sides first, then fold the bottom half up, then fold the tab down over it and secure it with a piece of scotch tape. (You can also tuck the tab in the little "envelope" at the top to avoid having to use tape, as is shown in the graphic.) Voila! You now have a working flashlight.

In addition to the projects described above, other options include paper masks, paper lanterns, storybooks, and zines. More or less any traditional paper-based makerspace project can be enlivened with the addition of some copper tape and LED bulbs! Consider, too, the option of getting creative with battery and bulb arrangements using alternative materials such as duct tape. The duct tape bracelets pictured below and inspired by Amy Quinn's book *Making Electric Jewelry* (Cherry Lake Publishing, 2017) are always a huge hit at maker events!

CONCLUSION

Paper circuitry is a fantastic way to instill self-confidence into young makers. The first time they get an LED to light up they will express the tell-tale signs of eager excitement. This low-tech activity will feel more high-tech than it is, inspiring some to go beyond paper circuitry and learn more. And indeed, the skills gained from learning circuitry on paper can be transferred to other kinds of circuitry and other contexts as well. If makers enjoy this activity, they may also like learning to use conductive thread to sew wearable electronics, or perhaps soldering actual wires together to create circuits that way, or maybe even programming LEDs with Arduinos. Paper circuitry is a foundational activity for teaching makers about electricity in an accessible way.

Makers proudly model their avant-garde light-up bracelets, inspired by Amy Quinn's book *Making Electric Jewelry*.

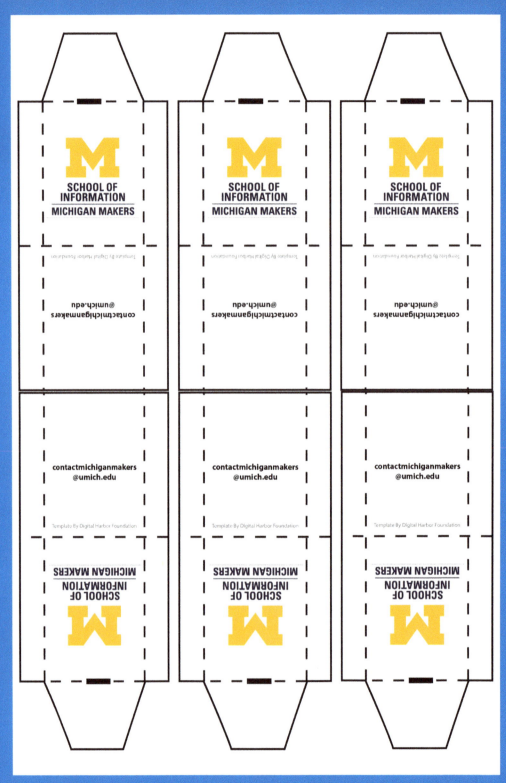

Former graduate student research assistant Mayank Khanna adapted the original cardstock template provided to us by Baltimore's Digital Harbor Foundation. You can download these templates as a PDF at http://makinglibraries.si.umich.edu/handbook.

PAPER CIRCUITS   215

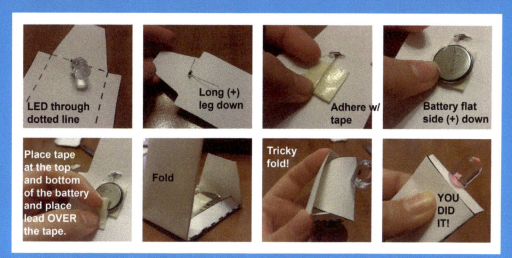

Flashlight instructions created by Amber Lovett

To re-create a bracelet like this in your own makerspace, simply poke the LED leads through the duct tape just as you would with paper and affix each LED to its own battery as detailed above in the simplified greeting cards activity. Fold the LEDs into place, then cover up the battery on the back with another piece of duct tape. Add adhesive Velcro to fasten.

Jimmy McLaren, maker coordinator at the Benzonia Public Library, created this cardboard robot to advertise for a community cardboard challenge event.

CHAPTER 19
CARDBOARD CHALLENGES

Tori Culler

Many of the best library makerspace activities rely on the use of cheap, everyday materials to spark creativity and engender new ways of thinking. Cardboard challenges are a perfect example of this in action. The basis for a cardboard challenge is simple: makers are given an assortment of cardboard and tools and are encouraged to prototype products for any number of uses—be they practical, abstract, or decorative. Cardboard challenges can be designed in any number of ways depending on your community. You can provide your makers with a specific prompt, for example, or opt for a more free-flowing drop-in environment. No matter the format, such events are usually filled with energy and excitement. Fully functional arcade games, makeshift weaving looms, full-size playhouses, and playful costumes are just a few examples of the kinds of items that your makers may come up with.

Beyond the sheer fun-factor of creating with such a highly manipulable material as cardboard, doing so instills some of the essential skills of making. By observing the innumerable possibilities of creation in themselves and others using items that are normally thrown away or recycled, makers may begin to view the world around them a little bit differently, envisioning new ways to upcycle what is usually considered waste. Furthermore, they stand to gain a lot in the way of learning the principles of Design Thinking.

Design Thinking is a problem-solving process that was conceived by the IDEO design group and has gained traction across the globe in many educational and corporate settings. This process consists of a series of phases in which makers confront a problem, research the problem, brainstorm potential solutions, and create and test prototypes of products to solve the problem. A carefully considered cardboard challenge can lead makers of all ages through this process from start to finish within the span of a few hours, leaving makers feeling accomplished, self-efficacious, and creatively satisfied.

GETTING STARTED

While the materials needed for a cardboard challenge are relatively straightforward, advanced planning is needed to provide yourself enough time to find or order the right items for your community's needs.

- A variety of cardboard
    - ☐ Corrugated/rigid (think: boxes used for packing and shipping)
    - ☐ Paperboard (as in: the kind of boxes that cereal, crackers, and the like come in)
    - ☐ Poster board (similar to the paperboard described above; great for big, cheap pieces!)
    - ☐ Egg cartons
    - ☐ Toilet paper, paper towels, wrapping paper tubes
- Cutting tools
    - ☐ Scissors
    - ☐ Box cutters, X-Acto knives, and/or utility knives
    - ☐ Makedo cardboard cutting tools (http://makedo.com)
    - ☐ Canary knives[1]
    - ☐ A box cutting power tool, such as Zipsnip[2]
- Fastening tools
    - ☐ Hot glue guns
    - ☐ Packing and/or duct tape
    - ☐ Plastic rivets or screws, such as those from Makedo[3]

---

1 For example, http://bit.ly/canary-knives.
2 See http://bit.ly/zip-snip.
3 See http://bit.ly/makedo-screws.

- Decorative elements
    - ☐ Markers
    - ☐ Acrylic paint
    - ☐ Printed duct tape or washi tape
    - ☐ Glitter
- Miscellaneous items to have on hand
    - ☐ Brown paper bags
    - ☐ Newspaper
    - ☐ Junk box items
    - ☐ Design Challenge prompts
    - ☐ Labeled recycling bins for scraps

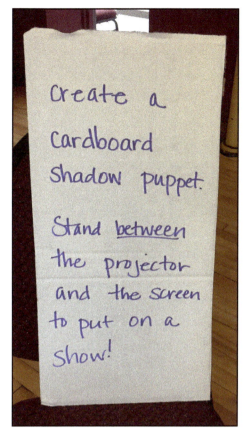

The trick to a good cardboard challenge is providing a good balance of open-ended making and just the right amount of structured guidance.

When it comes to collecting your cardboard, be creative in soliciting donations. Ask for parents to help contribute by saving their boxes. IKEA, as it turns out, has a history of donating its used cardboard for the very purpose of helping kids think creatively (O'Brien 2018)! You can also try asking restaurants, grocery stores, appliance stores, and recycling centers for their gently used cardboard. And don't forget that having a variety of cardboard on hand is key—a mixture of heavy and thin cardboard will lend best to the design studio environment.

In considering cutting tools, be sure to consider the skill level and safety concerns you may have for your maker community. While cardboard is very versatile, it can be tough to shape with just scissors on hand. Fortunately, there are a number of tools that are specialized for cutting cardboard, though they tend to be rather sharp and may not be the safest option for younger children. The company Makedo (https://www.make.do/) sells kits for working with cardboard that include plastic saws and other tools that are kid friendly. A YouTube review weighing the pros and cons of various cardboard manipulating tools can be found here: http://bit.ly/cardboard-tools.

POTENTIAL PROJECTS

As has been mentioned, a good way to get started with cardboard in your makerspace is to consider hosting a cardboard challenge that incorporates the elements of Design Thinking. If this sounds interesting, you can check out

At the Benzonia Public Library's Cardboard Challenge event, we used a shower curtain, a digital projector, and a small IKEA clothing rack to create a show puppet screen. The shadow puppets were cut from cardboard scraps.

https://cardboardchallenge.com/ to get inspired, learn more about hosting an event, or find an event nearby. You can also follow the Design Thinking process as described below to guide your makers through an experience:

Step 1. Identify a Problem

This step can be approached in a number of ways. You can give your makers a specific prompt around a real-world problem that can be solved by creating a product or thing. It could be something as silly as "Make the perfect cat tree for cats to play on" or something as serious as "Design the safest possible car." You can also leave this more open, asking participants to define their own problem based upon something that matters to them.

Another option is to use our Design Thinking Game. In this game, makers randomly draw cards from two different stacks that feature pre-written prompts. One stack of cards, for example, has statements like: "Create a house for a . . ." or "Make a communication device for a . . ." The second stack of cards contains subjects, such as "Ninja," "Mermaid," "Teacher," "Doctor," and "Student." See Chapter 31 for details.

Some makers really enjoy working with cardboard using our Design Thinking Game. Here is a variation on "build a house for a fairy" in progress.

Step 2. Research, Observe, and Interview

In this step, makers should think more deeply about the problem. If their prompt is based in reality, you should encourage them to think about products already on the market that may address the problem and how these products could be improved based on what users need. If their prompt is a little more fantastical, encourage them to ask thoughtful questions nonetheless. What *would* a mermaid need to communicate? Who would they be communicating with and for what purpose?

Step 3. Synthesize and Focus

This is the part of the process where makers should begin thinking about what particular aspect of the problem they would like to address. What patterns did they see emerging in the research phase? What specific part of the problem do they want to focus on? If they are designing a safe car, for example, what kind of car are they going to design and for whom?

Step 4. Brainstorm

This part is simple: makers should think up as many possible solutions as possible, sketching up the results for the most promising ones. Depending on how your makerspace is set up and the goals you would like to achieve, makers could be working alone or in groups at this stage.

Step 5. Prototype

And finally: makers get to dive in to creating whatever product they have decided on with cardboard! They should be encouraged to get creative with the materials and remember that the object they are creating is likely a mock-up or prototype and not a final product.

Step 6. Test, Adjust, Test Again

Once makers have drafted their first prototype, they should test it out themselves and with members from their target users if possible. At the very least, they should get a bit of feedback and make some tweaks so they can get a feel for design as an iterative process.

Even though the cardboard mock-ups makers create in cardboard challenges may not end up surviving for very long past the event itself, go big or go home is still a good motto to live by! Here, Jimmy McLaren, maker coordinator at the Benzonia Public Library, shows off his creativity.

Following the above steps is a surefire way to introduce some structure into your cardboard challenge event. It is by no means, however, the only way to conduct such an event. Another option is to simply provide the space and materials for makers to come in and be inspired, creating to their hearts' content.

In our most recent iteration of the cardboard challenge activity, for example, we had makers work together to build a cardboard city. The only structure we provided was an outlined city map made of painters tape that delineated roads and city blocks. Makers then filled in the empty space with cardboard houses, a farm, a soccer field, and even a helipad for their town rocket launcher! In this way, makers were not only able to explore creating prototypes with a new medium, they were also able to meaningfully contribute to a group effort. As is evident, then, the possibilities for cardboard challenges are truly endless.

For more information on using Design Thinking in makerspace activities and planning cardboard challenges with your particular audience in mind, see Kristin Fontichiaro's articles in Teacher Librarian *for December 2016 and April 2017, respectively.*

224 PROJECTS AND PROGRAMS

One of the many cardboard homes lining our cardboard city's streets at an event at the Ypsilanti District Library's Michigan Avenue Branch. This one even features a "stained glass" window!

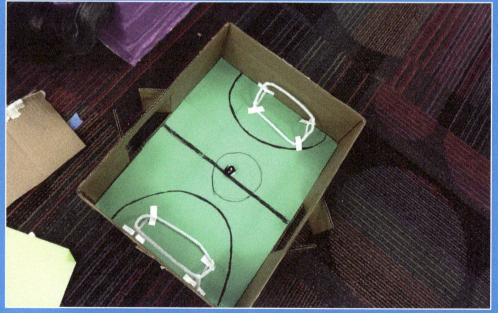

The town soccer field in all its glory at the Ypsilanti District Library's Michigan Avenue Branch.

REFERENCES

Fontichiaro, Kristin. 2016. "Inventing Products with Design Thinking: Balancing Structure with Open-Ended Thinking." *Teacher Librarian*, December, 53.

Fontichiaro, Kristin. 2017. "Planning a Community Cardboard Challenge." *Teacher Librarian*, April, 51+.

O'Brien, Kyle. 2018. "Ikea Finds Practical Use for Its Cardboard Box Waste in Helping Kids Create Toys." *The Drum*, June 20. Retrieved July 11, 2019, from https://www.thedrum.com/news/2018/06/20/ikea-finds-practical-use-its-cardboard-box-waste-helping-kids-create-toys.

Intimidated by knitting? Don't be! Finger knitting is a great introduction for all ages. By mastering a few simple steps makers will be churning out their own handmade knitwear in no time.

CHAPTER 20
KNITTING AND CROCHET

Tori Culler

Needlework crafts such as knitting and crochet are timeless additions to any well-rounded makerspace. While many may think of these activities as less stimulating than other kinds of exciting things that go on in makerspaces, knitting is actually a perfect representation of the culture of the maker movement. By learning to knit, makers are empowered to create and design things that add value to their own lives and those of the people around them. Simply by mastering a few basic techniques and developing the courage to experiment, the possibilities open to knitters are expansive. What starts as knitting items for yourself or your family and friends can quickly translate into participating in charity knit drives[1], contributing to a public art project[2], or even starting a social movement.[3]

GETTING STARTED

The good news is that you don't even have to be an expert needleworker to provide knitting and crochet opportunities in your makerspace. All you really need to get started is yarn and a pair of scissors. Finger knitting and finger crochet allow you to learn and teach the basics without the need for specialized needles and hooks, though these implements can easily be added at any point. This makes needlework crafts an accessible addition to your

---

1 See https://www.craftsy.com/knitting/article/crocheting-and-knitting-for-charity/.
2 See https://www.craftsy.com/knitting/article/how-to-yarn-bomb/.
3 See https://www.pussyhatproject.com/our-story/.

makerspace given that they can be adapted to a variety of skill levels for all kinds of makers, though we recommend trying this one out with kids around age six and older.

When deciding what kind of yarn to buy, nearly anything you can purchase at your local craft supply store will do, making this a low-cost activity to start up as there are many options available in bulk. In general, a standard, worsted weight yarn is best, though thicker yarns may make stitches easier to see for beginners. "Worsted" is a merely a fancy word describing the thickness of standard acrylic yarn (see photos below for reference). You will also want to avoid yarns with lots of extra frills and adornments for starter projects. Further, reading the labels on your yarn choices is wise, as this will tell you what kind of fibers it is composed of and whether or not it is machine-washable or able to withstand exposure to heat. Most mass-produced yarns are acrylic and are fine for most uses, for example, but if makers are wanting to create something for the kitchen (such as an oven mitt or dishrag) you'll want to look for a cotton or wool yarn instead.

If you are purchasing needles and hooks, needles that aren't too small or too large are best. Every knitting pattern will call for a specific needle size, but in the beginning when makers are just playing around, having a variety of tools on hand in the mid-size range is best. For knitting needles, look for those labeled as U.S. size 7–13 (4.0mm–9.00mm). And for crochet hooks,

Examples of yarn "weights" or thicknesses. On the left is a very thin sock weight yarn, in the middle is a standard worsted weight yarn, and on the right is a chunky weight yarn. Aim for the middle of the road worsted weight yarn for beginning projects.

look for those in the range of H–L (5.00mm–8.00mm). Thrift stores often have a jug of needles and hooks so you can build your collection at low cost. A yarn or tapestry needle is also good to have on hand for finishing projects and tying together loose ends.

HOW TO LEARN

Once your materials are gathered, there are several options for beginning projects and teaching makers. You could bring in local needleworkers, offer print resources, or consult online tutorials.

By asking around for volunteers, you may be surprised to find people in your area who are willing to share their time and expertise. Learning one-on-one from an experienced knitter or crocheter is an especially helpful way to pick up the craft. While it is certainly possible to learn on one's own, getting real-time advice from someone who is patient and willing to help can mitigate much of the frustration that beginners may face. Try asking around in parent circles, local yarn shops, and retirement centers to get started. Keep an eye out, too, for left-handed knitters and crocheters who can help provide special guidance to left-handed makers.

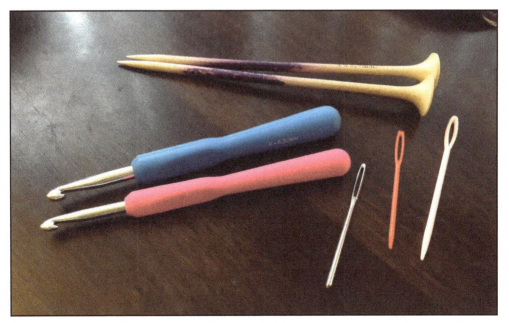

Crochet hooks and knitting needles will be clearly labeled either on the packaging or the tool itself; look for the specifications described above. Pictured on the far right here are also tapestry needles which are sure to come in very handy in the construction of any knit or crochet projects!

If reaching out to community members proves fruitless or is inaccessible for your makerspace, begin looking to other resources such as print and online materials. Most public libraries still have large selections of crafting books and magazines in circulation, including those based in knitting and crochet. Such print tutorials are a time-tested way of learning, though following the diagrams in these sources can be tricky.

The most common way for makers to learn on their own is by watching video tutorials. YouTube is full of knit- and crochet-based channels that provide accessible tutorials to people of all ages and skill levels. The beauty of learning through YouTube videos is that learners can take things at their own pace, pausing and rewinding at leisure until they master the steps.

PROJECTS

Before tackling knitting or crocheting with needles and hooks, it is advisable to begin with finger knitting or crochet. Finger knitting allows makers

Finger-knitted bracelets in progress at Mitchell Elementary School in Ann Arbor, MI.

to use one hand as a miniature loom while manipulating the yarn with their other hand. The result is thin strips of flexible fabric that can be fashioned into bracelets, necklaces, belts, headbands, keychains, and more. These are the perfect kinds of projects that can bring beginning knitters the satisfaction of being able to complete a project in a single sitting. In the case of finger crochet, on the other hand, makers simply use their index finger as a makeshift crochet hook and are able to create larger, more dynamic fabric swatches that can be built into a number of projects, including scarves, blankets, bags, and more.

Check out the following YouTube playlists for each of these options:

- Finger knitting: http://bit.ly/knit-finger
- Finger crocheting: http://bit.ly/crochet-finger

An example of a finger crocheted scarf. Made entirely without the use of any needles or hooks!

For makers who are ready to jump into the league of traditional knitting and crochet with tools, the best place to start is by mastering the basic stitches. For knitting, the two stitches upon which everything is built are the knit and purl stitches. By combining the two, any number of patterns are possible. For crochet, the most basic starting point is the single crochet stitch. In either case, starting out with a two-dimensional project such as a scarf, bracelet, or bookmark is a good way to master these skills while quickly seeing the fruits of one's labors result in a functional object.

To get started viewing some examples of knit and crochet stitches, visit the following YouTube playlists:

- Basic knitting stitches: http://bit.ly/basic-knit-stitches
- Basic crochet stitches: http://bit.ly/basic-crocheting-stitches

Once makers have mastered the basic needlework skills, there are a number of knitting and crochet online communities to consult for free and low-cost patterns. One such example is www.ravelry.com. When searching for patterns on Ravelry, users can apply a number of useful filters, including that of difficulty level.

CONCLUSION

In the end, the thing to remember about incorporating knitting and crocheting into your makerspace is not to be intimidated! All you really need is yarn, a pair of scissors, and some form of tutorial. These needlework crafts can add a lot of value to your space, providing makers with an invaluable practical skill that will ignite their creativity.

And bear in mind, too, that many of the benefits of knitting and crocheting go beyond just the practicality of creating wearable fabrics. The experience of learning to follow and create knitting patterns imparts many of the higher-order thinking skills involved in STEM disciplines, including pattern

Finger-knit accessories are for everyone . . . even stuffed reindeer!

recognition and algorithmic thinking. Some of the first "programming" that ever happened, in fact, happened on knitting machines.

But perhaps one of the best cases for teaching makers to knit is that once they get in the groove of things, it is an excellent form of self-soothing. On the whole, knitters self-report being more relaxed and clear headed than non-knitters. Needleworking is gaining prominence as a therapeutic technique, due to its ability to enhance feelings of self-control, self-expression, purpose, and social support. (See Kristin Fontichiaro's article on making as self-soothing for additional information.)

What's more is that knitting and crochet can be turned into a regular creative practice for makers to help bring joy to others as well. If they find that they have a knack for it and want to do more with their newfound handicrafts, makers can consider forming regular knitting group meetings and/or knitting for charity projects. Examples include Project Linus[4], which accepts donations of handmade blankets for children in need, and the Snuggles Project[5], to which needleworkers can donate handmade items to brighten and comfort the lives of shelter animals and their caregivers.

Clearly, then, it is well worth the time to invest in needlework crafts within your makerspace. At the least, it can serve as a respite for makers. And best-case scenario, it teaches them a variety of skills that will last a lifetime that they can use to contribute to the well-being of others.

REFERENCES

Fontichiaro, Kristin. "Making as Self-Soothing: The Power of Stitches." *Teacher Librarian*, June 2018. Pp.53–56.
Laskow, Sarah. 2014. "Before Computers, People Programmed Looms." *The Atlantic*. Retrieved from https://www.theatlantic.com/technology/archive/2014/09/before-computers-people-programmed-looms/380163/.
Peruzza, Nadia, and Elizabeth Anne Kinsella. 2010. "Creative Arts Occupations in Therapeutic Practice: A Review of the Literature." *British Journal of Occupational Therapy, 73*(6), 261–268.
Riley, Jill, Betsan Corkhill, and Clare Morris. 2013. "The Benefits of Knitting for Personal and Social Wellbeing in Adulthood: Findings from an International Survey." *British Journal of Occupational Therapy, 76*(2), 50–57.

---

4 See https://www.projectlinus.org/about/.
5 See https://www.snugglesproject.org/about/index.html.

Makers are always proud to show off items that they've sewn themselves! Sewing is a great foundational exercise that can boost makers' confidence and find its way into many other making activities.

CHAPTER 21
SEWING

Tori Culler

The wonderful thing about teaching makers how to sew is that it is much more than just a one-off afternoon activity. Sewing is a basic crafting skill that can aid makers in a variety of makerspace activities, but it is also a life skill that will serve them in numerous practical ways as well. Learning to sew can be both a meditative, creative practice as well as a self-serving one in that sewing can be used to mend tears in all manner of fabrics, from camping equipment and sailboat sails to dresses and jeans. Learning to work with a variety of fabric types is an example of an application of sewing which allows makers to combine elements of expressive design with functional design.

It is also worth noting that sewing is a skill that naturally builds on itself and can help facilitators slowly build makers' self-efficacy over time. The child that is terrified of a sewing machine at first may eventually work themselves up to giving it a go if they start with sewing felt pillows using larger, blunter needles by hand. The agency makers will feel at being able to use tools they were once intimidated by is one of the highlights of the maker experience.

GETTING STARTED

Before beginning, it is worth taking stock of your community's needs and skill baseline. Luckily, sewing is an activity that is easily scalable. For younger

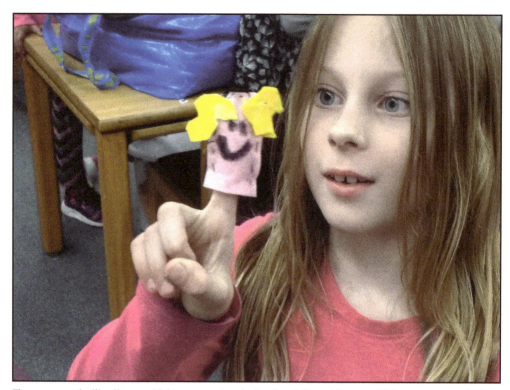

Finger puppets like these which are constructed using felt and larger stitches are a good place to start for those new to sewing. They make up quick, letting makers see the fruits of their labors early on in the process and inspiring them to keep going.

kids or even older kids and adults that have never sewn before, starting with **embroidery thread or yarn** and **tapestry needles** on **felt** can be a good place to begin. These items are more easily manipulable for children who are still getting the hang of their fine motor skills, and they make what is happening with each stitch easier to see for beginners.

Another entry point is projects made with **cotton fabric**, also known as quilt fabric or quilting cotton. You can find this woven fabric a craft supply store, local quilt or sewing shop, Jo-Ann's, Michael's, or even some Walmarts. Use standard **hand-sewing needles**—you can get multipacks for about $6 and have enough for an entire classroom of makers. These smaller needles can be more hazardous and are harder to use for children under age five. It's a good idea to pre-thread batches of needles if you anticipate your crowd will need assistance in this area. This minimizes the amount of time you spend threading needles for beginners during an activity.

There are numerous types of hand stitches that makers can learn for different purposes and at different skill levels. A running stitch, for example, is a simple

Sewing machines are useful when you are creating garments. In a Making in Michigan Libraries workshop at the Coopersville Area District Library, a participant's first sewing machine project was learning to make these boot covers for cosplay out of a secondhand pleather jacket.

stitch to start with that can be used for binding two pieces of fabric together or to create a bunched or ruched effect. A back stitch can be handy when you need to create a stronger bond between two fabrics. And a blanket stitch can be used to create or reinforce edges. Demonstrations of each of these three stitches can be found here: http://bit.ly/basic-hand-stitches. For more on basic hand-sewing stitches and handy infographic, see: http://bit.ly/9-basic-stitches.

In our experience, there is more pleasure in hand sewing than one might expect, but the time may come when your young patrons are ready to tackle projects that use a sewing machine. Especially if you anticipate a large number of workshop attendees, it's tempting to stock up on multiples of the cheapest machines you can find. Be aware that these "starter" machines often cost less because they have fewer features that can be helpful for novice sewers. We own these two models:

- **Brother CS6000i computerized sewing machine** ($150).[1]
  We chose this model because it has some features found on more expensive sewing machines, like speed control, a large sewing table to stabilize fabric, a walking foot for quilting, a free "arm" making it easy to sew around sleeves and hems, and many custom stitches and feet. However, it is made with plastic parts, so its longevity may be shorter.

---

1 https://www.amazon.com/Brother-Quilting-Stitches-Auto-Size-Buttonholes/dp/B000JQM1DE.

- **Janome 2212 sewing machine** ($190).[2] This machine was highly-rated because of its durability and metal-part construction. While it lacks some of the stitch variety of the Brother, it is reliable and made to last.

You may also want to invest in a sewing box. Sewing boxes can be bought pre-filled with necessary material, or you can buy a standard empty one and fill it with the tools and supplies you need. Common sewing supplies include:

- **Sewing scissors designed for fabric** (we like Fiskars, which are about $10/pair if bought on sale), both for left-handed and right-handed sewists. We keep these separate from our scissors for all other projects because cutting paper or other materials with sewing scissors can dull the blades quickly. You need sharp blades to cut fabric!
- **Pinking shears**, which cut the ends of fabric into a zigzag pattern so the edges will not fray or ravel
- **A flexible measuring tape** for taking people's measurements
- **Rotary cutters**, which are like pizza-cutting tools for fabric (not recommended for young children)
- **Self-healing mats** for rotary cutters, which give you a safe surface for your rotary cutters
- **Rigid acrylic rulers**, which help you measure out quilt blocks or self-drafted pattern pieces
- **Polyester or all-purpose thread**, which works for the great majority of basic sewing projects
- **Hand-sewing needles** of various sizes
- **Tapestry needles** for embroidery or stitchery projects
- **Machine needles** (universal works for almost all projects, though if you are sewing with knits, then special ballpoint needles may be more effective)
- **Thimbles** to protect fingers while hand sewing, doing denim or upholstery repair, or some embroidery projects
- **Beeswax or thread conditioner**, which you run the thread through to prevent it from tangling while sewing by hand
- **Embroidery hoops** of various sizes for cross-stitch, embroidery, or visible mending

---

2   https://www.amazon.com/gp/product/B015YCBNOU/.

- **Pins** for holding fabric layers together. We prefer yellow-headed pins for quilting. Their extra length makes them easy for going through multiple layers.

POTENTIAL PROJECTS

Once makers have a command of a few different kinds of stitches, they can begin applying them to different projects in numerous combinations. Many things can be made out of felt using the larger needles and thicker thread or yarn as mentioned above. One great project to start with is felt pillows and stuffed toys. Pillows are especially great because a four-sided shape is simple enough to start with. Later, you can encourage students to draw shapes—like their initial or the outline of an animal—and create pillows, stuffed ornaments, or toys out of them. Remind them to add seam allowances to their drawings. A common error is drawing images that are too small for tiny fingers to manipulate—think big!

As has been mentioned, another great starter project for people of all ages but especially younger kids is finger puppets. These allow for a lot of

A stuffed toy made from secondhand T-shirts in a Making in Michigan Libraries professional development workshop at Coopersville Area District Library.

240 PROJECTS AND PROGRAMS

Finger puppets, seen here at Mitchell Elementary School in Ann Arbor, Michigan, are good introductory sewing projects because they can be completed in a single sitting, which is important for impatient makers eager for a finished project.

expression and playfulness, and can easily be scaled up to creating larger hand puppets if makers really take to it. In lieu of patterns, we encourage children to trace around their finger, then add seam allowance before cutting. Felt fabric is an ideal choice for this because it does not fray, so a short line of stitching around the perimeter is all it takes to get to a complete project. It can be tough to talk beginning sewers out of making enormous stitches. Finger puppets gently nudge sewers to take small stitches—otherwise, their finger will poke through large ones! We have been surprised at how effectively this lesson is learned with minimal nagging. Consider using craft or hot glue to quickly attach additional pieces. (Surprisingly, fabric glue does not hold felt together well.)

A fun option to consider as makers move on from felt and into more intermediate levels of sewing is to repurpose different types of fabrics to make interesting items. Moving into projects that use sewing needles and the cotton fabric, makers can begin by making some of the same items mentioned above that they tried out with felt and thicker thread such as pillows, stuffed toys, and puppets. But here they can also begin experimenting with making some clothing items and accessories. They could start small scale by making pants, shirts, dresses, and bags for dolls, and then graduate to making these items for people. A thrift store run wherein you gather different kinds of clothing items such as flannel, denim, cotton T-shirts, and leather can serve as a great materials base for makers to begin experimenting with.

Michigan Makers at Scarlett Middle School in Ann Arbor, Michigan, create pillows as an introduction to sewing.

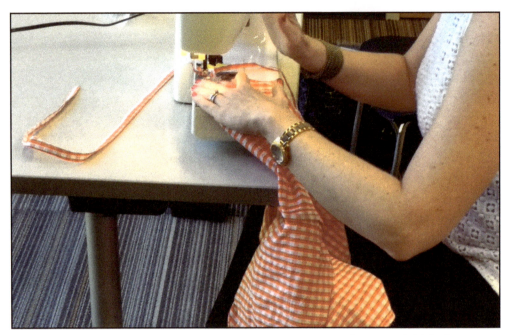

A sewist at a Making in Michigan Libraries workshop at Coopersville Area District Library converts a men's button-down shirt into an apron. Secondhand shirts like these are a bargain for stocking a makerspace because you can get yardage much cheaper than at the fabric store.

They can repurpose these items to make products that feel store-bought, but still unique and maybe even a little luxurious.

VARIATIONS

Another ideal sewing-based project for a makerspace is to have a mending workshop. This would be an event during which makers learn how to use sewing skills to fix torn fabrics. This would be another time when loading up on thrift store clothing items of various fabric types would prove helpful. You can either distress the clothing beforehand yourself by creating random cuts and tears in the clothing or you can have makers do so as part of the process. The overall idea will be for makers to learn the technical skills of mending while having fun creating a new, patchworked item. Some public libraries in Michigan are offering occasional mending sessions staffed by volunteers, who offer to repair clothing while patrons browse the library.

In this vein is also visible mending and utility stitching, such as Japanese boro repair and kantha stitching from India. As Kristin Fontichiaro writes in the June 2018 issue of *Teacher Librarian*, these are:

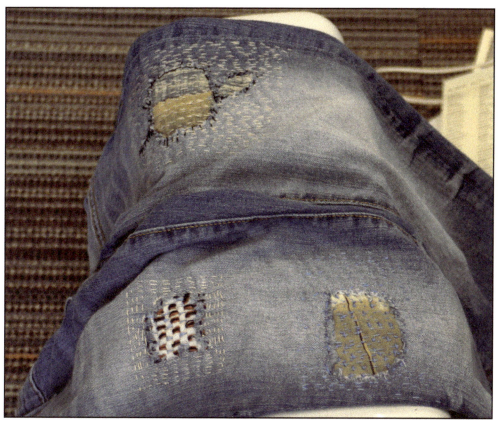

A participant at a Making in Michigan Libraries project at the Coopersville Area District Library showed off her boro denim repairs.

terms that refer to rows of densely placed, highly visible running stitches that can either repair or enhance the look of fabric. Irregularities in stitch length or spacing are considered part of the charm of the work instead of a flaw, making this kind of work particularly forgiving for novices.

The repetitive nature of the stitches can also have a calming effect on participants, making it a good counterpoint to more high-energy activities.

Makers who take to this or sewing in general can begin to look at sewing-adjacent activities, such as embroidery and cross-stitch and even, as covered elsewhere in this volume, knitting and crochet.

Many public libraries have been delighted at the popularity of sewing nights. In some cases, the library provides a location to which sewists can bring their own projects but work in a collaborative setting.

CONCLUSION

As is evident, then, sewing offers no shortage of potential activities for makers and can lead naturally into a variety of other activities while building crucial skills and self-efficacy in the process. What's more is that sewing can be combined with other common makerspace elements to create a truly special experience. Makers who are also familiar with circuitry concepts, for example, can begin experimenting with conductive thread to create expressive electronics that they can wear. For an excellent video introduction to soft circuits and e-textiles, see http://bit.ly/soft-circuits-etextiles.

Sewing is more than just a craft: it's a skill that everyone can benefit from. The child who is learning to sew a felt pillow today could one day be a successful fashion designer, or they could even be the medical professional suturing wounds. But no matter the possible outcomes, everyone has to master the basics first.

REFERENCES

Fontichiaro, Kristin. 2018. "Making as Self-Soothing: The Power of Stitches." *Teacher Librarian*, June. 53+.

A young maker begins fashion hacking a T-shirt.

CHAPTER 22
FASHION HACKING

Alyssa Pierce

Fashion hacking can be a great activity to add to your library's repertoire of making activities. It combines the expertise of crafters and tech-minded makers, and can help draw more girls and women into a makerspace. It also empowers makers, giving them practical as well as creative skills.

So what is fashion hacking anyway? Here, we define it as the act of taking a pre-existing item of clothing and changing it. That change can take many different forms and includes activities like altering the hem or sleeve length, making a stuffed animal out of the item, tearing the item into strips to make yarn, or taking the item apart and reassembling it into a tote bag. Though we use the term fashion hacking, there are many names for this trend, such as refashioning, altering, upcycling, or making-do.

These movements arose to take advantage of the surplus of used clothes in the world today. The fashion world used to have 4 fashion cycles a year, but now there are typically at least *12* fashion cycles in a year. The need to keep up with these fast-changing trends means that clothes are now being made cheaply, quickly, and in great volume. Many of these end up being donated to thrift stores, but only 10–20% of the items donated at a thrift store stay on site. The other clothes are bundled up and sold to companies that ship them to sell in the third world. There, the amount of exported clothes is often overwhelming and can be harmful to the local economy and the environment, as most of the countries lack facilities to process textile waste. This leads to landfills full of textiles, most of which do not decompose well. Some of your participants will feel bad "destroying" what they see as perfectly good garments, which is understandable, so being able to explain this context to them may help some participants feel more comfortable with the activity. (For more on the worldwide phenomena of clothing overload, please see the slide deck at bit.ly/fashion-hacking.)

Beyond making use of overly abundant used garments in the world today and diverting them from landfills, there are many other benefits to fashion hacking programs. Those who develop higher-level skills can generate income by taking hemming or tailoring jobs. They provide people with access to styles and trends that they may not be able to otherwise afford. It can also help people express themselves in ways that buying from big box stores cannot supply. This kind of programming can help people develop confidence and agency, especially with teenagers who are trying to build their own self-identity. It can also help low-income members of your community; for those who may not be able to afford a new piece of clothing when the old one wears out, knowing how to fix or alter their old clothes can give them a sense of power and dignity. In addition to that, supplying used clothing that people can take home once they alter it can relieve some of the stress and pressure that they may be experiencing regarding their appearance. For those working with kids, fashion hacking projects can supply a fun, meaningful, and affordable activity that the kids can take home once they are done!

Especially for libraries with smaller budgets, fashion hacking can provide an exciting program for a low cost. Donations can provide the majority of your materials. Local thrift stores can also be a good resource, especially if you can work out a deal with them for their unsold merchandise. In addition to those establishments, putting out a bin in the library, or sending a call for old clothes in a newsletter, can also be a good way to get a stockpile of old clothes. This technique can work especially well if you are looking for old T-shirts.

GETTING STARTED

A great beginning fashion hacking activity can be making bags out of T-shirts (see https://thethingswellmake.com/recycled-t-shirt-bags-review-of-7-ways/ for several pattern options). T-shirts are a great material for beginning fashion hackers because the fabric will not unravel if left unhemmed. With just some fabric scissors and imagination, a T-shirt can become a cape, a wig, bracelets, yarn, a knight's tabard, or a skirt! (Editor's note: For more ideas about repurposing T-shirts, see the "Costume Creation Lab" chapter.) You can also use T-shirts as blank canvases for stenciled T-shirt designs using digital cutting tools like Silhouette or Cricut.

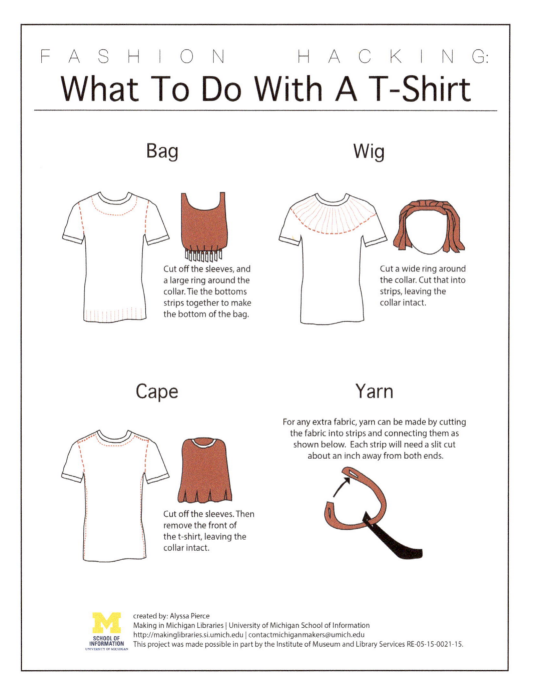

ANATOMY OF CLOTHING

For teens or adults, it can be an exciting challenge to study the shape of the individual pieces in an existing garment, then deconstruct the garment and remake it in new ways. I use the term "Anatomy of Clothing" to describe this process. As shown on page 251, novice garment refashioners can benefit from seeing garments as *modules* that can be moved and repurposed in novel ways, such as a sleeve becoming a belt. For initial Anatomy of Clothing activities, consider using men's button-down shirts. They contain more fabric than women's clothing, making them ripe for refashioning. I've created a Pinterest board at https://www.pinterest.com/bookbinder12/fashion-hacking/ with some of my favorite fashion hacking ideas. There are additional inspirations in the Resource List below to help you discover more ideas. Happy Hacking!

BLOGS FEATURING REFASHIONING OR FASHION HACKING

Starred sites are no longer being updated but still have an archive worth visiting.

- **Charity Shop Chic*** (https://charityshopchic.net)
- **Confessions of a Refashionista** (http://awesomesauceasshattery.com)
- **DIY Clothes by Tringa Osmani*** (http://diyclothes.net)
- **Refashionista*** (http://refashionista.net)
- **New Dress a Day*** (http://www.newdressaday.com)
- **Collective Gen (formerly A Pair and a Spare)** (https://collectivegen.com/category/style/diy-style/)
- **Refashion Co-op** (http://refashionco-op.blogspot.com)
- **Little Did You Know*** (http://littledyknow.blogspot.com/p/before-after.html)
- **Makery by Portia Lowrie** (http://www.makery.co.uk)

FASHION HACKING:
The Anatomy of Clothing

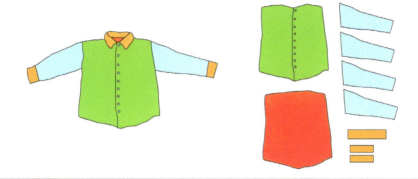

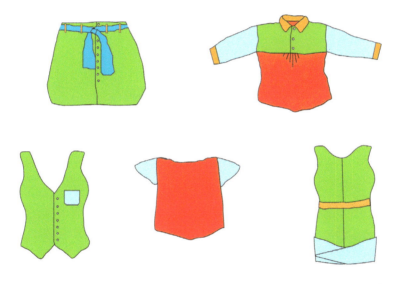

created by: Alyssa Pierce
Making in Michigan Libraries | University of Michigan School of Information
http://makinglibraries.si.umich.edu | contactmichiganmakers@umich.edu
This project was made possible in part by the Institute of Museum and Library Services RE-05-15-0021-15.

Costume Creation Lab at the Benzonia (Michigan) Public Library in 2017.

CHAPTER 23
COSTUME CREATION LAB

Kristin Fontichiaro

When the calendar turns toward October, our thoughts often go to Halloween, and when spring arrives it brings class plays to it: both mean costumes! Libraries can help! Along with our colleagues at the Benzonia (Michigan) Public Library, we have developed Costume Creation Lab as a way to make costume creation fun and free for participants. In this chapter, we look at how you might host an event like this in a public library or in a school library during or after school hours.

SETTING THE STAGE FOR YOUR LAB

A Costume Creation Lab is, essentially, a room temporarily converted into a costume shop and prop-making studio. Not only are there donated costumes to adopt and wear as-is, but there are also abundant supplies that makers can use to concoct their own finery and accessories. The space is staffed with knowledgeable, friendly volunteers who can share expertise and enthusiasm—and document the event with photos. Our lab has the components below.

Empty Tables

Set out empty tables and chairs where students or families can work. Real-world tailors often ask their customers to stand on small boxes, so the tailor doesn't have to work on the floor—so you may see participants standing on chairs as others measure them.

Mirrors

If you have mirrors in your space, you will avoid incessant requests for school library bathroom passes or crowded bathrooms in public libraries! We use inexpensive full-length mirrors (ask for loans), set them atop a chair, then bungee-cord them to the backs of chairs.

Costumes and Clothing

Display donated or thrifted clothing and costumes on hanging racks. Some items may be adopted as-is, a comfortable option for those who want to get in on the fun but don't like creating costumes from scratch (or those who have never been able to have what they see as the luxury of a store-bought costume). If your local thrift stores or rummage sales have sales or by-the-bag prices, use this as an opportunity to stock up on formal wear, Western wear, scrubs, and other evocative items. Even extra-fuzzy fleece can summon prehistoric or zoo vibes! We wash all clothing beforehand to minimize musty thrift-store odors and maximize hygiene. Post a sign inviting creators to take what they need, alter it to fit, or hack it into a new creation. Last year, the tulle from a prom dress was used to create eyeholes for a Minecraft character mask! Paper dulls scissors quickly, so acquire some fabric-only scissors that cut easily through fabric. Look for Fiskars shears (about $10 a pair).

T-Shirts

T-shirt costumes are cheap, easy to find or request as donations, and perfect for beginner fashion hacking projects because knit fabric doesn't fray or ravel. Try these:

- **Skirt:** Step into the neckband of a T-shirt. Pull it up to your waist, so that the neckband becomes the waistband. Tuck the sleeves into the armholes and stitch the ends closed for "pockets."

- **Knight's Tabard:** Just inside the shoulder lines, cut straight down either side of a t-shirt.

- **Cape:** Cut the sleeves off of a T-shirt. Then carefully cut on the front side of the shoulder seam, so that the seam stays attached to the back, then cut around—but keep the neckband. Carefully cut down either side of the torso of the shirt. You'll be left with just the back shirt piece and the attached neckband. Place the neckband over your head for a cape.

- **Beanie:** Cut off the sleeves of a short-sleeved, adult T-shirt. Pull the sleeve, like a tube, across your head. Which side fits better? Rubber-band the other side closed.

- **Elf Hat:** Need "Elves and the Shoemaker" costumes? Try the beanie technique with a long-sleeved T-shirt for a hat that hangs down your back.

- **Wig:** Cut off a long sleeve to see which end grips your head more easily. That end is your headband. Start at the opposite end and cut fringe until you are about 2" away from the edge of the headband.

- **Cuff:** Use the same technique with a short-sleeved T-shirt sleeve. Wrap it around your wrist twice to serve as rock band cuffs, fairy bracelets, or animal paws.

- **Belt:** Trim off the bottom hem of T-shirts, resulting in a loop of fabric. Cut open the loop to create a long strip. Tie it around you for a quick belt.

- **Hair Braid:** Weave three hems together to create a braid for Rapunzel's long hair.

SEWING

While some kids enjoy picking out a costume as-is, others may need or want alterations. A few sewing machines and volunteers can facilitate this. You'll also want fabric scissors, pinking shears for quick and dirty seams that won't ravel, pins, extension cords, elastic, thread and needles for hand sewing, and measuring tapes. Scissors tend to wander away from the sewing station, but volunteers can keep them close at hand by tying them around their necks. We use men's ties as lanyards, because the weight of the scissors is well-balanced and won't pull on the volunteers' necks. Try to keep the focus on

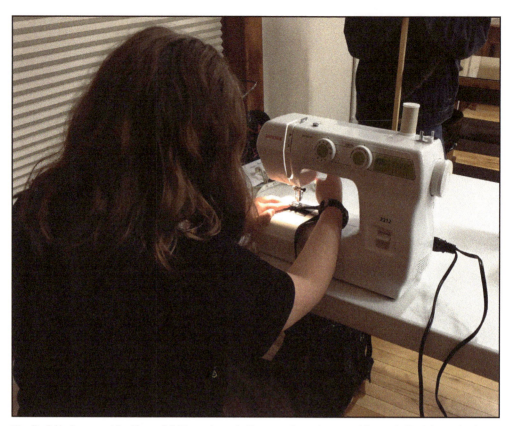

We find that a combination of DIY sewing stations and sewing machines staffed by volunteers works well at events like these.

alterations, not from-scratch costumes, as it may not be realistic to make an entire costume from scratch given the number of kids visiting your lab at any one time.

CARDBOARD

In our work with the Benzonia (Michigan) Public Library, we've seen cardboard converted into everything from dragon wings to beaks, shin guards, and horses for cowgirls (see Chapter 19). Be prepared in advance to advise students whether it's OK in your school or community to create paper swords, shields, guns, or other weapons.

Hit up the local recycling center or ask the school custodian to save boxes for you. The bigger the pile, the more it will fuel kids' imaginations. If there are only a few pieces, it will create a sense of "I can't afford to mess this up" rather than creativity.

Created with the help of Jimmy McLaren, maker coordinator at the Benzonia Public Library, this cardboard horse was the perfect partner for this cowgirl.

Use Makedo cutting tools (similar to the orange plastic knives sold for pumpkin carving) with younger learners to support self-sufficiency. Demonstrate different methods of assembling cardboard, such as Erin Riley's wonderful handout found at https://erinriley.weebly.com/uploads/2/1/0/8/21080698/cardboard_inventory_v2.pdf.

You may also set aside some utility knives, X-Acto blades, or box cutters for use by older students or adults, if permitted at your school. I carry mine in my pocket instead of leaving it out, so I always know where it is if small children are around.

For younger students, staff this area with an adult who can use or model safe use of a glue gun. Glue guns have the fastest-drying glues, so they are the most efficient choice if you are doing this activity many times in a day. Low-temperature, small glue guns will do the trick. Wood glue is another alternative, though slow drying time may hinder completion rates. (Use a tablecloth and/or floor tarp to catch drips.) Alternatively, use Makedo tools and screws to hold pieces together.

ANTENNAS AND EARS AND TAILS, OH MY!

Students making animals will need ears, tails, antlers, or antennae to complete the look. Try cutting a pig's ear on the fold of a piece of pink felt. Wrap

Benzonia Public Library director Amanda McLaren helped this girl make her dream costume, complete with a purple wig made out of ribbons and yarn.

the ear around a plastic headband and secure with fabric glue. Use pipe cleaners (another method of fashioning ears as well as antennae for insects and weird robots) as well as rope or yarn for tails and manes. Hair elastics can help secure these creations to the body.

PAINT

I like the look of plain cardboard, but if you are well staffed and have room to store drying creations, set up a paint station with water-based tempera. As with wood glue, cover furniture and flooring with tarps or tablecloths to make cleanup easy. Alternatively, provide construction paper that can be glued on to add color, or use wide-tip markers (make sure they are washable for young kids).

JAZZ IT UP!

No costume is complete without the last-minute accessory. Scrounge last year's lost-and-found and prewash gloves (for animal paws, snowboarders, lumberjacks, or high society). Get out the leftover Mardi Gras beads, funky

If you incorporate a painting station, be sure to have paint shirts and drop cloths on hand.

The Jazz It Up station features hats, scarves, and other accessories. We find that people use this space to shop with the intention to complete a costume or to just play around with what they find there.

sunglasses, and old conference badges. Wigs and hats are fun . . . but may also transmit lice. (Yuck.) Silk or polyester scarves are endlessly versatile for pirate or cowboy kerchiefs, prairie-style or Patricia Polacco babushkas, capes, slings, and more. Set up a "boutique" by hanging items along wooden drying racks, so students can be inspired by your offerings.

PROTOTYPE IT!

Feeling hesitant about how this event will roll out? Schedule a session with a single class or your Teen Advisory Board in advance of working with large groups, so you can work out the details.

CONCLUSION

A Costume Creation Lab is a chance to bring the entire school community together in the communal art of creation and celebration. Consider hosting this event after hours or even during parent-teacher or student-led conferences as a way to bring joy to what, for many families, can be a stressful occasion. Enjoy!

An earlier version of this chapter appeared as "Costume Creation Lab" in the October 2018 "Makerspaces" column of Teacher Librarian. *Special thanks to Edward Kurdyla for permission to reprint it here. Special thanks to Jean Hardy, ethnographic researcher on the Making in Michigan Libraries project, for staffing the original Jazz It Up with Jean station. Additional thanks to the Benzonia Public Library, director Amanda McLaren, and maker coordinator Jimmy McLaren for piloting this project with us.*

A photographer practices using beach vegetation as a frame for capturing an interesting lake photo at Jeff Smith's Pro Photo Walk for the Benzonia Public Library in fall 2018.

CHAPTER 24
PHOTOGRAPHY

Sophia McFadden-Keesling and Kristin Fontichiaro

Documenting our lives through photography has become second nature to many Americans. People document by using their smartphones, DSLR cameras, point-and-shoot cameras, instant print cameras, and many more. With the advent of the smartphone and simple-to-use sharing apps, most of us carry a camera with us at all times. In this chapter, we'll discuss what photography programs worked well for Making in Michigan Libraries and cover some tricks for bringing digital photography into your makerspace.

FINDING AN INSTRUCTOR

Reaching out to photo experts in your community is a great way to get people involved in the library and relieve a little bit of stress on your end about having to learn a new skill. You may have in-house staff with expertise in photography or who are willing to learn from YouTube or subscribe to LinkedInLearning.com (formerly Lynda.com) or mybluprint.com. This could also be a good opportunity to reach out to your community for a guest instructor. It adds another level to a workshop if a professional in the field is leading it and can increase attendance!

Check with local community centers to see if there are any photography clubs that would be interested in facilitating a session. Local community colleges

A pro photo walk at Benzonia Public Library in fall 2018 helped patrons see beauty in the everyday, even in this back alley in Beulah, Michigan.

and universities are another good place to reach out to see if a photography instructor or promising student would be interested in running a workshop.

Consider, too, freelance portrait photographers who might enjoy setting up a small exhibit of their work in the library in exchange for a series of classes. They get extra publicity (and possibly extra work), and you get more attendees!

Additionally, there may be a photographer on the staff of the local newspaper who is looking to branch out. And if the photographer hosts the event, perhaps the newspaper will give it a bit of extra coverage!

TARGET AUDIENCE

A photography workshop can be geared to all ages because of how accessible and easy it is to pick up the hobby. However, you may wish to specify a particular audience given that different generations have different goals, software preferences, and equipment. For example, you could organize a workshop that attracts patrons who want more Instagram followers, whereas patrons who want better photos of their children might prefer a portraiture session. Tailor the focus of the event to your audience's needs and let a guest presenter know who is likely to attend. Having pre-registration for the event may help with planning and will allow you to collect email addresses and/or phone numbers so that you can send reminders to attendees before the event.

SAMPLE EVENTS

The Making in Michigan Libraries project worked with the Benzonia Public Library and photographer Jeffrey M. Smith to develop a pair of successful photography events. Jeff is a photographer and videographer at the University of Michigan School of Information (UMSI) who additionally does freelance and commercial photography. In his UMSI role, he has frequently documented Making in Michigan Libraries events and was already familiar with the Library. We planned two events for a single day: "Taking Better Portraits with Your Smartphone" and "Pro Photo Walk."

Taking Better Portraits with Your Smartphone

Jeff's workshop was timed to be early in the back-to-school season and focused on taking better portraits with smartphones. We focused on smartphones because a majority of Americans own one. (If this isn't true in your community, there are so many ways to adapt photography lessons for your community! Consider using library-owned tablets or disposable cameras, for example.) While it's easy to point one's phone and press the button to capture a photo, there are many tools built into the camera that may be less familiar to casual users. A focus on smartphones also enabled him to transition from shooting photos into other apps, like Instagram and Snapseed, which provided simple but powerful editing and sharing tools. In our workshop, participants much preferred Snapseed because it does not require a login, something to keep in mind if you work with youth under 13 who may not be allowed to use an app or with social media-shy patrons. By focusing on portraits, we could prioritize the kinds of photos patrons valued most, especially since we planned this workshop to take place near the beginning of the school year and before photo-heavy fall events like Halloween, Thanksgiving, and the winter holidays.

TAKE BETTER PHOTOS
WITH THE CAMERA/PHONE YOU HAVE

with pro photographer jeffrey smith
join us for one or both free workshops

taking better portraits with your smartphone
sat., sept. 22, 10am-noon, mills community house

In this workshop, you'll learn more about how to take better photos using your smartphone. You'll acquire some strateiges for improving your photos, have time to practice, get feedback from a pro, and learn how to make simple edits and photo enhancements using the Instagram app. Please bring your own phone.

pro photo walk
sat., sept. 22, 1:30 - 4:30pm, meet in front of ursa major

Grab your smartphone, point-and-shoot, or DSLR camera and join us for a walking photo tour of downtown Beulah. Photographer Jeffrey Smith will guide you through some great locations and photo shots. At the end of the tour, we'll head to the Mills Community House and Jeff will walk us through his photo roll and model how he decides which photos to keep and why. **In case of rain, please call the Benzonia Public Library at 231.882.4111 for updated plans.**

your instructor

Photographer Jeffrey Smith is a life-long Michigander whose love for nature, people, and storytelling fuels his passion for visual communication. He currently works as a photographer and video producer at the University of Michigan School of Information, by way of newspapers across the state.

This event is part of the Making in Michigan Libraries project of the U-M School of Michigan and is made possible in part by the Institute of Museum and Library Services RE-05-15-0021-15.

Flyer for the photography workshops.

After an introduction from library director Amanda McLaren, Jeff began the workshop with a PowerPoint presentation showing some of his professional work. This is a useful starting point because it establishes the credibility of the speaker and excites attendees about the artist who will be guiding them.

He then shifted his presentation into simple tricks and techniques for using a smartphone camera's built-in—but often unknown—features to improve images, followed by some hands-on practice and feedback to participants. Finally, he connected his smartphone to the data projector so that he could show real-time editing using Instagram and Snapseed.

Here are a few tips from his presentation. While we use an iPhone for these examples, you can find similar strategies for Android devices at https://www.mybluprint.com/playlist/5322/11462 (subscription required) and https://www.udemy.com/pro-mobile-photography-in-1-hour/.

Clean your lens. Try to avoid cleaning the lens with tissue paper or paper towel as they can leave residue or fibers on the lens. Lint-free microfiber cloths such as those you get with a new pair of glasses are recommended for cleaning camera lenses. In a pinch, you could use your shirt hem, but it is not ideal.

Put your camera in "Photo mode." Some smartphones have built-in filters like Apple iPhone X's Portrait mode. When just starting out, it's good to get used to standard Photo mode instead.

Turn off the flash. The iPhone's flash is too intense and often diminishes the quality of the photo. You'll want to play around with light sources to get the best picture possible, but for now turn off the flash!

Seek out natural lighting. Regardless of what you're photographing, lighting is key. There are three main types of lighting in a photo: front, side, and back. The placement is referring to the direction of the light. Front lighting is referring to light shown directly on the object you're shooting, making the shadows fall behind the object. Front lighting can sometimes make your subject look a little flat because of the lack of shadows on them. Side lighting means light is coming from the side, which allows shadows on the subject to be brought out. This can add more depth to your image. Jeff recommended having subjects stand near a window, where their face will be softly illuminated by natural light. Backlighting is where the light source is directly behind the subject of the photo. This can often lead to your subject appearing as a

Smith demonstrates how side light is ideal for portraits.

dark silhouette. While obscuring the face may not be desirable in all situations, it can have a cool artistic effect.

Hold your finger on the screen to focus. Click on the area you want to focus on with your finger. The app will adjust to make that the focus of the photo.

Use volume buttons to take the photo. The iPhone allows users to not only take photos with the button on the camera app but also with the volume buttons. This can be especially helpful

You can "tell" your smartphone camera to focus on a particular area of an image if you hold down your finger on that area of the screen.

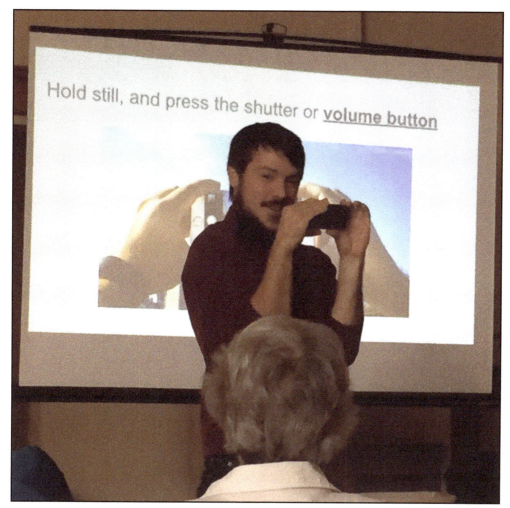

Keep your upper arms firmly to the side to stabilize the camera just before you take your shot.

when taking a selfie with an outstretched arm or while trying to steady the phone for a landscape shot.

Adjust your exposure level. You can change the exposure (the amount of light your lens lets in) to adjust how light or dark an image will appear by holding your finger on the focus area for a few moments. A "sun" icon will appear, indicating that you can change the exposure level. Slide your finger up and down to increase and decrease how much light you let into the photo.

Avoid the zoom. When the object/person you're photographing is nearby, Jeff suggests you "zoom with your feet rather than the zoom on your camera." The iPhone's zoom feature doesn't work in the same way as the zoom on a DSLR camera. Rather than zooming mechanically with the camera's lens, it uses "digital zoom," which uses software to focus in. This means that even if the smartphone camera allows you to focus in, you will lose image quality.

Rule of Thirds. The Rule of Thirds is a term that refers to the composition of a shot. It breaks down a photo into a 3×3 grid (as shown below) where the four intersecting lines are where it's suggested that you put the most important aspects of the shot.

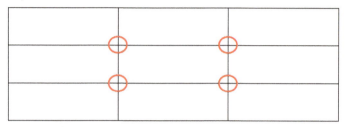

The Rule of Thirds is a quick strategy to help beginning photographers compose their shots more effectively.

Let's look at the Rule of Thirds in action. Below you can see the progression in the editing process of applying the Rule of Thirds to a photo already taken. While it is recommended that you try to apply the Rule of Thirds while taking the original photo, that doesn't always work out perfectly. The editing process is a photographer's best friend! The photos on page 271 show the editing process by applying the 3×3 grid to a photo, cropping it accordingly, and evaluating the final result. Keep in mind that while it's ideal to apply the Rule of Thirds when you are taking the photo, you can always use the technique when you are editing photos later on. Most digital editing tools—including the simple cropping tools built into your smartphone's default photo app—allow you to straighten or crop images quickly. Although the Rule of Thirds can help us think differently as we compose or edit an image, Jeff would remind us that sometimes it's worth breaking rules, too!

Editing. Built-in camera apps usually have minimal editing options. Introducing free photo editing apps such as Snapseed or Instagram can expand the user's customization capabilities. If your audience already uses Instagram, then a review of its built-in editing tools may be a good fit. In our workshop, where the attendees reported low Instagram use and lack of interest in sharing portraits online, Snapseed was preferred because it does not require posting to social media and does not require an account.

RULE OF THIRDS IN ACTION

Public domain photo by "Counselling" on Pixabay.com, uncropped. Notice how the top of the basket cuts the image in half, which is less pleasing to the eye.

Here is the original photo with the 3×3 grid provided by the editing software as an overlay.

Using the software's cropping tools, you can easily move the grid around to consider alternate compositions before cropping.

We ultimately chose this cropping angle, which placed the three large balls of yarn along the center vertical third.

Our final, cropped image.

Pro Photo Walk

Photo walks are where an expert (or someone who feels confident enough with a few photography tricks) takes a group around the community to take pictures. The "pro" takes the group to predetermined locations to help patrons practice their skills with lighting, perspective, framing, the Rule of Thirds, landscape shots, and action shots. At each location, the pro talks through how they would frame the shot, models some sample images, and leaves time for the participants to practice and receive feedback. Photo walks have both learning and social components and are a lovely way for beginners and experts to see their community in new ways.

When we held this workshop, Jeff met participants at a popular downtown corner. He then took us to a back alley. An alley seems like a rather unphotogenic locale, but he told us that he had selected locations that people wouldn't initially think of as "picturesque" in order to really hone in on the idea of perspective and framing. Such locations could be an abandoned building, a field of weeds, or a hole in a fence.

A hole in the fence can provide an unusual frame for the vegetation growing inside.

In addition to his alley walk, Jeff chose locations with lots of contrast in light, differing elevations, and the beach. It was a sunny day, which can make things a bit difficult for new photographers—cloudy days are often ideal for taking photos because you don't have to worry about the angle of the sun and harsh lighting. Make sure you plan for the weather and decide in advance what your rainy day plan is. You might consider hosting multiple walks in different seasons or extending this activity by hosting a gallery of printed photos.

As he led the walk, he explained why he chose particular locations, then walked participants step-by-step through the shots he took, gave them time

Jeff shows participants how standing higher on a hill can change one's perspective.

to take photos, and answered questions along the way. He showed the group how to frame the picture to include the beautiful blue wall behind a building (for maximum contrast against skin color) and how to crop out the unsightly dumpster.

We spent about two hours on our Pro Photo Walk through downtown Beulah, Michigan. We then returned indoors to the Benzonia Public Library, where Jeff reviewed his photos, talked through why he thought certain photos were better than others, and applied some simple edits using Photoshop Elements. While that software isn't free, tools like Fotor.com, Gimp.com, and Picmonkey.com all provide some editing tools at no cost.

CONCLUSION

Regardless of age and level of experience, photography is a fun and accessible hobby. As Benzonia Public Library director Amanda McLaren pointed out, it's a creation genre that attracts males and older makers to your events, which can serve as a desired counterbalance with knitting or crafting events that mostly attract women and youth.

Photography events can help your patrons create positive memories while promoting artistic expression. We hope you'll enjoy bringing photography into your maker toolkit as much as we did!

To learn more about the work of photographer Jeffrey M. Smith, please visit his website at http://www.jeffreysmithphoto.com, follow him on Instagram at @jmsmith802, or view his past work for the Making in Michigan Libraries project at https://www.flickr.com/photos/michiganmakers/albums/72157688355346493 and https://www.youtube.com/watch?v=VQcF8iphvfA.

A stack of completed zines.

CHAPTER 25
ZINES

Kristin Fontichiaro

As our Michigan Makers and Making in Michigan Libraries work matures, we notice a surprising trend: that even as school library makerspaces are doubling down on STEM and technology, many kids are increasingly drawn to non-digital forms of making. Non-digital activities—sewing or toy takeapart, Shrinky Dinks or glass etching, junk box creations or photo frames—appeal to kids' sensory appreciation, can call on prior knowledge to facilitate easier customization of materials to meet personal expectations, and give them the option to take home their creations (often as gifts for others).

Our after-school and community programs are designed to try to best replicate the spirit of community makerspaces, a social, supportive environment where makers decide what to make. Because our program is not exclusively STEM-focused, we continue to experiment with non-technological, open-ended, take-home stations that make room for maker customization and choice.

While we had previously had mentor-led comics creation (culminating in a pair of ComicCon-styled exchanges) and a collaborative *Choose Your Own Adventure* project, these had dried up when their champions had graduated. But when Kalamazoo (MI) school librarian Laura Warren-Gross told me she had created a zine-making kit for her daughter's holiday present and current Michigan Makers mentor and bullet journal aficionado Sarah G. Swiderski showed me her copy of Emily K. Neuberger's 2017 *Journal Sparks: Fire Up*

Your Creativity with Spontaneous Art, Wild Writing, and Inventive Thinking, we decided it was time to bring story-making back into our extracurricular maker program.

If you have the flexibility to consider maker projects beyond STEM kits, are eager to amplify diverse voices, or simply want to broaden the range of activities available to makers, zines may be for you.

WHAT ARE ZINES?

Zines are small, handmade magazines with pages commonly 4.25" × 5.5"—a quarter-sheet of copy paper—that reflect topics or themes of significance to the creator. They first became popular in the preinternet 1990s and often were an avenue for voices not welcomed or recognized in mainstream culture, including underground movements, feminism, minority culture, LGBTQ issues, poetry, and more. (Today's BoingBoing.net site had its origins as a zine.) The author or artist would write, collage, paint, cut-and-paste images, or more, then take the originals to a copy machine, where they could be

The fine tips on these Stabilo-brand markers help create detail on the tiny pages of the zine.

reproduced cheaply. The result is a work that looks intentionally home-made—in fact, a zine with too much polish might be seen as inauthentic. Because of their unique perspectives, production values, and subject matter, '90s zines were collected by some public and academic libraries, most noticeably Barnard College. In fact, Barnard curates a list of zine collections by state at https://zines.barnard.edu/zine-libraries.

GETTING STARTED WITH ONE-PAGE ZINES

Since 2018, zines have been having a small resurgence, and we find that a simple zine made of a single piece of copy paper is an excellent starting point. Because it is limited to eight tiny pages, writer's block is less likely to set in, and a single "issue" can be completed in a single 90-minute session. We notice that some makers determine they need more space, and they add pages as they see fit.

Zines require few supplies[1]:

- **pencils** for those who like to prototype first
- **black gel pens** for a firm dark line that photocopies well
- **white copy paper** (8.5" × 11" is standard, but any size will work)
- **glue sticks** for collages
- **scissors**
- **fine-point markers**
- **drawing books** (we're partial to the Ed Emberley classics for elementary zine makers)
- **journal prompt reference books**
- **colorful washi tape**
- **a safe place** where kids can turn in completed zines for copying
- **old catalogs or magazines** for collages and illustrations

Start by folding and cutting the zine. Elementary-aged kids can be disoriented by how to do this, so if you cannot staff this table yourself to demonstrate in person, you may also want to set up a laptop or tablet with a YouTube video showing how to fold and cut the books. The one at http://bit.ly/makerzine is useful for all ages because it has no audio, making it perfect for English Language Learners. Remind them to keep their zine folded as they draw.

---

[1] See http://a.co/3PrZQ8A for the specific items we use.

We honor zines' original function as one-of-a-kind passion publications, so we do not assign topics. (We find that some kids are downright exhilarated by the ability to choose.) Simply placing drawing books or books with suggestions for journal entries on the table can help patrons identify what it is they want to create and give them ideas about whether their zine will prioritize text or art or a combination. We do make some samples ourselves, with our names on the front cover, to show that we, too, are writers and to show various ways in which drawings, collages, and text can be deployed within the zine format, but almost no creator will model their zine on ours. (Please.)

When completed, a single-page zine can be unfolded, with all of the mini-pages appearing on a single side of the paper. You won't even need a photocopier that makes double-sided copies! First, make sure participants know where they can "turn in" their zine for copying so it doesn't get lost in the shuffle of supplies. Remind them to put their name on the front "cover," and on the zine's blank side, ask them to write their class or homeroom plus the number of copies needed. Some are reluctant to give up temporary custody of their creation; in that case, we use the free scanning app Scannable to email ourselves a PDF copy. This method can be a little tricky if your copier will not print to the edges of the paper, so you may need to shrink the copy size down to 90%–95% in order for the entire image to print. Make enough copies for makers to share at school and with family. Give the copies to the creator, who will assemble each copy for distribution.

ZINEFEST

A ZineFest is an event where zine creators swap and autograph one another's work. Among adults, zines are sold (often for just more than the cost of copying), but you can maximize diversity and inclusion if your makerspace can cover the cost of copies. If you don't have the funds for every participant to receive a copy of everyone else's creations, limit the number of copies per maker and give each recipient a limited number of tickets they can exchange for zines.

Have each author create a cardstock table tent with their name and zine title. You can invite them to bring tablecloths or props related to their publication, but again, keep in mind that the ability to execute on this may exacerbate the privilege gap in some populations. Remind attendees of prosocial zine etiquette: being polite and respectful of the author, not offering suggestions or "improvements" unless asked, and requesting (not demanding) an

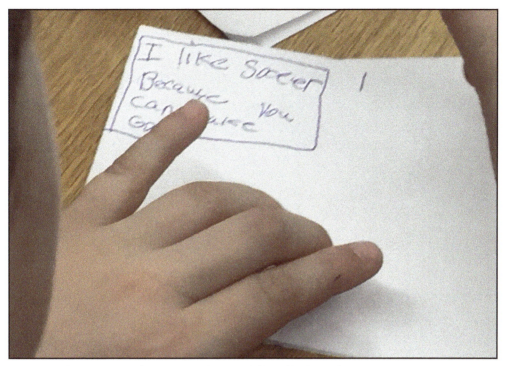

Zines should reflect the authentic interests and hobbies of their creators.

autographed copy. Split the class in half, with half sitting behind their tent with their zines and the other half visiting the tables. Halfway through, switch roles. Snacks and readings are commonplace when authors come together, though certainly not essential.

EXTENSIONS

If single-page zines take off in your library, consider these project extensions:

- Collaborate with an art teacher on mini-lessons on calligraphy, design, or new media such as watercolor or collage to build the visual toolkit of creators. The online craft site Creativebug.com has a video discussing alternate construction methods and various media.[2] Collaborate with the English Language Arts teacher on an extension unit around a tour of an online zine collection (remember that some topics may not be suitable for young learners!), discussion of book publishing methods, historical framing around marginalized voices and underground media, and more.

---

2 Requires monthly subscription: https://www.creativebug.com/classseries/single/how-to-make-zines.

- Collaborate with a classroom teacher on developing a zine library featuring diverse voices from around the school as well as "anchor texts" featuring outstanding examples of writing traits such as voice, language, or interplay of text and illustration.

- Update a "parts of the book" lesson by having authors include requisite sections in their zine . . . just remember that the *content* choices should still be theirs!

CONCLUSION

We find that zines are surprisingly engaging for the youth we work with—and for us, too, as we work alongside them. Hope you'll find the same!

An earlier version of this chapter appeared as "Zines" in the March/April 2018 "Makerspaces" column of Teacher Librarian. *Special thanks to Edward Kurdyla for permission to reprint it here. Thank you to Laura Warren-Gross, Ben Rearick, Tori Culler, Sarah G. Swiderski, Sarah Cramer, Rachel Moir, and the staff of the Benzonia (MI) Public Library for helping to plan maker activities for writers.*

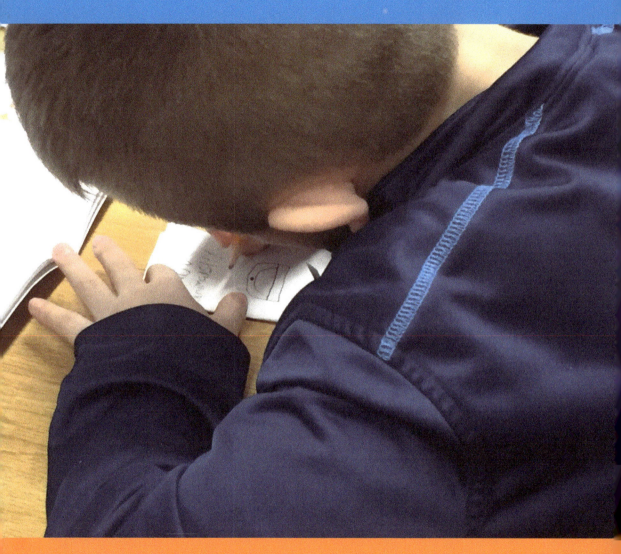
A student at Mitchell Elementary School in Ann Arbor, Michigan, creates his first zine.

CHAPTER 26

20 WAYS TO MAKE A ZINE

Sarah G. Swiderski

Need zine ideas? These themes are meant to spark your creativity and help you come up with your own ways to make a zine. You should feel free to tweak or change these prompts in any way you want. Enjoy and happy zine making!

#1: 10 FACTS YOU NEED TO KNOW ABOUT ME

What better way to introduce yourself than to give someone a zine? Make a zine with 10 facts you think everyone should know about you. These can include how old you are, your favorite hobbies, or a secret talent. You can even include magazine cutouts of your favorite things. The tough part will be deciding which 10 facts to include!

#2: ME IN 10 YEARS

Benjamin Franklin once said, "If you fail to plan, you are planning to fail." Make a zine about your plans for the future and who you will be in 10 years! Where will you live? What will you be doing? How will you look? Most importantly, how will you do all of this? Plan your future so you can turn your dreams into realities.

#3: TEACH SOMEONE SOMETHING

Are you really good at something? Has anyone ever told you they wish they could do what you do? Then this way to make a zine is perfect for you. Make a zine to teach someone something. This can include pictures and written instructions. You can teach someone how to make a craft, about the rules of your favorite sport, or even something simple like how to tie your shoes. What better way to share your smarts than with a zine?

#4: ANIMAL MASH-UP

Let your imagination run wild like an animal with this way to make a zine. Pick two animals and imagine what it would look like if they were combined! After you have your animal mash-up, make a zine about it. Include facts about where your animal lives, what it eats, and its personality. You could even tell a story starring your animal mash-up. Don't forget to draw a picture of what your animal looks like.

#5: WRITE WITH MAGAZINE LETTERS

For this way to make a zine, use only letters cut out of magazines to spell the words of your zine. You can use the letters to make a zine about whatever topic you would like, just be sure to only use magazine letters to write the words!

#6: WRITE A SEQUEL TO YOUR FAVORITE BOOK

Have you ever wished your favorite book didn't have to end? Do you find yourself wondering what happened to the characters after the story ended? With this way to make a zine you can continue the story. You can continue the story by writing a sequel in a zine. How will you continue the story? Will you draw pictures to tell the story? Will you only use words? Some combination of the two? How you create the zine sequel is up to you!

#7: PACK FOR YOUR DREAM ADVENTURE

Think of a trip you would like to take and the adventures you would want to have. What will you need on this trip? What kinds of clothes will you wear?

Plan your trip by creating a packing list in this way to make a zine. Write down everything you think you might need in your zine and tell what adventure you will need each thing for!

#8: MAKE A TOURIST'S GUIDE TO YOUR NEIGHBORHOOD

Sometimes your neighborhood may seem boring because you pass by the same building, streets, and other places every day. Remember how wonderful and interesting your neighborhood is with this way to make a zine. Create a zine that will guide tourists around your neighborhood: a tour guide! Point out the major landmarks in your neighborhood, like is there a great big tree on the street? Are there any fun places you like to go? Use this zine to tell about how wonderful your neighborhood is.

#9: IMAGINE YOUR SCHOOL AT MIDNIGHT

Five days a week you go to school, but you are only there during the daytime. What does your school look like at midnight? Imagine your school at midnight and show and describe it in your zine. Do the desks creak? Does the classroom pet come out and play? Reveal your school's secret nightlife!

#10: MAKE A TIME CAPSULE

Back to the future! Make a zine about what you would put in a time capsule that will be opened 50 years from now. What are some things that you want the people in the future to know about today? What do you think people from the future want to know about today? You can use newspaper clippings, pictures, and magazines to illustrate your zine or you can draw what you would want to include. Tell the story of today to the future through your zine.

#11: MAKE SOME NOISE

Reading is a quiet activity but with this way to make a zine you can change that. Make a zine that makes noise when you read it. It doesn't matter how you do it, just be sure you create a ruckus that will make people wonder what you are reading!

#12: I SPY

I spy with my little eye a great way to make a zine! Create a series of jumbled-up pictures and hide clues and images. Challenge your readers to find what you have hidden. Think of this zine as being similar to a find and point book. Be sure to get creative with how you hide your clues. This zine is as fun to make as it is to read!

#13: IDEAL GROCERY LIST

Have you ever gone to the grocery store with a grown-up and you asked to get your favorite cookies and the grown-up said "not today" or just plain "no"? Well in this way to make a zine, there is no such thing as "no." If an adult told you they would buy whatever was on the grocery list, what would you put on the list? Want to put all kinds of sweets on your grocery list? Go for it! Maybe you would like to get the ingredients for your favorite dinner? Put it on the list. The only rule is that you have to be able to buy it in the grocery store. Create your ideal grocery list!

Washi tape is a popular accessory for zines, as shown at the Benzonia Public Library's Behavior Incentive Day.

#14: A SCIENTIST AND INVENTOR'S NOTEBOOK

Pretend you've just discovered a kooky scientist and inventor's notebook filled with all of his or her wonderful and fantastical discoveries and creations. What kind of ideas or notes do you think are inside? Maybe, there are specimens of rare and exotic plants with notes about where he or she found them. Perhaps, there are schematics for a new flying machine. Fill your zine with the whimsical and scientific ideas that you might find in a scientist and inventor's notebook.

#15: RECIPE BOOK

Don your apron, because this way to make a zine will take you to the kitchen! Create a zine about your favorite recipes. These recipes might range from beef Wellington to boxed macaroni and cheese. Maybe you have a special chocolate chip cookie recipe or a trick for making banana bread that doesn't cave in on itself. Your recipes might be funny or they might be simple quick meals. They might be salty and they might be sweet. If you like to make it and eat it, put it in the zine!

#16: WHAT LIVES UNDER YOUR BED

This way to make a zine will take you where no zine has gone before: into the mysterious world of under your bed. Are there just smelly socks and spiders under there or is that where you hide secret treasure? Do monsters live under your bed or is it just dust bunnies? Make a zine about what literally lives under your bed or what you imagine is there. You can include pictures, drawings, and maybe even samples of what you find there. Give your readers a peek under the bed with this zine!

#17: DICTIONARY

According to the dictionary, a sneeze is defined as "to emit air or breath suddenly, forcibly, and audibly through the nose and mouth by involuntary, spasmodic action." Thank goodness someone came up with a word for a sneeze! If someone hadn't, people would have to say, "she had to emit air or breath suddenly" instead of "she had to sneeze."

Unfortunately, sometimes words just don't or can't describe what you want them to. People sometimes have to use long complicated explanations to describe what they want to communicate (kind of like you would have to if there wasn't a word for sneeze). For example, there is not a good word to describe that fantastic feeling of popping Bubble Wrap. Can you make up a single word to describe that feeling? Or maybe you wished there was a word for the type of laughter that follows after your friend squirts milk out his or her nose. Can you think of a word for that too? In this way to make a zine, create your own dictionary with words you create yourself to describe things, feelings, actions, people, and more that currently do not have a one-word description.

#18: POETRY

This way to make a zine is perhaps one of the classic ways to make a zine. Create a zine filled with poetry. These might be poems you write yourself or written by others. Just make sure you have permission to put someone else's poems in your zine or tell who wrote the poem and where you got it from.

You can include a variety of poems in your zine. The poems might be about your everyday life or they might be about wondrous adventures. The poems might rhyme or they might not. Poetry is like a zine in that there is no wrong way to make it. Poetry is as unique as the zine that holds it. Find your inner poet in this way to make a zine!

#19: ULTIMATE RANKING OF DINOSAURS ... OR SOMETHING ELSE

Tyrannosaurus rex, Triceratops, and Brontosaurus are all fantastic types of dinosaurs that sadly no longer roam the Earth. Even though they are gone, they are not forgotten. In this way to make a zine, create an ultimate ranking of the top 10 dinosaurs. When you are ranking the dinosaurs, make sure you explain in your zine why you ranked each of the dinosaurs the way you did. Is it because of what they eat, how big they are, or something else?

Dinosaurs not your thing? Pick something else to rank! It could be types of music, famous athletes, even colors. If there are different kinds, you can rank it!

#20: YOU DECIDE

You have tried all the other ways to make a zine? Now, decide for yourself how **YOU** will make a zine. Will you use just pencil to create sharp drawings or magazine clippings in screaming color? Will you write your words or cut them out of a magazine? There is no wrong way to make a zine. You decide in this way to make a zine!

REFERENCES

Biel, Joe, and Bill Brent. 2017. *Make a Zine* (3rd ed.). Portland, OR: Microcosm Publishing.
Emberley, Ed R. 2002. *Ed Emberley's Complete FunPrint Drawing Book* (1st ed.). New York: Little, Brown and Company.
Hirschmann, Kris. 2018. *100 Screen-Free Ways to Beat Boredom* (1st ed.). I. Elisa Paganelli. Hauppauge, NY: Barron's Educational Series, Inc.
Smith, Keri. 2011. *Finish This Book* (1st ed.). New York: Penguin Group Inc.
Till, Kera. 2013. *Dottie Polka's Vintage Collection* (1st ed.). New York: Little Bee Books.

Reprinted with permission from Sarah G. Swiderski's Twenty Ways to Make a Zine *site at https://sites.google.com/umich.edu/twentywaystomakeazine/home.*

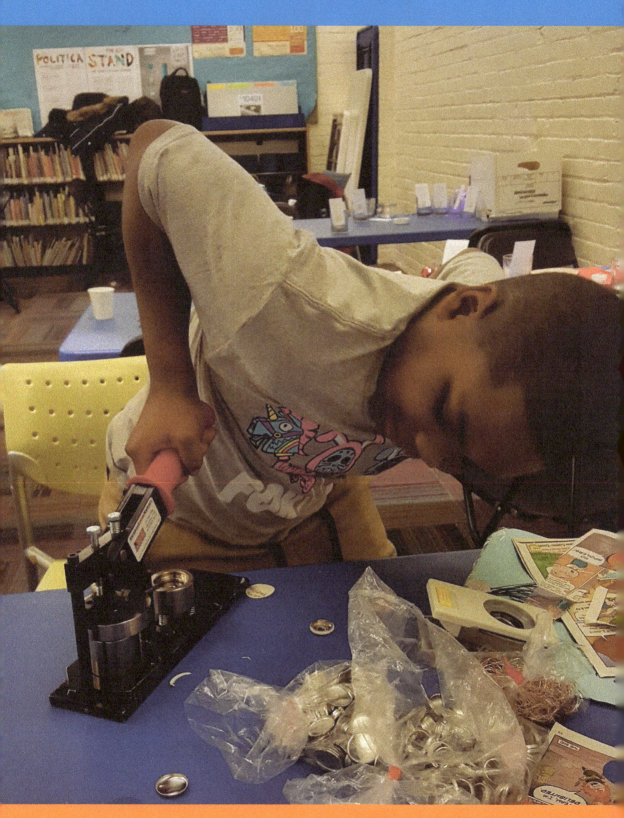

A button maker shown here at the Ypsilanti (MI) District Library's Michigan Avenue Branch, is easy, fast, low-cost, and satisfying for makers.

CHAPTER 27
BUTTON MAKING

Nicole Sype

People of all ages enjoy finding or creating images to be turned into a fashionable accessory. Buttons can be worn on clothing, put on backpacks, used within a larger craft, and/or given out as prizes. But how do you make quality, wearable buttons? The answer is an easy-to-use machine: a button maker! Button makers allow for various levels of creativity, making it accessible for almost every age. They allow children the opportunity to create something with their hands and learn how to use a new tool. They can be used in youth and teen programming and are a great addition to any makerspace. The best part about them is that literally any image (within the size constraints) can be used. In this chapter, we'll go through what button makers are, who can use them, and ideas for making buttons. Be warned, button making is incredibly addicting!

WHAT IS A BUTTON MAKER?

Button makers are small machines that make creating buttons extremely simple. Button makers are sold individually or in kits (which include all of the supplies needed to make your own buttons). The price range for the kits are around $400–$650 depending on what size buttons you want. For the Making in Michigan Libraries project, we purchased a 1″ button maker from American Button Machines because we heard rave reviews about its ease of

We paid about $350 for this 1″ button maker from American Button Machines.

use and durability. We chose the 1″ size because the buttons could be glued to specialty jewelry findings or attached to magnets.

WHO CAN USE A BUTTON MAKER?

Pretty much anyone! There are only a few steps, and your button maker will come with simple instructions. The most time-consuming part for you will most likely be locating materials to get or create images from, while the user will likely spend the majority of their time choosing or creating their image.

Save your damaged and weeded books: the pictures or text can be cut out to create unique buttons. (If you use images from paperback book covers or

At the Ypsilanti District Library, these 1" buttons were made from images taken out of discarded picture books and comic books.

other thick paper, you may need to omit the clear Mylar button "cover" for the image to fit into the button's layers.) One of our Michigan Makers, Tori Culler, suggests looking at thrift shops, Friends of the Library book sales, and used book sales for illustrated books or comics. Also, try adding to a picture, illustration, or section of text by coloring it or writing over it with a Sharpie. If someone is a talented artist, they can create their own piece of art to turn into a button (if your machine is finicky, make a button from a color copy of the art instead of the original). Pre-sized outlined images can be provided for people to color in. Users can also take their own pictures and edit them before sizing them and printing them out.[1]

When users have found or created an image that needs to be cut out, they can use the graphic punch included in the kit or a Fiskars hole punch (which

---

1 http://www.teenlibrariantoolbox.com/2016/06/makerspace-button-maker-challenges/.

Here we see a four-year-old child getting the hang of using the button maker at the Ypsilanti District Library.

He was soon able to use the button maker without any assistance.

Ypsilanti District Library makers use a graphic punch to cut out the image they want. Using the punch upside-down allows makers to preview their image prior to cutting it out.

is what we use—we hold it upside down to preview the button in the punch's metal shape). Once the image is cut out, you'll follow the instructions that come with the button maker and then enjoy your new button!

A BUTTON MAKER IN YOUR MAKERSPACE

Whether you're planning a makerspace for children, teens, or adults, a button maker is a guaranteed crowd pleaser. Its ease of use allows it to be an independent activity with minimum guidance. People will love searching through books and comics or creating their own piece of art to make a button with. The creative options are endless and with the variety of crafts, apps, and games that can be paired with button making, you and your patrons will never get bored.

KEEP GOING!

To learn more about button making, including a sample set of instructions for self-serve use of the button maker as well as Design Challenge cards,

You can't make just one!

see Karen Jensen's blog post, "MakerSpace: Button Making Is All the Rage (the Complete Button Making Index)" from *School Library Journal*'s Teen Librarian Toolbox (http://www.teenlibrariantoolbox.com/2017/07/makerspace-button-making-is-all-the-rage-the-complete-button-making-index/).

You can also find other libraries' experiences with button makers at these URLs:

- https://ontarianlibrarian.com/2015/03/10/teen-button-makerspace/
- https://greenelibrary.info/makerspace/button-maker/
- http://makerbridge.si.umich.edu/2014/12/guest-blog-post-buttonmakers-as-pop-up-making/

Button makers appeal to all ages. Here, teens at Scarlett Middle School in Ann Arbor, Michigan, work together to make creative buttons.

The Mid-Michigan Library League makes this MakerBot 3D printer available for loan to its many rural library members. Here, it is being used at the Houghton Lake (MI) Public Library.

CHAPTER 28
3D MODELING AND PRINTING

Caroline Wack

3D printers have come to symbolize makerspaces for some teachers and librarians. With help from 3D modeling software, makers can watch their ideas materialize from thin air, becoming tangible representations of their creativity and engineering skills. In addition to the symbolic value, 3D printers are useful tools for creating durable, professional-looking products. Depending on the maker's age and expertise, 3D-printed projects can range from small trinkets downloaded from the internet to elaborate, customized designs with real-world utility.

WHAT IS 3D PRINTING?

When people talk about 3D printing, they're actually describing multiple steps and workflows. First, a maker uses 3D modeling software—often with a drafting software called CAD driving things behind the scenes—to develop a model. The maker then exports that file into a printable format, in most cases with the .stl or .3gs extension. (Check your printer's software to know which formats it can accept.) Be aware that making simple shapes is relatively easy, but drafting something custom and precise, like a new part for one's vacuum cleaner, may require significant time and expertise. (Note that using an existing, downloadable model from an online repository like Thingiverse.com or MyMiniFactory.com bypasses the modeling stage.) Next, the file is uploaded or opened in your printer's software. While some printers, like MakerBot, have their own proprietary software that can be downloaded online at the manufacturer's website, there is a class of printers that uses open-source printing software like Cura. Finally, the printing software communicates with the 3D printer itself via a printer cable. You may need to keep your computer tethered—with sleep mode disabled—to the printer for the duration of the print, which can be minutes for a charm-sized print or hours for something the size of a soda can. Some newer model 3D printers allow you to transfer the file to the printer itself via Wi-Fi or an SD memory card instead.

HOW DOES A 3D PRINTER WORK?

Watching a 3D printer at work is often an awe-inspiring experience. 3D printers create objects using a process known as *additive manufacturing*, meaning that the object starts from nothing and generally builds into an object. (The opposite, *subtractive manufacturing*, starts with raw materials and removes portions until the desired object is achieved. Think of Michelangelo starting with a large piece of stone and, from it, carving excess away until the *David* is all that it is left.) The printer feeds filament (a rigid plastic "cord" made out of PLA or ABS plastic, depending on what kind your printer is designed to accept) into a heating chamber, then *extrudes* a thin, threadlike width of plastic out of it. The plastic is laid out on the build plate in thin rows, building layer after layer until your object takes shape before you. Think of your printer as a tube of toothpaste that squeezes out melted filament instead of paste!

Some printer software lets you send several objects to print at once. This is great if your printer runs reliably, because you can set it once and then walk away. If your printer is finicky, however, laying out multiple objects at once can actually mean that if something goes wrong, you have several aborted objects. In that case, you may be more successful printing one job at a time.

DO YOU NEED A 3D PRINTER?

A 3D printer may not be appropriate for every makerspace. It is difficult for several makers to share a single 3D printer at one time, which limits their effectiveness in classroom settings or scheduled library programs. Also, because the printing process takes so long, a printer may not be able to finish even one large print in a session. 3D printers also require a significant financial investment from a school or library—in addition to the initial cost

Mayank Khanna, former graduate student research assistant for the Making in Michigan Libraries project, introduces 3D printing to students at Scarlett Middle School in Ann Arbor, Michigan.

of purchasing a printer, you will have to purchase filament (we like Solutech brand, which has a wide range of colors and a below-average price point; available via Amazon.com) and be ready to fund the cost and time for the inevitable repairs. Consider reaching out to nearby makerspaces, schools, or libraries to see if you can match their model, which may give you in-town support when your printer acts up or needs repair.

Finally, your makers can 3D print objects even if you do not have a 3D printer. Patrons or students can create a digital model then upload it to a site like Shapeways.com, a company that will, for a fee, print their creations using plastic, metal, or even ceramic. The completed project is shipped back to the creator.

GETTING TO KNOW YOUR 3D PRINTER

When you first acquire a 3D printer, you'll want to get to know its mechanics. The best way to do that is to download some pre-made designs from sites

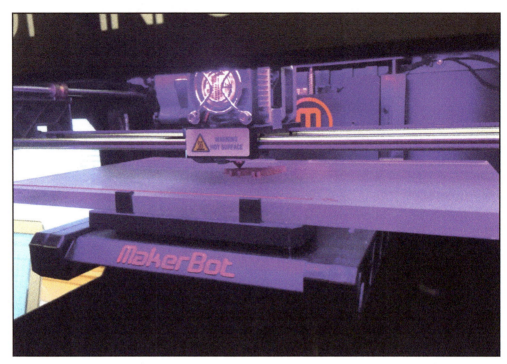

This 3D print is being made without a raft, or the disposable foundation layer that can help your printed objects stay adhered to the build plate during printing.

like Thingiverse.com or MyMiniFactory.com and see how your printer works. Printing 3D objects can be challenging, so spend a week or so just exploring with pre-made objects.

For example, designs that have a cantilevered or "overhang" section (such as a figure of Pinocchio with his outsized nose) can be tricky to print because the 3D printer will be printing the nose in mid-air. In cases like these, you'll want to play with your printing software's "supports" feature for this. Supports are rough foundations onto which those cantilever portions can rest. Later, the supports are snipped off with nipper-style pliers and the resulting underside of the object is sanded down. Be sure to sand in a ventilated area and wear a mask.

Another printing challenge can occur when you are 3D printing an object that is quite small on the bottom, like a chair or the legs of a small animal. In this case, there may not be enough filament being laid down to adhere well to the build plate. In this case, you don't need supports; you need a *raft*, a rough base with a texture similar to a Triscuit cracker that is wider than the base of the object. After printing, use pliers to pry off the raft from the object and sand the resulting rough spots with sandpaper.

So where can you quickly get your hands on some projects with which to practice printing? Luckily, there are a handful of online repositories where volunteers upload their designs and allow others to download, modify, and use them.

ONLINE OBJECT COLLECTIONS

Thingiverse.com

Thingiverse is an online community, sponsored by MakerBot, for makers who are interested in 3D printing. Users can "friend" or "follow" other users to see what they are creating, and join communities ("Groups") based on location, interest, profession, or purpose. Users can also upload their own 3D printable designs ("Things") to the site, where they are searchable and usable by other Thingiverse members. Thingiverse gives its users control over how their Things are used—they can allow other users to freely use and customize a design, they can allow free use without customization, or they can require payment for the use of their designs.

There is also an educational component to Thingiverse. Thingiverse Education is a sub-community where teachers, librarians, and other educators can share projects and tips for teaching 3D printing. There are over 100 free lessons available for educators through Thingiverse Education. In addition, the site runs Design Challenges, encouraging users to explore new tools or uses for their 3D printers and rewarding them with new 3D printers, filament spools, or subscriptions to design tools.

Thingiverse is not a design tool in itself, so we will refrain from going into too much detail here. It is a useful place to search for pre-existing designs of all levels and to find community and support when creating your own designs.

MyMiniFactory.com

Similar to Thingiverse, MyMiniFactory.com has thousands of designs that users can download and print. This platform also offers community forums and design competitions, and objects downloaded from MyMiniFactory.com are tested and guaranteed to be printable. Unlike Thingiverse, MyMiniFactory.com also has a paid tier for some designs.

306 PROJECTS AND PROGRAMS

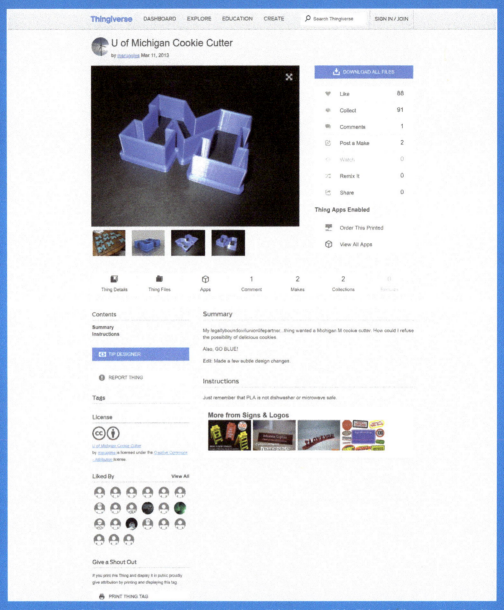

A University of Michigan cookie cutter posted on Thingiverse. This Thing is licensed under the Creative Commons–Attribution license, which means that other Thingiverse users are free to use and share this Thing as long as they give attribution to the original creator. Makers can choose which Creative Commons license they assign to the Things they upload to Thingiverse, which gives them the power to determine how others use and credit their work.

Cultural and Science Model Repositories

An increasing number of repositories are cropping up that help you replicate art, culture, and science models. These include:

- **Smithsonian Institution:** Ancient Roman art, Air and Space Museum models, and natural science. https://3d.si.edu/

- **National Institutes of Health:** Medical models. https://3dprint.nih.gov/

- **NASA Models:** Models from NASA's collection, including lunar surfaces and artifacts. https://nasa3d.arc.nasa.gov/models/printable

MODELING TOOLS

If you decide that a 3D printer is right for your makerspace, you will want to be aware of the design tools available to you. This section focuses on 3D modeling tools rather than the software that is used to run the printer, which will vary based on your printer model. These tools were all tested on a MakerBot Replicator 2.

CookieCaster.com

Cookie Caster (cookiecaster.com) is a website that creates 3D-modeled cookie cutter designs from user sketches. It's an especially good tool for younger children, because the design process is fairly simple and children can then use their designs in real life.

Makers have two options to create sketches:

- They can draw something freehand by clicking in the drawing canvas. Each click creates a blue point that is connected to the previous point by a straight line. Once the shape is closed, users can add curves to the lines by clicking and dragging the yellow dot in the center of the line, sliding the dot down the line to create uneven curves if needed. Users can also move the vertices of the lines by dragging the blue dots.

- Makers can upload an image to the drawing space and create a shape by tracing the image (we've found that this feature can be finicky with some browsers and images). Cookie Caster will automatically outline that object. The lines can be manipulated further by clicking and dragging the blue vertices or the yellow centers of the lines, just as in freehand drawings.

Once makers are satisfied with their shape, they have two options to download a file for use. First, they can set their preferred size and click "download now" on the right side of the screen. The 3D file will immediately download to the maker's computer. Or, if makers wish to share their design with others, they can save it to their Cookie Caster account by clicking "save it" in the lower right corner of the drawing canvas. If they are not logged in already, they will be prompted to log in or register for a free account, and then name their design. They can then download the design as above, but the shape will be saved to a gallery of community creations.

Makers who don't care to make their own cookie cutter can browse through the Cookie Caster gallery. Every cookie cutter saved on the site goes into the gallery, so makers can download and print other people's projects if they

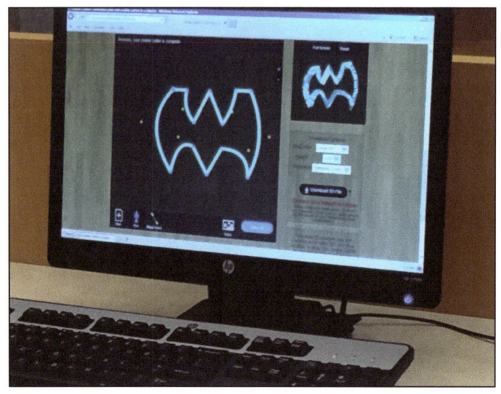

CookieCaster.com in use at a Making in Michigan Libraries workshop at Coopersville High School in Coopersville, Michigan.

wish. The same is true in reverse: if makers save their objects, other people will be able to find and use their designs. And while the obvious use of the creations on this site is to cut out cookies (or Rice Krispies Treats, as our colleagues at the Michigan Avenue Branch of the Ypsilanti District Library have done!), you can also use the completed projects as zipper pulls or key chains. Make them tiny if you need to print them same-day!

Cookie Caster is a fairly simple tool, with few advanced features. Some limitations of the tool include:

- There is no search feature in the gallery.

- Makers can only create polygons, so there is no way to design cutouts within a cookie—lines cannot intersect. There is also no way to create a part of the cookie cutter that is a shorter length, which would leave an indentation in the cookie for an illustrative effect.

- The sizing options are set to increments of a half-inch between 2 inches and 5 inches, although the size of the final printout can be changed in the software that controls the printer.

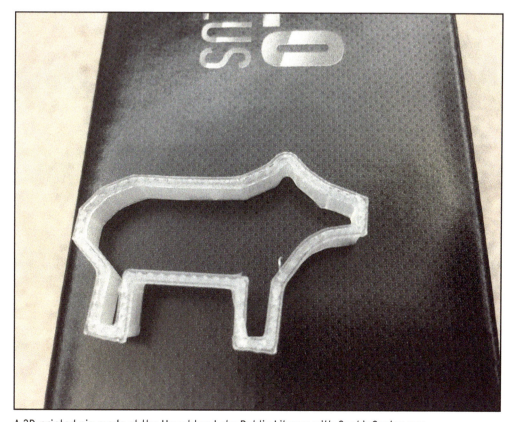

A 3D-printed pig made at the Houghton Lake Public Library with CookieCaster.com.

These limitations may not matter much to a total beginner, but once they gain a little experience, makers will want some more control over the design process. The following tools offer more customization.

Pxstl.com

Another site that facilitates a quick design process for beginners is Pxstl.com. This site, developed by John Pariseau of the University of Michigan College of Engineering, provides users with an empty grid. Clicking in the boxes of a grid colors them in black and represents what will be printed. Click "Preview" to see your design in 3D instead of on the 2D grid; adjust the size of your grid under "Settings." As with Cookiecaster.com, you can download the completed design (look for "Generate Design" from the panel that appears once you begin designing) in .stl format when completed.

This site is limited to straight edges and uniform heights, but it's a good option for time-limited programs. Consider setting out books showing traditional knitting or beading patterns and challenging your patrons to replicate or modify a pattern using the Pxstl grid. As long as patrons leave at least one white box open in their design, they will be able to string their completed object with a ribbon, chain, or leather cord for one-of-a-kind jewelry, suncatchers, or holiday ornaments.

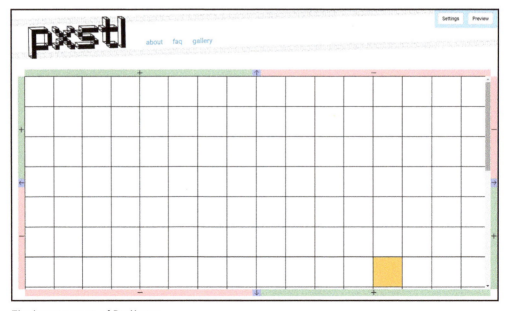

The home screen of Pxstl.com.

3dslash.net

Earlier, we mentioned that 3D printing is an example of additive manufacturing, where you build layers of material to create an object, as opposed to subtractive manufacturing, where you start with a material and remove pieces of it to get the object you want. 3dslash.net is a tool that lets you try a little bit of both.

The "Classic" mode of 3dslash.net provides users with a 3D model of a block. Users can then "carve" at the block using a hammer tool. Each click of the hammer tool removes a smaller block from the 3D model, creating empty space. Users can set the size of the blocks that they are chipping away, and, with paid subscriptions, can unlock the smallest block sizes and new ways of removing material—for example, removing entire lines or curves at a time. When makers are satisfied with their creation, they can download it or share it on Facebook, where their friends can comment on or even rework their models. Other modes allow users to build blocks on an empty plate (similar to Pxstl.com, but with the option to build in three dimensions), upload a .stl file and remove blocks from the existing design, or remove blocks from a logo or text that has been converted into a 3D model.

This tool is great for users who are looking for more flexibility than Cookie Caster or Pxstl.com may offer, but who still need support. The grid layout

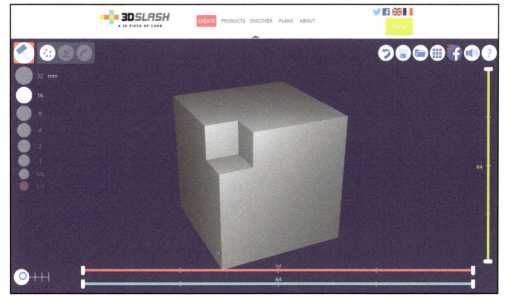

The classic mode of 3dslash.net.

makes it easy to see where you are adding or subtracting blocks, and how big your addition or subtraction is relative to the size of the whole model. Encourage students to pretend that they are carving a statue—what are the limitations of doing this task digitally, and what are the affordances?

Tinkercad

If you're looking to create something completely custom, then you will need to move into CAD design software. Professional CAD software like Rhino or Fusion 360 can be complicated and expensive. Luckily, Tinkercad, made by AutoDesk, is a free, robust, and simplified version of Fusion 360. Tinkercad is a 3D modeling tool that allows users to combine basic shapes, text and numbers, characters, and connectors to form a design. Users can create everything from trinkets to tools using Tinkercad. The control that users have over the shapes and the limitless combinations of objects mean that users are only constrained by their own creativity, and the detailed tutorials that are available make it accessible to most makers.

There are four tabs on the top of the screen in Tinkercad. The main design process takes place in the first tab, labeled "design." This tab consists of a Workplane in the center of the screen, controls for the Workplane on the left-hand side, and a menu of shapes on the right. Users select a pre-set shape from the menu on the right and set it on the Workplane, where they can resize it on any (or all) of its axes, move it around the Workplane, and combine it with other shapes. Clicking on the shape reveals even more options for customization: depending on what the shape is, users can set the font, the bevel size, or the number of "steps" in a curve, among other options. They can also choose to make their shape a "hole" rather than a "solid," which means that it will create negative space in the design. Users can also choose to permanently join two objects so that they move and scale together using the "group" feature. Free tutorials available in Tinkercad explain each of these processes in greater detail.

The other tabs on the top are labeled "blocks," "bricks," and "shape generators." Blocks and Bricks take the design that the user created in the Design tab and show what it would look like if it were instead built with either blocks or LEGO. Users can then re-create their designs using blocks or bricks that they have on hand to save time. After all, it can take hours for a 3D model to print, but only minutes to check dimensions via a quick LEGO assembly! Users can set the level of detail on the screen, and then use the "layers" function to get a step-by-step tutorial for re-creating their designs with these everyday materials.

For users that are not satisfied with the shape options available in the Design tab, Tinkercad also has the option of creating new shapes using JavaScript, located in the Shape Generator tab. Users who are already familiar with JavaScript may enjoy this increased flexibility, but because the shapes are already so customizable, most users will not need this option.

Tinkercad offers powerful and flexible design options for beginners. The focus on joining different elements to create new, unique designs will appeal to makers of all levels.

Some makers may want to use Tinkercad to replace a broken part. You may wish to have a few pairs of digital calipers on hand to facilitate this. These are precision measuring tools that will help makers match the size of an existing object to the size of the designed object in Tinkercad. Most 3D printing and modeling software defaults to displaying in millimeters, not inches, so choose a caliper with a built-in digital display that can measure in both inches and

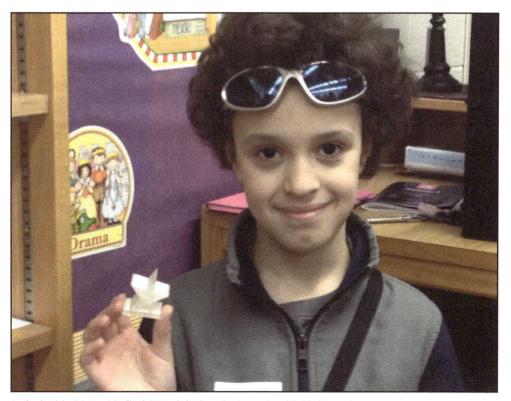

A student holds up his first 3D-printed project, made with Tinkercad.

millimeters. The Home Depot sells a model for $14 that is worth consideration (https://www.homedepot.com/p/Steel-Core-6-in-Stainless-Steel-Electronic-Digital-Caliper-with-LCD-Display-30902/301118028).

CONCLUSION

3D modeling and printing can be an exciting part of your makerspace that draws in many visitors and allows makers to gain skills in tech and engineering. Be sure to do a careful needs assessment before committing to this in your makerspace, and be aware of the cost in time, money, space, and materials. If you do decide that a 3D printer is appropriate for your space, take advantage of the resources in this chapter to make 3D printing accessible for a wide range of ages and skill sets.

A young maker at the Ypsilanti District Library studies Dash, a robot created by Wonder Workshop.

CHAPTER 29
ROBOTS

Caroline Wack

Makerspaces are often touted as a way to prepare learners for careers in STEM. We've discussed how the benefits of makerspaces are actually much more nuanced than this, but it is still important to provide these tools in your space—they bring people in, they are educational, and they are fun!

Robots, which we're defining as pieces of technology that can move on their own or respond to remote commands, are one way to introduce STEM into your makerspace. Children of all ages love playing with robots—it's exciting to watch something move with no apparent outside stimulation! There are a multitude of robots available at a variety of price points and levels of complexity, so there are many potential options for your makerspace. With these tools, you can teach lessons on circuitry, programming, construction, and design, among many other things.

SUGGESTED ROBOTS

Below are some types of robots that you might consider as you create your makerspace. Keep in mind the ages and interests of learners in your space, as well as financial constraints, as you acquire technology. Some of these tools require apps to operate; can you afford tablets or smartphones in addition to the robot? Will makers take advantage of the more complicated features available in more expensive robots, like programming and sensors, or do they prefer simply to have a toy to drive around? These factors may influence the sort of technology you have in your makerspace.

BrushBots or BristleBots

One example of a simple first robot does not require any application or computers to run. It needs only a small vibrating motor (you can find these on Amazon for around $1 each by searching for "cell phone motor" or hack the motor inside an electric toothbrush from the dollar store), a coin cell battery, some electrical tape, some double-sided tape, and something relatively small and flat that can be used as the robot body. Many people prefer small scrubbing brushes or the bristly heads of toothbrushes—hence the names BrushBot and BristleBot—but any small item with a flat surface will do. At Michigan Makers, we've used plastic insects and 3D-printed stingrays as robot bodies.

Stick the motor to the robot's body and tape the motor's wires ("leads") to the battery, making sure to match up the positive side of the battery with the positive wire ("anode") and the negative side of the battery to the negative wire ("cathode"). The motor will begin to vibrate. Wrap the leads and battery

Making robots with 3D-printed stingrays at the Ypsilanti District Library.

tightly in electrical tape. Using double-sided tape, attach the battery to the robot's body and set it down on a flat surface. It will begin to skitter across the surface of the table as the motor vibrates.

Have makers experiment with placing the battery and motor in different places on the robot's body—different weight placement can make the robot go in different directions. You can also have makers decorate their bots with pipe cleaners, googly eyes, and Sharpies to make their robot uniquely theirs. Consider combining these motors with a junk box and letting makers explore going beyond robots—one student at the Ypsilanti District Library found a plastic headband and made herself a "massage headband" using these motors.

An advantage of these simple creations, unlike commercially-made robots, is that makers can take them home at the end of the session.

Ozobots

Ozobots are small, round robots that makers can program to move in one of two ways. The first way is typical for robot toys: there is an Ozobot app, where makers can drive the bots or build programs using Blockly.[1] The second way is more unique: users can draw paths and color codes for the robots using markers included with the purchase. Using built-in sensors, the Ozobot will follow paths drawn by these markers. The codes, which are colored right into the path, make the robot change its behavior—for example, speeding up or turning right at the next intersection. Ozobot markets this as a screenless method of teaching coding, and indeed these color codes teach children important concepts like cause and effect and debugging. However, some coding concepts such as if/else logic (which allows a program to do different things, depending on the input) and loops (which allow a program to repeat until certain conditions are met) are not able to be represented through color coding the way they are with Blockly.

The drawing element of Ozobot makes it a playful entry to robots for younger makers, combining a craft that they are already familiar with and a technology that they are sure to be excited about. Have makers draw their names (in cursive, so the letters connect), smiley faces, houses or trees, or anything else that they already like to draw. As they grow more confident, they

---

[1] Blockly is a computer program that teaches programming skills. It allows users to create single commands, like "move forward 10 rotations" or "spin 90 degrees to the right," and then drop them into blocks of code to create programs.

Maker mentor Nicole Sype works with a maker with Ozobots during a Michigan Makers Family Night at the Ypsilanti District Library.

can draw things specifically for the Ozobot, like mazes or obstacle courses. You can even work with kids to connect each of their individual paths to one another, spreading out for several feet along the floor.

As of the time of this writing, basic Ozobots can be purchased for $60 each. See https://shop.ozobot.com for purchase information.

MeeperBOT

MeeperBOT is a small, app-controlled vehicle. Similar to Ozobot, makers can drive a MeeperBOT via the app (which has four different drive modes) or build a program using Blockly in order to execute many directions at once—for example, driving forward, turning 90 degrees to the right, driving forward again, and then spinning in place.

A maker from Mitchell Elementary holds up a MeeperBOT and LEGO creation.

The real advantage of MeeperBOT is that the top of its car is a brick platform, so makers can build structures on top of the car with LEGO or other brick construction toys. This makes for endless activity possibilities. Makers can build claws or cages on the front of their robots and collect items scattered across the room, they can build towers on their BOTs and battle each other, or they can hold races and see if adding structures and weights to their BOTs speeds them up or slows them down. This makes the MeeperBOT a tool useful for far more than just programming; the construction component teaches engineering, Design Thinking, and problem solving, among other skills.

At the time of this writing, MeeperBOTs can be purchased for $55 each. See https://meeperbot.com/collections/bot-2-1 for purchase information.

Dash

Dash robots are made up of four balls—one ball, the head, rests on a tripod formed of the other three balls. Like MeeperBOT and Ozobot, Dash can be controlled from an app. Its functionality, however, is far greater. In addition to moving, Dash can make sounds, flash colored lights, and use sensors to navigate—all controlled from the app. These sensors in particular make the Blockly portion of this app more robust than other tools we have reviewed—by generating input, the sensors allow if/else loops in the programming. For example, makers can instruct Dash to turn out of the way if it senses an obstacle in its path.

There are many different accessories available for Dash, including a xylophone, a gripper, a launcher, and brick connectors, which are controlled through separate apps (all apps are free). All of these accessories have their own affordances and could be used to adapt Dash for many different activities. Keep in mind that accessories will add extra cost. Note too that Wonder Workshop, which produces Dash robots, also produces companion robots called *cue* and Dot. We have found that Dot robots, while cheaper than Dash, have more limited functionality; we have not yet worked with *cue*. It may be worth evaluating which robot would work best for your space:

At the Benzonia Public Library, one maker built a LEGO car for a Dash robot to pull.

see https://www.makewonder.com/compare_robots/ for a chart comparing these three robots.

At the time of this writing, Dash can be purchased for $149.99 each. See https://www.makewonder.com/robots/dash for purchase information.

Code-a-Pillar by Fisher-Price

Public librarians we met were eager to hear about robotics options for the very young. The Code-a-Pillar is a set of plastic segments that, combined, create a caterpillar with serpentine action. Young learners can grasp the concept that commands, placed in various sequences, are executed in different ways.

At the time of this writing, the Code-a-Pillar is $49 at https://www.barnesandnoble.com/w/toys-games-fisher-price-think-learn-code-a-pillar/29908219.

Code and Go® Robot Mouse Activity Set

While some educators have expressed a preference for the similar BeeBot robot kit, we found that Code and Go® was a better-scaffolded tool for the same or lower price. Youth can arrange the maze blocks provided, then program the mouse to navigate the path. As with Code-a-Pillar, this tool is a good fit for preschool through early elementary.

At the time this book was written, this product was available for $59.99 at https://www.learningresources.com/code-gor-robot-mouse-activity-set.

LittleBits Kits

LittleBits are single-function parts ("Bits") that snap together. Depending on how they are snapped together, you can form different inventions—for example, a button, an LED, and a power source might snap together to form a flashlight. While you can buy Bits individually, if you're trying to grow your robot collection it may make sense to buy LittleBits Kits. Kits consist of Bits and other parts that have been specially selected for a purpose—for example, making music, exploring space, or building superhero technology. Makers using these kits get to experience building and customizing a robot

A LittleBits KORG Music kit in use at Mitchell Elementary School in Ann Arbor, MI.

before playing with it. And thanks to Bits like the Bluetooth Bit, the Arduino Bit, and the Code Bit, makers aren't just building self-contained machines; the robots constructed with LittleBits can connect to the internet and be reprogrammed to function differently than they were intended to. LittleBits kits represent endless possibilities for makers interested in technology, electronics, and programming!

The cost of LittleBits kits varies, but expect to pay about $100–$200 for most kits. See https://shop.littlebits.com for purchase information. Keep in mind that if your Bits break, you can contact the company for free replacements.

CONCLUSION

There are many more robots available for makerspaces—these are just the ones that we've used and enjoyed at Michigan Makers. While the variety is exciting, it may make it difficult to choose the tools that do end up in your makerspace. Remember to think about what your learning goals beyond programming are—while most of these tools have a drag-and-drop coding component, it is likely that children will prefer to just play. What affordances does each robot have that will make it useful for your learners?

The result of a Design Thinking session in Benzonia, Michigan, was this new and improved set of tools for a firefighter.

CHAPTER 30
DESIGN THINKING AND DESIGN CHALLENGES

Ben Rearick

What is Design Thinking and how can libraries use it? Design Thinking is an iterative problem-solving process that elicits needs and wants about a range of possible solutions. It can be adapted to fit any setting and solve any kind of problem. Makerspaces can use it to teach makers problem-solving skills like identifying a focus, brainstorming solutions, and testing ideas.

Originally promoted by IDEO, a product design company, Design Thinking has grown to influence many different institutions and can be used anywhere. The most memorable example of using Design Thinking on a large scale came from an ABC Nightline piece on IDEO's redesign of the shopping cart in 1999.[1]

TEACHING DESIGN THINKING

As Design Thinking is a process, not a checklist, it's important to teach it in a way that allows participants to go through the process as they learn. Participants who have finished a session with us often said Design Thinking was a way to teach people how to be creative. We hope it allows already creative

---
1 See https://www.ideo.com/post/reimagining-the-shopping-cart.

people to channel their energy, while giving the more structured folk an opportunity to be flexible with their experiences. To teach Design Thinking, it's imperative to walk people through one cycle of the process. Giving time for reflection at the end of each step can allow participants to gain a deeper understanding which can be built up over many sessions or one longer session. See Kristin Fontichiaro's 2016 *Teacher Librarian* article on Design Thinking for librarians for more detail, and read on for some information about how we have used this process in the Michigan Makers project (Fontichiaro 2016).

IDENTIFY A PROBLEM

Essentially, the problem is real-world, community-oriented, or something that affects the participant. It's recommended that the problem shouldn't be too emotionally involved for the participant, as they will have a solution in mind already—for instance, a student shouldn't be asked to solve a problem with homework, nor should a teacher suggest recommendations on classroom space (Zielezinski 2016). It's important to give kids the opportunity to learn the *stages* of Design Thinking, rather than rush to a solution. It can be helpful to think of genres of problems, allowing people a wide range of possible issues to address while keeping them in the same ballpark.

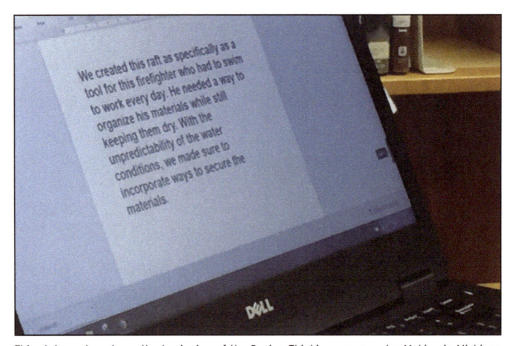

This statement captures the beginning of the Design Thinking process at a Making in Michigan Libraries workshop in Coopersville, MI. Makers have identified the needs of the person they were designing for and have begun to brainstorm some potential solutions.

The framing of the problem can be wide (What can we do about the opioid abuse crisis in 2017?), allowing participants to hone in on where their expertise lies. Or it can be narrower, to allow for a tighter exploration of solutions. Our favorite example of a narrower framing is to say, "How might we improve a vehicle dashboard?" created by our colleague Kamya Sarma. A dashboard is something that most adult participants (in Michigan, anyway!) deal with every day, yet unique solutions have come out of every session we've had. Even a narrow focus like improving a dashboard can lead to solutions that ultimately are about training new owners or changing how windshield wipers sense that they need to activate.

RESEARCH, OBSERVE, AND INTERVIEW

For this stage, and for many of the following stages, we recommend putting participants in pairs or groups. Design Thinking is never done alone, and the diversity of opinions moves participants forward in their thinking. It also teaches great 21st-century skills of communication, collaboration, and decision-making in teams.

Research can take place online as participants gather information about ways people have attempted to solve the problem in the past. We don't want participants to rehash what's already been done; we want novel, creative experiences—that's what making is all about! Gathering background information is essential to see how professionals have focused on solving different issues, while sometimes ignoring others.

Observing how people use the product or experience the problem in real-time can be among the most useful data for participants to gather. Going out to observe a dashboard in use, either through a walkthrough by the owner, or even by a short test-ride shows how the product is actually used. It's important to get firsthand information as it is tough for people to summarize or generalize their experience.

In asking questions, the participants can interrogate how or why something is being done in the way that it is. Eliciting the reasons behind automatic actions can reveal assumptions and design choices. As design thinkers, it is important to empathize with the people being designed for. Oftentimes the people being designed for are the designers, or participants, themselves—it can take courage to reach out and connect with other people you are designing for, and we like to keep it simple!

SYNTHESIZE AND FOCUS

If we take a wider lens approach, this step can be substantial. Groups need to decide on the issue they will address with their solution in future steps. We encourage participants during this step to use their data and research, instead of any preconceived notions they may have had about the subject coming into the discussion. This is another reason why picking something with less emotional engagement to start with is suggested.

BRAINSTORM POSSIBLE SOLUTIONS

Many participants will want to jump to brainstorming right away, but it's good to move to this step together. Frequently, we will have people individually list as many possible solutions as they can think of. We encourage outlandish solutions, solutions which approach the focus from many different angles, in order to get the creative juices flowing—don't worry about feasibility at this point! Some participants will have one suggested solution in mind, but it can help to isolate the brainstorming step to teach people to come up with as many as they can. In isolating it, the presenter could ask for ideas on something unrelated, encouraging everyone to suggest as many as possible and highlighting the strengths in a wide variety of suggestions. Then, the participants could move back to the focus they had decided on and apply that same tactic to their own issue.

CHOOSE ONE IDEA AND PROTOTYPE IT

Whether by group vote, or by common suggestion, each group can move on to creating a prototype of their selected idea.

After all the work that the group has put in, it can begin to feel like they've reached a final product, but it's important to remind them that a prototype is just the first iteration of their solution. We love to use non-precious materials that can be added and taken away at will, so participants understand this isn't a final product. Some of our favorite materials include cardboard with Makedo, LEGO, Strawbees, and our ever-present, ever-provocative junk box.

TEST, ADJUST, AND TEST AGAIN

Making a prototype that's able to give you feedback is essential. Whether it's through a short presentation to the other groups, or through giving it to someone and seeing how they use it, feedback can come in a variety of forms.

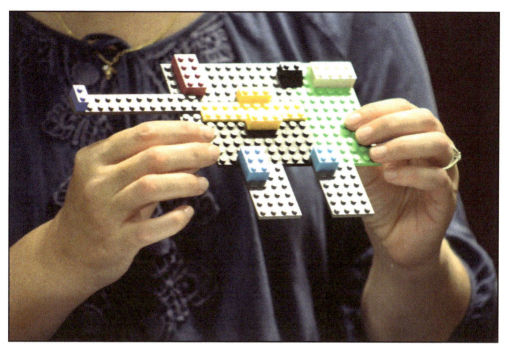

The beginning of a LEGO prototype at Making in Michigan Libraries Day of Design Thinking workshop at the Niles (Michigan) District Library.

Tenets from Design Thinking can also be used for individual, discrete Design Challenges. These can be as simple as a 15-minute introduction to a longer program or the focus of an hour-long program.

A Design Challenge can be a way to balance open-endedness and structure, allowing for participants of any age to come up with a solution that fits their interest and skill set. Design Challenges have three features: an audience, a challenge, and an optional constraint.

An audience is the person, animal, group, occupation, or fictional character the person will design for. This narrows the band of Design Thinking, allowing designers (students, patrons, community members, even employees!) to work from previous knowledge, thus shortening the time required for research or observation.

The challenge itself is a key component. It is important for the challenge to not be too specific, but rather be able to be interpreted in multiple different ways.

Finally, an optional constraint can be added that specifies an additional requirement for the design of the object.

In an effort to lighten the workload for librarians, our team created a Design Thinking Game that works extremely well when paired with different types of materials used for prototyping. Included in this handbook, the game consists of challenge cards (orange), audience cards (yellow), and constraint cards (red). We recommend printing these cards out on cardstock, or laminating them, as they will get a lot of use! Additionally, some pictorial versions were also made with icons from the Noun Project (thenounproject.com) which are free to use with attribution. Our thought was these pictorial cards could be used with those who weren't yet literate, but what we've found is they open up interpretations by others in exciting ways. When excitement, engagement, and interest are the goals, we'll take what can get where we can get it! Similar games have been produced and attached to products by Strawbees, LittleBits, and even LEGO, but having a free standalone game that can be used with any material is really beneficial. See the next chapter for more information about how the Design Thinking Game is played.

REFERENCES

Fontichiaro, Kristin. 2016. "Inventing Products with Design Thinking: Balancing Structure with Open-Ended Thinking." *Teacher Librarian* 44(2), 53–55, 63.

Zielezinski, Molly. 2016. "Finding Your Fit: Empathy, Authenticity, and Ambiguity in the Design Thinking Classroom." In *Taking Design Thinking to School*, edited by S. Goldman and Z. Kabayadondo. New York, NY: Routledge.

Workshop participants in a workshop held at Niles District Library in Michigan used the Design Thinking Game with cardstock, cardboard, and Makedo screws to invent a new storefront for a plumber.

CHAPTER 31
DESIGN THINKING GAME

Kristin Fontichiaro

This is an easy way to ease into Design Thinking with makers of all ages. It begins to develop the critical Design Thinking skill of *empathy*, or thinking of others. The goal is to get the wheels turning and then to use paper and pencil or common engineering materials to prototype. We have used this activity with individual makers and small groups and with students from kindergarten up through research administrators at our university. You can choose the amount of time available for this activity and determine whether it's the main course or merely an *hors d'eouvre* prior to a different main activity.

DECIDE WHICH CARD DECK YOU WANT TO USE

You can download the decks at http://makinglibraries.si.umich.edu/handbook. The Words deck includes three types of cards: users, inventions, and an optional constraint card. The Pictures deck is wordless and only has user and invention cards. But don't be fooled—the images may yield more complex inventions than you might think!

DECIDE WHICH TOOLS YOU WANT STUDENTS TO USE FOR PROTOTYPING

Here are some commonly-used tools: sketches, paper models, cardboard and Makedo screws, LEGO, Tinkertoys, junk boxes, Strawbees, or

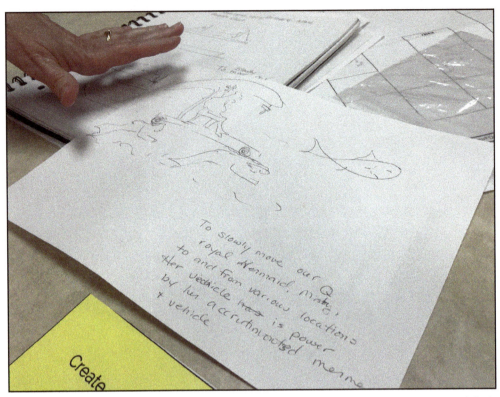

Participants in a Design Thinking workshop at Coopersville Area District Library sketch out their potential solution to a mermaid challenge.

MadewithChrome.com. If students are unfamiliar with how the tools are used, schedule some time for them to explore the tool and its features prior to playing the game.

DECIDE HOW YOU WANT TO ORGANIZE PLAY

For example, you can give an entire class the same challenge and have them work individually or in small groups to complete the challenge. Alternatively, you can give each student or group its own challenge. Give each designer or team one yellow and one orange card. Yellow cards represent the type of invention to create (and are deliberately vague to maximize diversity in inventions); orange cards represent the target user.

GIVE BRAINSTORMING TIME

Give each player/group time to think about the characteristics and probable needs of the user and what features the invention would need to have to be

Maker facilitators in an Ann Arbor workshop use Strawbees and LEGO to communicate their mermaid designs.

compatible with the user. If you feel students need more challenge, introduce the red (constraint) card, which adds an element of tension for students to resolve with their design.

GIVE PITCH-BUILDING TIME

Now you can add English Language Arts skills practice. Let students know that they will need to "sell" their product's usefulness to the group. Generally, this is a short oral presentation in the form of an advertisement, but it could also be framed as a social media pitch, a short video, a poster, or a brochure. Just keep in mind that you want to keep the focus on student problem-solving, not on extended ed tech time. Here are some questions for students to consider: What features make their invention so useful for their target consumer? Why should people care about their invention? What would motivate someone to find this product helpful? What problems does this invention solve for the user? What other features of the advertising genre (e.g., music or jingles, presenter charisma, sound effects, humor, demonstration of features, taglines, snappy language, etc.) might help sell the message?

HOST THE PITCH!

Ask each designer/group to share their invention pitch with the group.

GATHER FEEDBACK

If time allows, follow each pitch with some constructive peer feedback and time to upgrade the prototype of the invention.

ASSESSMENT OPTIONS

If grading is desired, consider evaluating the *pitch* and not the *product*. (This preserves students' wild ideas when designing.)

We hope you find the Design Thinking Game to be a flexible, often-used tool in your maker toolkit—it has been for us!

The game in action at a workshop co-hosted with Coopersville Area District Library.

APPENDIX A: WHAT'S IN YOUR COMMUNITY'S DREAM MAKERSPACE?

Needle and Thread

- Finger knitting
- Crochet
- Sewing by hand
- Sewing by machine
- Machine embroidery
- Needlepoint/crewel
- Ribbon embroidery
- Cross-stitch
- Boro/kantha/utility stitching
- Quilting
- Tailoring and alterations
- Patternmaking
- T-shirt refashioning
- *Project Runway* challenges
- Fashion hacking
- E-textiles
- Sewing machine
- Embroidery machine
- Serger
- Industrial sewing machine for upholstery
- Hand puppet making
- Spinning
- Weaving
- Freezer paper T-shirt stencils
- Fabric printing: Spoonflower.com or GreenParkStudios.com
- T-shirt stenciling using stencils from a Silhouette Cameo or Cricut machine

A ball of yarn made out of repurposed clothing at a Frankenmuth (Michigan) fashion hacking event.

Paper

- Origami
- Quilling
- Scrapbooking
- Zines
- Paper airplanes and gliders
- Gift wrapping
- Hand-drawn comics (consider hosting a comics swap or ComicCon-type event to show off completed projects)
- Collage
- Decoupage
- Silhouette/Cricut machine
- Shadow puppets
- Papier-mâché
- Paper marbling
- Body-tracing art
- Tiny books (You can use what you have made as endpapers for one-of-a-kind books!)
- Letterpress
- Printmaking

Making magazine page collages at Michigan Makers at Scarlett Middle School in Ann Arbor, MI.

Writing

- Choose Your Own Adventure
- Six-word memoir
- Story Cubes
- NaNoWriMo, PiBoldMo
- Blogging and web design
- Google Docs → export as ePub
- BookCreator (iPhone/iPad)
- DIY publishing: Lulu, CreateSpace, Smashwords, Scribd.com, Espresso Book Machine

Cooking

- Kitchen Knives 101
- Make fresh salsa
- Make smoothies
- Cookie decorating
- Cake decorating
- Freezer jam

Gardening

- Seed exchange
- Bonsai pruning
- Floral arranging
- Tool exchange
- Community gardening

Building and Construction

- LEGO
- K'Nex
- Lincoln Logs
- Tinkertoys
- Marshmallow launchers
- Cardboard box creations and Makedo kits
- Rube Goldberg machines

A LEGO prototype built by a Mitchell Elementary student.

Science

Make your own musical instruments

Paper airplane trajectories

Make your own speaker

Design your own bubble wand

Microscopes, telescopes

Magnifying glasses

Hydroponics

Science Olympiad teams

Oobleck

Slime (try magnetic slime, too)

Circuits

Snap Circuits

Squishy Circuits

LittleBits

Circuit Blocks (http://www.ciplearningstore.com/circuit-block-sets)

Conductive ink, such as BareConductive.com

Paper circuits

Chibitronics

Light-up/electric jewelry

Mentor Sarah Cramer works with a Mitchell Elementary School student in Ann Arbor, Michigan, to create a LittleBits invention.

Programming, Coding, and Robots

- HTML
- Python
- Ruby on Rails
- Java / JavaScript
- https://scratch.mit.edu
- Scratch Jr. app
- Hopscotch app
- Kodeable app
- Daisy the Dinosaur app
- Wio for Internet of Things (https://www.seeedstudio.com/Wio-Link-p-2604.html)
- Arduino microcontrollers
- Raspberry Pi minicomputers
- LEGO Mindstorm
- Makey Makey
- Dash & Dot robots (makewonder.com)
- MeeperBOT
- Ozobot
- Sphero
- FIRST Robotics
- Vex Robotics
- BrushBots and BristleBots

Digital Preservation

- VHS to DVD/digital converter
- Cassette to digital audio converter
- Flatbed scanner

Audio/Music Production

Finalemusic.com

LittleBits/KORG music kit

Dash and Dot with xylophone extension

Music Tools
(see aadl.org/musictools)

Garage Band

Audacity.com

Podcasting apps like Anchor or SoundCloud

Flat (flat.io) collaborative music

Chrome Music Lab
(http://g.co/musiclab)

Musical instruments for checkout (analog or digital)

Video Production

Production Room

Green Screen

MovieMaker

iMovie

FinalCut Pro

A group of Scarlett Middle School students experiments with Makey Makey.

Animation Tools

GoAnimate.com

Xtranormal.com

Shadow Puppet Edu app

MyCreate stop-motion app

Digital Comics

Pixton.com

Makebeliefcomix.com

Photo and Image Editing

Pixlr.com

Picmonkey.com

Adobe Photoshop

Canva.com

Adobe Illustrator

Inkscape

Graphic Design

Canva.com

Picmonkey.com

Adobe InDesign

Adobe Illustrator

Web Site Creation and Design

Wordpress.com

Wix.com

Google Sites

Weebly.com

3D Modeling and Printing

3Doodler pen

3D printer

3Dslash.net

AutoDesk 123Design

Tinkercad.com

Sketchup.com

Maya or Blender software

Thingiverse.com

http://n-e-r-v-o-u-s.com/labs/

cookiecaster.com

embossify.com

Using CookieCaster.com 3D modeling software to create cookie cutters at a Michigan Makers event at Mitchell Elementary in Ann Arbor.

Entrepreneurship and Fundraising

- Etsy
- Kickstarter
- Zazzle
- CafePress
- Society6
- Shapeways
- IndieGoGo

Miscellaneous

- Rubber band bracelets
- Shrinky Dinks
- Duct tape wallets
- Junk box challenges
- Art boxes
- Candle making
- Decorative painting
- Furniture refinishing
- Photography
- CNC router, laser cutter, StepCraft
- Button making
- Pulled String Art (see https://tinkerlab.com/how-make-captivating-pulled-string-art/)
- Board game design
- Glass painting or etching

A board game design activity at a Michigan Makers workshop at Peter White Public Library in Marquette, MI.

APPENDIX B: PROJECT PERSONNEL AND PARTNERS

A good makerspace is an environment conducive to collaboration and collegiality, and since our project began in 2012, we have been fortunate to have worked with a wonderful and diverse group of individuals and organizations.

Making in Michigan Libraries Senior Personnel

Kristin Fontichiaro,
Principal Investigator

Silvia Lindtner,
Co-Principal Investigator

Jean Hardy,
Graduate Student Research Assistant

Mayank Khanna,
Graduate Student Research Assistant

Sophia McFadden-Keesling,
Graduate Student Research Assistant

Ben Rearick,
Graduate Student Research Assistant

Kamya Sarma,
Graduate Student Research Assistant

Caroline Wack,
Graduate Student Research Assistant

Michigan Makers After-School Sites

Bright Futures Program of Eastern Michigan University at Ypsilanti Community Middle School
(R.J. Quiambao, Natalie Turner)

East Middle School, Plymouth, Michigan
(Rachel Goldberg)

Mitchell Elementary School,
Ann Arbor, Michigan
(Jan Duncan, Kevin Karr, Matt Hilton)

Scarlett Middle School,
Ann Arbor, Michigan
(Salvatore Barrientes, Anne Colvin)

Michigan Makers Family Nights and Senior Summer Camp

Ypsilanti District Library,
Michigan Avenue Branch
(Joy Cichewicz)

Longitudinal "Deep Dive" Partnerships as Part of Making in Michigan Libraries Project

Benzonia Public Library
(Amanda McLaren, Jimmy McLaren, Michelle Leines, Kathy Johnson, and many wonderful volunteers)

Niles District Library
(Nancy Studebaker-Barringer, Laura Hollister, and volunteers)

Making in Michigan Libraries Workshop Sites

Alpena County George N. Fletcher Public Library, Alpena, Michigan

Ann Arbor District Library, Ann Arbor, Michigan

Benton Harbor Public Library, Benton Harbor, Michigan

Benzonia Public Library / Grow Benzie, Benzonia, Michigan

Coopersville Area District Library, Coopersville, Michigan

Frankenmuth James E. Wickson District Library, List Elementary, and Frankenmuth High School, Frankenmuth, Michigan

Houghton Lake Public Library, Houghton Lake, Michigan

Niles District Library, Niles, Michigan

Nottawa Township Library, Centreville, Michigan

Peter White Public Library and Northern Michigan University, Marquette, Michigan

Pickford Community Library of the Superior District Library, Pickford, Michigan

Public Libraries of Saginaw, Saginaw, Michigan

University of Michigan School of Information, Ann Arbor, Michigan

West Iron District Library, Iron Mountain, Michigan

Making in Michigan Libraries Workshop Staff

Kristin Fontichiaro
Amber Lovett
Quenton Oakes

Alyssa Pierce
Ben Rearick
Kamya Sarma

Senior Summer Camp at Ypsilanti District Library, Michigan Avenue Branch

Killian Carucci, doctoral student

Michigan Makers Mentors

Mary Corcoran
Sarah Cramer
Tori Culler
Kelsey Forester
Sharona Ginsberg (honorary)
Mollie Hall
Audrey Huggett
Amana Kaskazi
Stephen Liu
Amber Lovett
Shauna Masura (co-founder)
James McDaniel
Rachel Moir
Meg Morrissey
Caroline Mossing
Sandy Ng

Quenton Oakes
Terence O'Neill (co-founder)
Katherine Pittman
Alyssa Pierce
Alyssa Pisarski
Ellen Gustafson Range
Alexandra Quay
Samantha Roslund (co-founder)
Sarah G. Swiderski
Nicole Sype
Amelia Thompson
Mari Monosoff-Richards Thurgate
Purva Kulkarni Yardi
Theo Zizka
Jessica Schmidt Zubik

We are grateful to Jeff Sturges, founder and conductor of Detroit's Mt. Elliott Makerspace, for his mentorship throughout the book. From the moment Kristin walked into his space, she wanted to create environments that were as loving and cozy as his were. He later spent many hours talking with Michigan Makers staff to unpack his lessons learned, many of which were incorporated into Chapter 3 of this book.

This book and the Making in Michigan Libraries project are made possible in part by the Institute for Museum and Library Services RE-05-15-0021-15 and the University of Michigan School of Information's Founders Fund. Early Michigan Makers initiatives were funded by the University of Michigan's Third Century Initiative and a $1,000 grant from the Michigan Association for Computer Users in Education given to East Middle School in Plymouth, MI. We are grateful to Blanche Woolls for her review of the manuscript and to Jimmy McLaren for copyediting and indexing assistance.

IMAGE CREDITS

Kristin Fontichiaro vi, 2, 11, 12, 13, 15, 18, 19, 22, 23, 34, 37, 40, 47, 48, 52, 54, 56, 58, 61, 68, 87, 89, 91, 95, 97 (based on a design by the University of Michigan School of Information), 98, 104, 106, 112, 115, 118, 120, 123, 126, 132, 136, 143, 148, 154, 157, 160, 173, 174, 186, 188, 190, 191, 192, 194, 196, 210, 213, 215 (bottom), 219, 220, 221, 223, 224, 226, 230, 234, 236, 237, 239, 240, 242, 243, 246, 256, 258, 260, 262, 264, 266 (via Canva.com), 266, 268 (top), 269, 272, 276, 278, 281, 284, 288, 300, 304, 308, 309, 313, 322, 326, 328, 331, 334, 336, 337, 338, 340; **Cherry Lake Publishing**: 4; **Caroline Wack** 28; **Jeff Smith, University of Michigan School of Information** 31, 85, 252, 257, 258; **Amber Lovett** 39, 82, 110, 215 (top); **Jean Hardy** 74; **Jay Jackson, University of Michigan School of Information** 99; **Ben Rearick** 159 (design: Canva.com), 170, 241, 321, 341, 342, 347; **Michigan Makers** 180, 324; **Tori Culler** 202, 205, 207, 208, 209, 211, 228, 229, 231, 232, 234; **Amanda McLaren** 216; **Sophia McFadden-Keesling** 268 (bottom), 270, 271 (overlays), 273; **public domain via Pixabay.com** 271; **Nicole Sype** 292, 294, 295, 296, 297, 298, 299; **Sandy Ng** 303; **Jeremy Little, University of Michigan School of Information** 93, 316, 318, 320; **University of Michigan Photography** 343; **Mayank Khanna** 345; **Alyssa Pierce** 249, 251, 348; **Thingiverse.com** 306; **John Pariseau, pxstl.com** 310; **3Dslash.net** 311.

INDEX

123Design software, 346
3D modeling, 87, 123, 129, 158, 175, 301–314, 346, 347
    See also MyMiniFactory.com; Thingiverse.com
3Doodler pen, 346
3D printing, 4, 5, 7, 8, 11, 14, 21, 29, 36, 47, 57, 60, 62, 63, 64, 69, 86, 87, 118, 119–124, 129, 139, 150, 158, 175, 300–314, 318, 346
    See also MakerBot Replicator
3dslash.com, 311
43 Folders, 62

AASL Framework, 172
ABC *Nightline*, 327
Activity Release, 71
Additive manufacturing, 302
Administrators, 46, 47, 75, 94, 124, 134, 153, 162, 163, 171, 335
Adobe software, 72
    See also GIMP software; Inkscape; Software
Adventure, 286, 287
After-school events, 10, 14, 38, 69, 77, 78, 93, 96, 101, 134, 142, 162, 277
Algorithmic thinking, 233
    See also Robots

All Hands Active makerspace, 5
Alpena County George N. Fletcher Public Library, 350
Amazon.com, 63, 199, 204, 303, 318
American Association of School Librarians, 164
American Button Machines, 72, 293, 294
American Community Survey (ACS), 22
"American Maker" (Chrysler video), 5
Americans with Disabilities Act, 62
Anatomy of clothing, 250–251
Anchor.fm for podcasting, 345
Android, 152, 267
Animation tools, 346
Ann Arbor District Library, 350
Ann Arbor Public Schools, 16
Annie E. Casey Foundation KidsCount, 38
App creation, 11
Appliance autopsy. See Toy takeapart
Arduino microcontroller, vi, 4, 10, 62, 92, 110, 150, 187, 213, 344
Art boxes, 347
Artist statements, 108, 109, 111, 185
"Ask three before me" strategy, 97
Assessment, 104, 105–111, 133–147, 161–178, 314, 338
Audacity.com, 345
AutoDesk, 312, 346

INDEX

Backward Design, 49
Badges, digital, 12–13
Badg.us, 12, 13
Bagley, Caitlin, 8
Baltimore County Public Schools, 57
Baltimore's Digital Harbor Foundation, 92
Bandwidth, 62
Banzi, Massimo, 5
BareConductive.com, 343
Barnard College, 279
Barriente, Salvatore, 349
Basement makerspaces, 5, 54, 59
BBC Micro, 3
Behavior, issues, 16, 49, 69, 71, 94–95
Behavior Incentive Day, 20, 288
Benton Harbor Public Library, 110, 250
Benzie Guild of Makers, 20
Benzonia Public Library, 19–21, 34, 37, 59, 136, 216, 220, 223, 252, 253, 256–258, 261–262, 274, 282, 288, 322, 326, 350
"Beware the Magical Object," 92, 113–117
Bing Preschool at Stanford, 172, 182
Biographical Sculpture, 185
Blackboard.com, 162
Blender software, 346
Blockly, 78, 84, 173, 319, 320, 322
Blogs, 3, 107, 142, 144, 145, 153, 162, 250, 340
  See also WordPress
Board Game Design, 17, 21, 23, 25, 27, 70, 182, 347, 348
  Events, 21
BoingBoing.com, 278
Bonsai, 342
BookCreator, 341
Book making, 29, 52, 340, 341
Boro repair stitching, 242, 243, 339
Bracelets, rubber band, 347
Brainstorming, 222, 230, 236
Bright Futures Program, 349
BristleBots, 318, 344
Brother sewing machine, 237

BrushBots, 318, 344
Bubbler lab (Madison Public Library), 77
Bubbles, 343
Budget, 7, 9, 24, 67, 75, 79, 116, 121, 130, 149, 150–153, 163, 248
Building and engineering as category of making, 158
Bulletin board, 43, 62, 162
  See also Whiteboards
Burke, John, 8
BusinessDecision database, 128
Butman-Fish Branch of the Public Libraries of Saginaw, 55
Button making, 18, 29, 69, 292–299

CAD (Computer-Aided Drafting), 123, 301, 312
  See also 3D printing; Tinkercad.com
CafePress, 347
Cake decorating, 341
Calipers, 313–314
Camaraderie, 30
Cameras, 4, 29, 72, 89, 137, 138, 151, 189, 263–274
Candle making, 347
Canva.com, 78, 192
Capacitors, 187, 188, 189
Cardboard, 10, 17, 18, 20, 27, 47, 55, 67, 79, 183, 216–224, 256–257, 330, 334, 342
Cardboard challenge, 20, 216–224
Caregivers. See Parents
Carts, 55, 167
Carucci, Killian, 29, 30, 31, 350
Cassette, conversion to digital audio, 344
Census, U.S. See American Community Survey (ACS)
Chain challenge, 184
Challenging the status quo, 100
Charging admission for events, 67–69, 76
Charisma, 94, 337
Charity Shop Chic, 250
Checklist, 16–162, 327

Chemicals, 86, 151, 166, 167, 189
Chibitronics, 206, 343
Chicago Public Library, 61, 72
Choose Your Own Adventure project, 93, 160, 277, 340
Chrome Music Lab, 345
Chrysler "American Maker" video, 5
Cichewicz, Joy, 29, 31, 32, 350
Cichewicz, Ricky, 118
Circuit blocks, 78, 343
Circuit boards, 92, 193–195
Circuits, 8, 27, 57, 78, 86–88, 115, 152, 158, 172, 174, 182, 187, 194, 195, 202–215, 317, 343
    Chibitronics, 206, 343
    Circuit blocks, 78
    In flashlights, 212–215
    LittleBits, 343
    Paper, 73, 86–87, 172, 203–215, 343
    Parallel, 206, 207
    Simple, 203–215
    Snap Circuits, 56, 78, 88, 115, 121, 150, 152, 172, 187, 202
    Squishy Circuits, 11, 12, 14, 135, 172, 174, 195, 202
    Templates for, 206, 207, 209
    See also Makey Makey
Circulation, 23, 40–41, 230
Citizen Science, 17
Civic organizations, 66
Classroom management, 80
CNC routers, 61, 347
Code and Go (Robot Mouse), 323
Code-a-Pillar (robot), 174, 323
Codecademy.com, 172
Coding, 8, 9, 10, 10, 57, 59, 78, 92, 114, 115, 143, 150, 151, 157, 158, 172, 174, 175, 319, 324
Cognitive issues, 30
Coin cell battery, 202, 206, 209, 210, 211, 212, 215, 318, 319
Colegrove, Tod, 8
Collaboration, 282, 329
    See also Mentors; Volunteers

Collage, 79, 158, 278, 279, 280, 281, 340, 341
Collective Gen, 250
Colvin, Anne, 349
ComicCon, 11, 14, 93, 277, 340
Comics, 11, 14, 43, 93, 95, 150, 277, 340, 346
Common Core State Standards, 164
Community Conversations (Harwood), 39
Community makerspaces.
    See Makerspaces
Community members, 19, 20, 32, 36, 37, 39, 40, 55, 65, 66, 230, 331
Community needs, 36–38, 39–40, 46, 53, 55, 64, 67, 74, 235
Computer programming. *See* Coding
Conductive ink, 343
Conductive tape. *See* Copper tape
Conductive thread, 213, 244
Confessions of a Refashionista blog, 250
Connected Learning, 90
Constellations of learning, 172
Constructionism, 8
Cookie Caster, 123, 307–310, 346, 347
Cookie decorating, 341
Cooking, 341
Coopersville Area District Library, 237, 239, 242, 243, 328, 332, 336, 338, 350
Coopersville High School, 308
Copper tape, 203–215
Corcoran, Mary, 351
Costa, Art. *See* Habits of Mind
Costume Creation Lab, 20, 249, 252–261
Cotton fabric, 236, 241
Coursera, 172, 175
Craigslist.com, 67
Cramer, Sarah, 93, 160, 282, 343, 350
CreateSpace, 341
Creating, 87
Creativebug.com, 281
Creative Commons Licenses, 134, 306
Crewel, 339
Cricut machine, 249, 339

Crochet, 78, 152, 158, 227–233, 243, 339, 340
Cross-generational learning, 90
    See also Multigenerational learning
Cross-pollination, 59, 77, 172
Cross-stitch, 78, 238, 243, 339
Cue robot, 172, 173, 322
    See also Wonder Workshop
Culler, Tori, 93, 189, 202–245, 282, 295, 351
Cura.com, 302
Current. *See* Circuits
Curriculum connections, 41, 43, 164

Daisy the Dinosaur app, 344
Dash and Dot robots, 59, 78, 79, 114, 115, 150, 152, 172, 173, 316, 322–323, 344, 345
    See also Robots
Data collection, 86, 105–111, 127–147, 161–179
Decoupage, 340
Delta College, 56
Demographics, 38, 46, 126, 128, 129, 166
Demonstration, 116, 137, 157, 237, 338
Derry, Bill, 8
Design Challenge, 117, 219, 305, 327, 331–332
Design Challenge cards, 117
    See also Design thinking game
Designer, 331, 333, 336, 338
Design studio, 84, 219
Design Thinking, 38, 85, 88, 143, 158, 174, 217–218, 220, 221–223, 321, 326–338
Design Thinking for Educators (IDEO), 38
Design Thinking for Libraries (IDEO), 38
Design thinking game, 185, 221–223, 332, 334–338
Dictionary, 289
Digital audio, 344
    See also LittleBits

Digital calipers, 313–314
Digital design, 78, 79
Digital fabrication, 47, 64
Digital Harbor Foundation, 214
Digital painting, 29, 30
District. *See* School districts
Documentation, 41, 72, 131, 133, 135, 141–146, 153
Donations, 67, 151, 152, 182, 183, 187, 189, 219, 248, 254
DonorsChoose.org, 121
Doorley, Rachelle, 172, 182
Double Union, 7
Dougherty, Dale, 5, 6, 7, 9
Dow Foundation, 56
Drawdio, 150
Drawing, 20, 174, 279, 280, 319
Drywall repair, 22, 23
    See also Home repair
DSLR (digital single-lens reflex) cameras, 134, 263, 269
Duct tape wallets, 347
Duncan, Jan, 349
Duxbury Free Library, 77
DVD, converter from VHS, 344
Dyson, James, 102

Eastern Michigan University, 349
East Middle School, 10–13, 14, 15, 47, 91, 99, 140, 143, 351
Edison, Thomas, 102
Educational standards, 8, 9, 36, 41, 42, 84, 105, 116, 164, 172
    See also Next Generation Science Standards; Science and Engineering Practices
Educational technology, 3, 8, 119–125, 203–215, 301–315, 317–325, 339–348
Educational trends, 113
EdX.org site, 45, 172
Electric bracelets, 18, 174, 213, 215
    See also Light-up bracelets

Electronics, 59, 70, 71, 79, 84, 89, 152, 194, 195, 213, 244, 314, 324
    See also Circuits; Robots
Elevator pitch or speech, 46, 109, 129
Elliott, Sean, 189
Emberley, Ed, 279
Embossify.com, 346
Embroidery, 4, 18, 29, 59, 78, 236, 238, 243, 339
    See also Crewel; Sewing
Emergency procedures, 69
Empathy, 85, 335
Empowering women, 29
Engagement, 16, 19, 41, 59, 76, 94, 141, 331, 332
Engineering, 8, 9, 41, 42, 57, 77, 78, 79, 120, 121, 141, 143, 152, 158, 301, 310, 314, 321, 335
Engineering Is Elementary, 77
English Language Arts (ELA), 164, 284, 337
Entrepreneurs, 5, 49, 121, 144, 201
ePub, 340
eRoominate, 20
Espresso Book Machine, 341
ESRI Tapestry tool, 38, 128
E-textiles, 339
Etsy, 49, 64, 347
Events, after-school, 10, 14, 38, 69, 77, 78, 93, 96, 101, 134, 142, 162, 277
Exit slips, 133, 142, 144, 162
Expectations, 4, 30, 53, 54, 69, 80, 94, 96, 99, 109, 277
Experimentation, 6, 102, 133, 143, 206
Exposure level, 269

Fab Labs, 8
Fabric, 10, 67, 69, 79, 86, 93, 151, 158, 182, 183, 231, 235, 236–244, 250, 254
    Scissors for, 238, 249, 254
Facebook, 26, 107, 134, 136, 162, 311

Facilitation, 3–33, 35, 54, 57, 60, 64, 65, 75–102, 113–117, 141, 165, 189, 235, 255, 263–264, 337
Family events, 19–21, 26–27, 29, 93, 217–224, 253–261, 320, 350
Fashion Hacking, 78, 136, 246–251, 339
Fayetteville Free Library, 8
Feedback, 38, 40, 100, 130, 136, 157, 222, 267, 272, 330, 338
Felt, fabric, 17, 235, 236, 239, 241, 244
Feminism, 278
Field of Dreams, 25, 65
Filament (for 3D printing), 67, 121, 122, 129, 302, 303, 304, 305
FinalCut Pro video software, 345
Finalemusic.com, 345
Finding an instructor, 263
    See also Mentors; Parents; Volunteers
Finger crochet, 230, 231
Finger knitting, 18, 78, 93, 226, 230, 339, 340
Finger puppets, 236, 239, 240, 241
First aid, 56, 166
FIRST Robotics program, 66, 344
Fisher Price, 323
Fiskars (scissors), 238, 254, 295
Flashlights, 212–215
Flatbed scanner, 344
Flat.io music app, 345
Fleming, Laura, 77
Flickr.com, 61, 134, 153
Floral arranging, 342
Foil tape. *See* Copper tape
Fontichiaro, Kristin, 3–153, 156, 161–178, 181–185, 187, 223, 233, 242, 253–283, 328, 335–337, 349, 350
Ford Motor Company, 5
Forrester, Kelsey, 91, 92, 351
Fotor.com, 274
Framework for K-12 Science Education: Practices, Crosscutting Concepts, and Core Ideas, 41

Frankenmuth High School, 89
Frankenmuth James E. Wickson District Library, 148, 158, 159, 183
Franklin, Benjamin, 285
Free to Make book, 6
Friends of Benzonia Public Library, 19–21
Friends of the Library groups, 163, 295
Funding, 32, 53, 56, 66–68, 76, 126, 127–131, 153
    See also Budget; Grants
Furniture, 59, 136, 163, 182, 259, 347
Fusion 360 software, 312

Gallery walking technique, 109, 111, 185
    See also Assessment
Game design, 11, 70, 82, 338
    See also Board Game Design
Garage Band, 345
Gardening, 342
Gardner, Howard, 91
George N. Fletcher Public Library, 350
Gift wrapping, 340
GIMP software, 72, 274
Ginsberg, Sharona, 351
GirlsWhoCode.com, 7
Glass etching, 60, 277, 347
Glass mosaics, 29
Glass painting, 347
Gliders, 14
GoAnimate.com, 346
Goldberg, Rachel, 10, 13, 47
Goodwill Outlet, 182–183, 189
Google Calendar, 63
Google Classroom, 162
Google Docs, 107, 340
Google Forms, 142, 144
Google Sites, 346
GQueues.com, 63
Graduate student, 32, 92, 93, 141, 190, 214, 303
Grants, 13, 14, 21, 46, 67, 76, 127–131, 163

Grantwriting and Crowdfunding for Public Libraries course, 131
Graphic design, 346
Graves, Colleen, 77
GreenParkStudios.com, 339
Green screen, 345
Greeting cards project, 206, 208, 210, 212, 215, 216
    See also Circuits
Gretchko Elementary, 57
Grover, Dale, 6, 59, 88
Guardians. *See* Parents
Guidelines, 80, 107, 109, 129
Guide on the side method, 92
Guiding principles, 102

Habits of Mind, 84–90
Hall, Mollie, 351
Hand sewing. *See* Sewing
Handspring Theatre Company, 2
Hardy, Jean, 24, 190, 261, 349
Harold Washington Library (Chicago Public Library), 61
Harwood Institute, 37, 39
Hasbro, 201
Hatch, Mark, 6
Helping Hands tool, 86
Herbert H. and Grace A. Dow Foundation, 56
Hess, Amanda Nichols, 144
Hewlett-Packard, 59
Hilton, Matt, 349
Hollister, Laura, 22, 25
Home Depot, 314
Home repair, 22–24, 26
Hopscotch app, 78, 344
Houghton Lake Public Library, 300, 309, 350
Hour of Code, 14, 78, 88, 172, 174
HTML, 343
Huggett, Audrey, 351
Humor, 94
Hydroponics, 343

Idea exchange, 99
    See also Maker Idea swap (event)
Identifying Community Needs for Public Library Management course, 45, 46
IDEO design group, 37, 38, 218, 327
IKEA, 219, 220
Illustrator, Adobe, 346
    See also Adobe software; Inkscape
"I'm a Pepper" song, 15
iMovie, 345
Inclusion, 4, 7, 280
InDesign software, 346
    See also Adobe software
IndieGoGo, 347
Inkscape, 72, 346
Instagram, 107, 113, 134, 144, 145, 153, 265, 267, 270, 274
Institute of Museum and Library Services (IMLS), 3, 4, 17, 18, 19, 21, 26, 27, 29, 159, 188, 192, 351
Instructional Strategies, 83–117, 161–178
Instruments. See Musical instruments
International Baccalaureate, 164
Internet of Things, 344
Inventory, 22, 53–72, 75–81, 113–117, 161–178, 189, 339–347
Invent to Learn book, 8
Investment, 66, 122, 150, 152, 185, 302
iPad, 29, 72, 114, 152, 341
iPhone, 85, 182, 267–269, 272, 341
ISTE standards, 164
    See also Educational standards; Educational technology

Jam, freezer, 341
James E. Wickson District Library, 148, 158, 159, 183
Janome sewing machine, 238
Java, 84, 343
JavaScript, 313, 343
Jazz It Up with Jean, 259–261
Jensen, Karen, 299
Jewelry, 29, 180, 182, 310, 343
    See also *Making Electric Jewelry*
Jo-Ann Fabrics, 236
Johnson, Cathy, 19, 350
Journals, 133, 142–144, 280
    See also Assessment
Journal Sparks book, 277
Junk box, 10, 14, 16, 17, 21, 68, 78, 86, 151, 153, 180–185, 190, 277, 330, 335
    Challenges, 180–185, 247
    Provocations, 181
    See also Design Challenge; Design Thinking

K-12 education, 43, 116, 185
    See also Assessment; Educational standards
Kallick, Bena. See Habits of Mind
Kantha stitching, 242, 339
Karr, Kevin, 96, 349
Kaskazi, Amana, 351
Khanna, Mayank, 93, 214, 303, 349
Kickstarter, 347
Klapperstuck, Karen, 69
K'Nex, 78, 86, 150, 342
Knitting, 20, 43, 49, 59, 69, 78, 93, 142, 143, 151, 152, 158, 226–233, 274, 339, 340
Knives, kitchen, 341
Kodeable app, 344
Kolb, Liz, 43, 44
KORG, 324
Kurdyla, Edward, 80, 117, 124, 131, 139, 146, 153, 168, 176, 185, 196, 261, 282

Lang, David, 7
Laser cutter, 55, 58, 61, 66, 347
Learning culture, 66, 102
Learning environment search, 18, 71, 90, 94

Learning from peers, 155–158
Learning styles, 91
LED (Light emitting diode), 86, 151, 188, 202, 204, 206, 207, 208, 209–213, 215, 323
LEGO, 14, 16, 20, 43, 78, 79, 86, 115, 117, 121, 133, 150, 152, 171, 312, 320, 321, 322, 331, 332, 335, 337, 342, 344
    Mindstorm, 78, 150, 174, 344
    Walls, 61, 79
    WeDo, 78, 174
Leines, Michelle, 19, 350
Lesson plans, 125, 142
Letterpress, 340
LGBTQ issues, 278
Liability, 25, 26
Libraries, vi, 7–72, 74–80, 85, 86, 87, 88, 93, 94, 96, 102, 105, 106, 110, 113, 116, 117, 118, 119, 120, 121, 122, 126, 128, 131, 133, 134, 136, 142, 144, 145, 148–153, 155, 157, 158, 159, 161–176, 183, 184, 190, 192, 196, 210, 216–224, 230, 237, 239, 242, 243, 247, 248, 252–261, 262, 263–274, 279, 281, 282, 288, 292, 295, 296, 297, 299, 300, 301, 302, 303, 305, 308, 309, 316, 318, 319, 320, 322, 323, 327, 328, 329, 332, 334, 336, 338, 348, 349, 350, 351
Library of Things, 22, 23, 24
    See also Niles District Library (NDL)
Library relevance and value, demonstrating, 8
Licenses, 72
Life skills, 84
Lighting, 59, 267
Light-up bracelets, 213, 215
Lincoln Logs, 117, 150, 342
Lindtner, Silvia, 349
LinkedInLearning.com, 263
Little, Jeremy, 320, 353

LittleBits, 7, 14, 55, 59, 72, 78, 88, 121, 152, 172, 187, 202, 323–324, 332, 343
Liu, Stephen, 351
Long-term projects, 100–101, 108
Love, 94
Lovett, Amber, 39, 83–111, 215, 350, 351
Lowrie, Portia. *See* Makery website
Lulu.com, 341
LulzBot, 121

Made magazine mockup, 34, 37
MadewithChrome.com, 336
Madison-Oneida Board of Cooperative Educational Services, 156
Madison Public Library Bubbler lab, 77
Magical Object Syndrome (MOS), 114–117
    See also "Beware the Magical Object"
Magnet making. *See* Button making
Magnifying glasses, 343
Maintenance, 26, 62, 119–125, 161–177
Makebeliefcomix.com, 78, 346
Makedo, 218, 219, 257, 258, 330, 334, 335, 342
Make magazine, 5, 9, 34, 37
Maker activities, 22, 35–51, 62, 66, 67, 75–81, 113–172, 181–336, 339–347
MakerBot Replicator, 2, 14, 121, 307
    See also 3D modeling; 3D printing
Maker community. *See* Makers
Maker culture, 5, 5, 17, 54, 80, 119, 127, 133, 149, 155
    Creation of, 35–73
    History of, 3–33
    See also Makers
Maker Education Initiative, 77
Maker Faire, 5, 9, 96, 151
MakerFest, 20, 96, 97
Maker heritage, 34
Maker Idea swap (event), 154–158

Maker-in-residence, 8
Maker Media, 9
    See also Dougherty, Dale; Maker Faire
Maker movement. *See* Maker culture; Makers
Maker Movement Manifesto, The, 6
Maker Reporter role, 101, 137, 138, 142, 145
Makers, 3–32, 34–49, 53–125, 133–147, 155–178, 181–337
    Definitions of, 47
"MakerSpace: Button Making Is All the Rage" (article), 299
Makerspaces
    Facilitation of, 3–33, 35, 54, 57, 60, 64, 65, 75–102, 113–117, 141, 165, 189, 235, 255, 263–264, 337
    Learning in, 83–111
    Purposefulness, 35–51
    Setting up, 53–74
    See also Maker activities; Makers
Makerspaces: A Practical Guide for Librarians, 8
Makerspaces column in *Teacher Librarian*, 117, 124, 131, 139, 146, 153, 168, 176, 185, 196, 261, 282
Makerspaces: Top Trailblazing Projects, 8
Makerspace Tune-up, 49, 161–168, 171–176
    See also Assessment
Maker vision, 48, 49
MakerWorks (Ann Arbor, MI), 5, 6, 59, 62, 66, 88
Makery website, 250
MakeShop, 8
    See also Pittsburgh Children's Museum
MakeWonder.com, 344
Makey Makey, 28, 46, 55, 114, 344, 345
Making and Learning workshops, 83, 89
Making Electric Jewelry, 213
Making in Michigan Libraries, 3, 10, 17, 18, 19, 21, 29, 39, 58, 77, 97, 126, 145, 155, 159, 190, 192, 237, 242, 243, 261, 263, 265, 274, 277, 293, 303, 308, 328, 331, 349–351
Making music, 27, 28, 323
Mann, Merlin, 62
Manufacturing, 5, 30, 200
Marginalized voices, 281
Marionettes, 2
Marketing, including examples, 22, 23, 31, 45, 97, 163, 192, 266
Marshmallow launchers, 342
Martinez, Sylvia Libow, 8
Massive Open Online Course (MOOC), 46, 99
Masura, Shauna, 3, 351
Mathematics, 9, 41, 141, 164
Matteson, Addie, 18
Maya software, 346
Maze, 135, 174, 184, 320, 323
McDaniel, James, 351
McFadden-Keesling, Sophia, 35–51, 263–275, 349
McLaren, Amanda, 19, 20, 258, 261, 274, 350
McLaren, Finn, 21
McLaren, Jimmy, 19, 20, 21, 34, 216, 223, 257, 261, 267, 350
McTighe, Jay, 49
Measuring learning, 105–111
    See also Assessment
MeeperBot, 172, 173, 320–321, 322, 344
Memoir, 340
Mending workshops, 242
Mentors, 5, 6, 13, 16, 17, 27, 70, 88, 91, 93, 94, 95, 96, 100, 101, 107, 152, 160, 184, 185, 189, 277, 320, 343, 349–351
Metacognition, 86
Metaphorical Sculpture, 185
Michelangelo, 302
Michigan Association for Computer Users in Learning, 13, 351
Michigan Makers Family Night, 26–28, 320, 350

Michigan Makers project, 3, 4, 6, 8, 10–15, 17, 26, 27, 29, 32, 47, 58, 70, 77, 88, 91, 92, 95, 96, 99, 101, 134, 140, 141, 142, 145, 151, 152, 155, 160, 182, 183, 189, 241, 277, 295, 318, 320, 324, 349–351
    See also Making in Michigan Libraries
Michigan ZoomIn, 17
Microcontrollers, 152, 158, 344
    See also Arduino microcontroller; Tech Box Tricks microcontrollers
Microcredentials. *See* Badges, digital
Microscopes, 343
Microsoft Office, 92
    See also PowerPoint
Middle school, 93, 138, 142, 172
Mid-Michigan Library League, 300
Minds-on, 87
Mindstorm. *See* LEGO: Mindstorm
Minecraft, 11, 93, 254
Mini Maker Faire. *See* Maker Faire
Mission, 10, 25, 53, 77, 88, 153, 161, 162
    See also Purposefulness
MIT (Massachusetts Institute of Technology), 8
    See also Scratch computer programming
Mitchell Elementary School, 14–18, 68, 95, 96, 98, 160, 180, 186, 230, 240, 284, 320, 321, 324, 349
Mobile makerspace, 56–57
Moir, Rachel, 93, 95, 282, 351
Monroe Township Library, 69
Moodle, 162
Morning Meeting model, 15
Morning messages, 96, 98
Morrissey, Meg, 351
Mossing, Caroline, 351
Motor homes as makerspaces, 56
MovieMaker software, 345
Mt. Elliott Makerspace, 5, 54, 73, 351
    See also Sturges, Jeff

Multigenerational learning. *See* MakerFest; Michigan Makers Family Night
Multimedia, 142
Multiple intelligences, 91
Music, 344
Musical instruments, 23, 342, 344
Music Tools (Ann Arbor District Library), 345
Mybluprint.com, 263
MyCreate stop-motion animation app, 346
MyMiniFactory.com, 88, 301, 304, 305

NaNoWriMo, 340
NASA models, 307
National Institutes of Health, 307
National Maker Plan, 119
National Research Council, 41
Natural materials, 182
Needlework, 158, 227–233, 339
N-e-r-v-o-u-s.com/labs, 346
Neuberger, Emily, 277
New Dress a Day blog, 250
Next Generation Science Standards, 9, 36, 41, 42, 84, 116, 164, 172
Ng, Sandy, 93, 351
Nightline, 327
Niguidula, David, 144
Niles Daily Star, 26
Niles District Library (NDL), 21–26, 36, 40, 59, 74, 126, 190, 192, 196, 331, 333, 334, 350
NoEndz, vi
Northern Michigan University, 350
Nottawa Township Library, 350
Noun Project, 332

Oakes, Quenton, 39, 350, 351
Oakland University Libraries, 144
Obama, Barack, 144

Ohm's law, 204–206
O'Neil, Terence, 3, 349, 351
One-on-one meetings, 100
Online object collections, 30
Oobleck, 343
Open-ended work, 101, 105
Open network, 90
Open-source, 4, 6, 72, 302
Origami, 14, 43, 57, 78, 152, 340
Ozobot, 78, 115, 152, 172, 173, 174, 319–320, 322, 344
    See also Robots

PACE model, 80, 101–102
Pain point, 109
Painting, 347
    See also Digital painting
Paper airplanes, 340, 342
Paper circuits. See Circuits
Paper crafts, 340
Paper flashlights. See Circuits
Papert, Seymour, 8
Papier mâché, 340
Parallel Circuits. See Circuits
Parental permission. See Permission slips
Parents, 39, 71, 96, 98, 153
Pariseau, John, 310
Partnerships, 21, 25, 30, 43, 63, 97, 149
    See also Mentors; Volunteers
Patience, 94
Patronicity.com, 67, 121
Patrons, recruitment of, 8
Pattern recognition, 233
Peer culture, 66, 90
Peer institutions, 39
Peer mentorship. See Mentors
Permission slips, 69–71, 134, 166
    See also Liability
Peter White Public Library, 350
Photography, 11, 20, 29, 31, 85, 93, 132, 133–139, *262–274*, 347

Editing, 14, 79, 93, 270, 274, 346
Permissions for, 72
Photoshop, 72, 274, 346
    See also Adobe software; GIMP software; Illustrator, Adobe
PiBoldMo, 340
Pickford Community Library, 39, 350
Picmonkey.com, 78, 79, 274
Pierce, Alyssa, 247–251, 350, 351
Pillows, sewing of, 239, 241, 244
Pinterest, 77, 113, 250
Pisarski, Alyssa, 351
Pitches (presentations), 109, 136, 144, 163, 184, 337, 338
    See also Assessment
Pittman, Katherine, 351
Pittsburgh Children's Museum, 8
Pixabay.com, 271
Pixlr.com, 93, 346
Pixton.com, 78, 346
Plano Independent School District, 55
Plemmons, Andy, 76
Plymouth, Michigan. See East Middle School
Podcasting, 345
Poetry, 150, 174, 278, 290
Policy development, 24
Portfolios, 111, 142, 144
Portraits, photographic, 265–270
PowerPoint, 91, 93
Power Tools for Women workshop, 20
Preddy, Leslie, 8
Presentation, 330
Pressures on institutions, 8, 75
Prime Time Reading, 27
Principals. See Administrators
Printmaking, 340
Problem solving, 89, 97, 117, 218, 321, 327, 337
Process journals, 107, 162
    See also Assessment
Production room, 345

Professional development, 17, 55, 119, 127, 155–159
Programmable objects, 158
Programming. *See* Coding
Programming for Everybody MOOC courses, 175
Project Linus, 233
Project Runway, 136, 339
Pro Photo Walk, 262, 264, 265, 272–274
Prop-making, 253
Proposals. *See* Grants
Protocols, 38
Prototypes, 102, 142, 143, 153, 182, 184, 217, 222, 260, 330, 331, 335, 338
Providing context and examples, 100
Provocations, 172, 182
Public data, 38
Public libraries / librarians, 30, 47, 53, 61, 72, 93, 96, 106, 145, 151, 230, 243, 253
Public Libraries of Saginaw, 55, 57, 58, 350
Public Library Management MOOC courses, 45, 46
Public relations, 43
Puppets, 2, 17, 21, 27, 54, 79, 88, 92, 152, 173, 241, 339, 340, 346 (app)
Purposefulness, 35–51, 119, 149, 233
Pxstl.com, 310, 311
Python (programming language), 99, 175, 343

Quay, Alex, 107, 184, 351
Quiambao, R. J., 349
Quilling, 340
Quilting, 339
Quinn, Amy, 213

Range, Ellen Gustafson, 351
Raspberry Pi (book), 4
Raspberry Pi microcomputer, vi, 3–4, 10, 344

Ravelry.com, 232
Rearick, Ben, 155–159, 282, 327, 349, 350
Recruitment. *See* Volunteers
Recycled materials, 78, 158
Recycling, 20, 124, 189, 190, 199, 219, 256
Refashion Co-op, 250
Reggio Emilia preschool movement, 182
Release forms, 26, 71
Reporter role, 101, 137
Reports, 162
Repositories, 307
Repurpose, 92, 153, 189, 241, 242, 249, 250, 340
Repurposeful Librarians, 19
Research, design, 218, 222, 329, 330, 331, 335
Resistance, electricity, 205, 206
Resistors, 187, 188, 203, 204, 206
Responsive Classroom, 96
Riley, Erin, 257
Robotics, 57, 317–324, 344
Robot Mouse, 174, 323
Robots, 20, 27, 78, 88, 92, 107, 112, 114, 115, 120, 142, 150, 152, 172–174, 206, 216, 316–324, 344
  See also BristleBots; BrushBots; Code-a-Pillar (robot); Cue robot; Dash and Dot robots; MeeperBot; Robot Mouse
Role of the instructor, 91
Root, Tom, 6
Roslund, Samantha, 3, 351
Rotary cutters, 238
Rubber band bracelets, 347
Rube Goldberg machines, 185, 342
Ruby on Rails, 343
Rule of Thirds, 270, 271

Safety, 60, 92, 166, 190, 193, 219
  Glasses or goggles, 190, 193
Sage on the Stage method, 92

Saginaw, Public Libraries of, 57–58
Saginaw Valley State University, 57
Salsa, 341
Sarma, Kamya, 39, 53–73, 329, 349, 350
Scanner, flatbed, 344
Scarlett Middle School, 132, 241, 299, 303, 345, 349
Schematics, 207
School districts, 39, 40, 41, 43, 57, 69, 94, 128, 134, 151, 152, 165, 172, 174
School librarians. *See* Libraries
School libraries. *See* Libraries
School Library Journal, 18, 299
School Library Makerspaces: Grades 6–12, 8
School makerspaces, 83
Science and Engineering Practices, 41, 42, 84, 116
    See also Educational standards
Science Olympiad, 93, 343
Scientist and inventor's notebook, 289
Scissors, 238, 254, 295
Scrapbooking, 340
Scratch computer programming, 10, 78, 99, 152, 172, 174, 344
Scratch Jr., 78, 344
Scribd.com, 341
Seed exchange, 342
Seesaw app, 144
Self-directed learning, 83
Senior centers, 39
Senior citizens, 29–32
Senior Summer Camp, 29–32, 85, 87, 118, 351
Sentence starters, 108
Serger, 339
Series Circuit. *See* Circuits
Sesame Street, 38
Setting expectations, 94
Setting up a makerspace, 53–81, 119–178
Severance, Charles (Chuck), 4, 99
Sewing, 4, 8, 10, 11, 14, 17, 20, 23, 43, 49, 57, 59, 78, 79, 84, 92, 158, 171, 173, 174, 213, 234–261, 277, 339

Sewing machines, 23, 29, 62, 67, 78, 79, 135, 150, 152, 172, 174, 235, 237–238
Shadow Puppet Edu app, 346
Shapeways.com, 64, 303, 347
Short-term projects, 100–101
Shrinky Dinks, 21, 86, 151, 277, 347
Silhouette die cut machine, 14, 29, 62, 67, 72, 79, 152, 249, 339
Silicon Valley, 141
Simple circuits. *See* Circuits
SketchUp software, 346
SkillShare, 22–26, 74
    See also Niles District Library (NDL)
Slime, 343
SMART goals, 172
Smartphones, 29, 31, 79, 136, 137, 153, 172, 181, 263, 265, 267, 317
Smashwords.com, 340
Smith, Jeff, 136, 262–274, 353
Smithsonian Institution, 307
Smoothies, 341
Snap Circuits, 56, 78, 88, 115, 121, 150, 152, 172, 187, 202, 343
Snapseed app, 265, 267
Snuggles Project, 233
Social issues, 29, 30–31
Social media, 107, 113, 162, 171, 337
Social support, 233
Society for Women Engineers, 66
Society6.com, 347
Socioemotional skills, 164, 165
Soft circuits, 244
Soft skills, 84, 172
Software, 72, 75–111, 119–125, 236–275, 301–325, 339–347
Solutech, 303
SoundCloud for podcasts, 345
Space, building, 57–59, 62, 63
Spatial learning, 91
Speakers, 343
Sphero, 78, 174, 344
Spinning, 339
Spoonflower.com, 339

Squishy Circuits, 11, 12, 14, 135, 172, 174, 195, 202, 343
Staffing a makerspace, 64–65, 66, 67
    See also Mentors; Volunteers
Stager, Gary, 8
Stakeholders, 32, 38, 88, 107, 111, 133
    See also Makers; Parents
Standardized tests, 163
    See also Assessment; Educational standards
Standard operating procedures, 66
Stand-up meetings, 108
Stanford University Bing Preschool, 172, 182
State University of New York at Oswego, 64
STEAM/STEM, 9, 10, 20, 36, 40, 47, 55, 56, 84, 113, 116, 133, 141, 150, 152, 155, 162, 163, 164, 165, 175, 232, 277, 278, 316
StepCraft, 347
Stop-motion animation, 11, 54, 91, 93, 346 (app)
Storage, 57, 58, 59, 60, 165, 167
Story Cubes, 341
Strategic plan, 43, 166
Strawbees, 78, 115, 117, 330, 332, 335, 337
String art, 347
Stuffed toys, 239, 241
Sturges, Jeff, 5, 73, 351
Subtractive manufacturing, 302
Superior District Library, 350
Support, 6, 88
Supportive environment, 277
Sustainability, 9, 66, 98, 148, 149–153
Swiderski, Sarah G., 277, 285–291, 351
SXSWedu, 119
Sype, Nicole, 189, 293–299, 320, 351

Table tents, 110, 280
Tablets, 79, 137, 167, 265, 279, 317
    See also iPad

Teacher Librarian (publication), 80, 117, 124, 131, 139, 146, 153, 168, 176, 185, 196, 223, 242, 282
Teaching, 3–117, 133–178
    With your hands behind your back, 99
    See also Assessment; Educational standards
Tech Box Tricks microcontrollers, 152
Technology. See 3D printing; Educational technology; Robots; Software
TechShop, 5, 6, 7, 9
Telescopes, 343
Thingiverse.com, 88, 301, 304, 305, 306, 346
    See also 3D modeling
Third Century Initiative (University of Michigan), 14
Thompson, Amelia, 351
Thompson, Emily, 64
Three-department rule, 64
Thrift stores, 67, 183, 229, 241, 242, 247, 248
    See also Goodwill Outlet
Thurgate, Mari Monosoff-Richards, 351
Ticket out the door assessment, 108
    See also Assessment
Time capsule, 287
Tinkercad.com, 62, 65, 87, 312–313, 346
Tinkertoys, 78, 115, 117, 150, 335, 342
Title: Subtitle assessment, 106–107
    See also Assessment
Tool exchange, 341
    See also Inventory; Library of Things
Tools. See Inventory
"Tools + Support + Community," 88
Toyama, Kentaro, 37
Toy takeapart, 17, 20, 24, 25, 27, 74, 92, 151, 156, 157, 187–201, 277
    Worksheet, 197–201
Train the trainers model, 98
Transformative learning, 90
Triple E Framework, 43, 44

T-shirts, 14, 20, 79, 151, 152, 241, 246, 248, 254, 255, 339
Turner, Natalie, 349
Tutorials, 137, 175, 229, 230
Twitter, 107, 120, 134, 153, 162

Underwater remote-controlled vehicles (ROV), 89
University of Michigan, 14, 20, 37, 306
    College of Engineering, 310
    Founders Fund, School of Information, 17, 26, 27, 351
    School of Information, 13, 45, 92, 97, 106, 129, 159, 188, 192, 320, 350, 351
    Third Century Initiative, 16, 351
University of Nevada, Reno, 8
University of Tennessee–Chattanooga, 64
Upholstery, 339
Upward Bound funding errors, 130
U.S. Census, 38, 128
    See also American Community Survey (ACS)
U.S. Commerce Department, 201
U.S. Department of Education, 130

Values, 94
Ventilation, 55, 60–61, 63, 304
Vex Robotics, 344
VHS to DVD converter, 344
Videography and video production, 133–139, 345
Vision, 64, 106, 121, 149
Visual documentation, 133–139
Voltage, 205
Volunteers, 25, 26, 65–66, 70, 92, 94, 151, 153, 229, 242, 253, 256, 305

Wack, Caroline, 3–33, 202, 203–215, 301–325, 349

Wallet, duct tape, 347
Walmart, 236
Wants, needs, and aspirations, 36–38, 39
    See also Community needs
Warren-Gross, Laura, 277, 282
Washi tape, 288
Water, access to, 60
Wearable electronics, 152, 213, 339
Weaving, 339
Web 2.0, 174
Web design, 340, 343, 346
WeDo by LEGO, 78, 174
Weebly.com, 346
West Iron District Library, 350
Westport Public Library, 8
Whiteboards, 15, 40, 47, 61, 62, 95, 96, 98
White House, 141
Wi-Fi, 62, 302
Wiggins, Grant, 49
Wikki Stix, 78
Williams, Josh, 5
Williams, Pam, 183
Wio, 344
Wix.com, 346
Wonder Workshop, 114, 316, 322
    See also Cue robot; Dash and Dot robots
WordPress, 144, 346
Workshops, 16, 19, 20, 21, 24, 26, 30, 37, 39, 54, 55, 65, 75, 83, 92, 106, 155–159, 175, 237, 242, 263, 264, 265, 266, 308, 331, 334, 336, 337, 338
    See also Mending workshops
Wreck lab. See Toy takeapart
Writing projects, 341
Written documentation, 141–146

Xbox, 182
Xerox, 88
Xtranormal.com, 346
Xylophone, 345

Yardi, Purva Kulkarni, 351
Yarn. *See* Crochet; Knitting
Young learners, 8
YouTube.com, 230, 231, 279
Ypsilanti Community Middle School, 56, 349
Ypsilanti District Library, Michigan Avenue Branch, 26–31, 54, 85, 87, 93, 118, 210, 224, 292, 295–297, 309, 316, 318–320, 351
Ypsilanti Middle School, 136

Zauel Branch of the Public Libraries of Saginaw, 57–58
Zazzle, 347
Zero to Maker: Learn (Just Enough) to Make (Just about) Anything, 7
Zielezinski, Molly, 328
Zines, 17, 20, 93, 174, 212, 276–291, 340
Zipsnip cutting tool, 218
Zizka, Theo, 351
ZONTA Club, 66
Zooniverse.org, 17
Zubik, Jessica Schmidt, 351

CPSIA information can be obtained
at www.ICGtesting.com
Printed in the USA
BVHW051018201220
595980BV00002B/2